Pageant of the

ROSE

A history of the rose in art, religion, legend, romance, poetry, prose and symbolism.

Pageant of the

ROSE

Jean Gordon

STUDIO PUBLICATIONS, INC.
in association with
THOMAS Y. CROWELL COMPANY
New York

CONTENTS

I   LEGEND   7

II   ROMANCE   808443   16

III   ART   31

IV   CHARMS AND PORTENTS   59

V   FRAGRANCE   69

VI   ROSE CURES, COSMETICS, AND COOKERY   80

VII   CUSTOMS AND FASHIONS   93

VIII ROSE GARDENS OF THE WORLD   105

IX   HISTORY AND HERALDRY   125

X   MARTYRS AND MIRACLES   146

XI   FAIRY TALES   159

XII   PROSE AND POETRY   175

XIII SYMBOLISM AND MYSTICISM   193

       ACKNOWLEDGMENTS   215

       BIBLIOGRAPHY   216

       INDEX   219

TO ONE
BORN IN JUNE,
THE MONTH OF ROSES

I

LEGEND

. . . and I write
How Roses first came red and Lilies white.
ROBERT HERRICK, "Hesperides"

ON THE antiquity of the rose, legends and geologists agree. Geologists trace its ancestry through millions of years. Legends place the creation of the rose in the glorious days when gods and goddesses walked on earth and mingled with mortals. These legends for the most part try to explain why, when, and where the rose was created, the reason for the various colors and the addition of thorns and moss.

The Greeks at first styled the rose, "the king of flowers," *basileus ton antheon*. Then about 600 B.C. when the poetess Sappho wrote her "Ode to the Rose" a transformation took place:

> "Would Jove a Queen of Flowers ordain,
> The Rose, the Queen of Flowers, should reign."

Since that time, with the exception of some Christians and Mohammedans who introduced masculine origins and other attributes, the sex of the rose has remained in every sense, feminine.

When the Romans took over the Grecian myths as part of the culture they inherited, the Grecian Aphrodite, goddess of love, became the Roman Venus, patroness of all lovers. So, too, the rose sacred to Aphrodite became the floral symbol of Venus. Into the numerous legends one can read at will the name of either. Whatever form they take, the stories linking the origin of roses to either of these goddesses are all compliments to their exceeding beauty. So comely was Aphrodite that the very water in which she bathed gave birth to the flower dedicated to her.

According to some sources, roses first appeared when Venus emerged from the foaming sea near the island of Cyprus, a scene immortalized by Botticelli. Anacreon, an Ionian Greek poet, famous for his light and graceful lyrics, wrote that when the sea was formed and proudly bore **Venus** on its billows, the earth, eager to show that it could equal the gods in the creation of beauty, produced the rose. When the gods saw the flower, they gave homage to its perfection by watering it with nectar.

Although the rose was the symbol of Venus and Aphrodite they are not the only goddesses associated with its creation. Flora, the goddess of flowers, overcome by the death of her favorite nymph implored the Olympian deities to change her favorite's mortal remains into an immortal flower that all others would have to acknowledge as their queen. The deities consented, and thus the rose was born. Apollo lent the vitalizing power of his rays; Bacchus bathed the flower in nectar; and Flora gave the petals their hue, withholding, however, all blue pigment as a color cold and suggestive of death; therefore there could never be any blue roses.

According to another classical myth the blush rose, once queen of all roses, was created in a different manner. In Corinth there lived a maiden Rhodanthe who was so beautiful that even "high-born kings were suppliants of her love." One summer day, annoyed by the persistent attention of three of her admirers she sought to escape by going into the temple of Diana. As the three impetuous young men stormed the temple, Rhodanthe appeared so beautiful that her attendants flung the statue of Diana from its pedestal saying, "Rhodanthe shall be our goddess! She shall replace Diana!" Apollo, driving his sun chariot overhead, was so incensed by this insult to his sister Diana that he turned the proud Rhodanthe into a rose and her attendants into thorns. As for the three rash suitors, one became a worm, one a bee, and one a butterfly—still seeking the rose!

Apollo is also associated with the creation of the rose in another Grecian tale. Finding a beautiful nymph asleep, he kissed her; and the nymph, aroused, evaded any further amorous attentions by transforming herself into a rose.

Probably even older than the Greek and Roman myths is the story revolving around the virtuous maiden Zillah. When she rejected the advances of an undesirable suitor, he proved his perfidy by accusing her of evil and unclean practices. At a trial, of which nothing is recorded save the verdict, she was sentenced to be burned at the stake. Miraculously the flames died down, consuming only the evil-minded suitor, the smoldering embers being transformed into roses, "the first that man ever saw."

Robert Southey pictures this scene in his poem "The Rose":

> "...the stake
> Branches and buds, and, spreading its green leaves
> Embowers and canopies the innocent Maid
> Who there stands glorified; and Roses, then
> First seen on earth since Paradise was lost,

Opposite page: "Birth of Venus" by Botticelli (Uffizi Gallery). The use of the rose in this painting suggests simultaneous creation of the flower.

Interesting rose formations in rose-colored rock and mineral. Above: A gypsum crystal aggregate "Desert Rose" from the Gobi Desert. Below: Marcasite rose in shale from Randolph County, Illinois. At left: A rose fossil estimated to be thirty-five million years old, found at Crooked River, Oregon.

(American Museum of Natural History)

Profusely blossom around her, white and red
In all their rich variety of hues;
And fragrance such as our first parents breathed
In Eden she inhales, vouchsafed to her
A presage sure of Paradise regain'd."

A parallel to the Hebrew tale of Zillah concerns the Persian religious teacher and prophet Zoroaster who founded the religion of Persia—dominant until the rise of the Mohammedans. When Nimrod, the powerful king of Babylon, heard of the birth of this long-expected prophet Zoroaster he became alarmed and ordered the child to be brought to him, whereupon the irate king had him thrown into a blazing fire. But before the eyes of the astounded spectators, the flames died down and the glowing embers were transformed into a bed of roses "whereon the child slumbered sweetly."

In Christian narratives, two origins are given for the creation of the briar rose. According to one, Judas hung himself on a thorn tree which then burst into bloom as a sign that the blood of Christ was shed even for sinners. The other version has the briar rose emerge from the crown of thorns worn by Christ at His crucifixion, the roses forming from His blood.

"Men saw the thorns on Jesus' brow
But angels saw the roses."

Another rose, variously called the Holy Night rose, the rose of Noel, Christ's bloom or the Christmas rose, is said to have been created by the angel Gabriel for an impoverished shepherd girl, Madelon. This young maiden had followed the shepherds to the manger in Bethlehem. As she stood weeping God pitied her and sent the angel Gabriel to comfort her.

"Why do you weep?" he asked.

"Because I have nothing to give to the Babe and His mother."

Hearing these words the angel touched the frozen ground with his staff and there appeared the lovely blossoms of the Christmas rose. Madelon picked these and took them to the infant Jesus.

The legend of the creation of the moss rose tells how unhappy the moss was, envying the fact that "roses grow so high and free, and blow so sweet and red, while I lie low and have neither scent nor flowers." Just then the Saviour entered the glade seeking relief from the heat and dust of the road. So cool and clean was the fresh moss beneath His fevered feet that:

". . . in grateful thanks His heart welled up
   To Him who all bestows.
There sprang from where He stepped, ere yet He passed,
   The first moss rose."

11

Centuries later stories of the origin of other roses were told in America. One of these is of the Cherokee Indians who regard all flowers as conscious, friendly beings whose beauty is a reflection of love and whose petals bring healing. The white blossoms known as the Cherokee rose had for them an additional message. It tells the Indians to remain together under the pine fringes of the forest and that no white man can inflict on them a sorrow that cannot be borne with patience and dignity.

These velvety white flowers that riot over brush and mountains have their romantic side too. Often called white sweetbrier roses, they are the only flowers that the young braves gather for their brides to garland their raven hair. The maiden who wears these flowers will live happily and securely with her chosen love.

Despite this happy promise, the birth of the Cherokee rose itself was anything but joyous. This legend tells of Tsuwenahi, a brave and handsome warrior who returning from an extended hunting trip found his settlement destroyed and his sweetheart Dowansa missing. His frantic search for her was ended by the Nunnshi, the little people, telling him that to save her they had turned Dowansa into a white rose with golden breasts. The following spring, the little people found the maiden blooming in purity, but she begged them to give her thorns to protect herself against those thoughtless people, including Tsuwenahi, who carelessly trampled on her flowers. In answer to her plea the little people covered every stem and branch with multitudinous prickles so sharp that even animals do not dare to eat them.

Another American story is of the Grant or blood rose and is comparatively recent as rose legends go. During the Seminole uprising in 1835–1836, John Grant lived with his youthful wife and young child in the western part of Jefferson County, Florida. One day, leaving them at home, he started for the village to buy supplies. En route he was killed by the Indians who then turned back to ambush his wife. Barricading herself indoors, Mrs. Grant fought off the attackers as long as she could, and then escaped through the cellar into the nearby woods. Hampered by the baby in her arms, Mrs. Grant was soon overtaken by the fleet-footed Seminoles. On the spot where she and her child were massacred, tradition places the first Grant rose. The flowers have incurving petals of blood color. They are among the few evil-smelling roses, their scent being sickly and unpleasant. Old-timers say that when the dew falls on the flowers and then drips off, it is pink-stained as if with blood.

The credit for the creation of two roses on the same occasion goes to the Mohammedans. When their prophet Mohammed went on his epoch-making, overnight flight from Mecca through heaven, he rode on his swift-as-the-wind, supernatural steed Al Borak. Alighting at dawn on the Kubbet es Sakra in ancient Jerusalem, both he and his horse were sweating profusely from their Herculean effort. From the perspiration falling to earth from the sacred forehead of the Prophet sprang white roses, while from the magic sweat of the panting Al Borak came yellow ones. This tale of Mohammed and Al Borak is indeed unique, for it is the only one accounting for yellow roses, although this color has been used for the highest symbolism of Western culture.

There are innumerable romantic versions as to how the color of the rose came to be red. According to one, the nightingale was a conceited bird who sang so sweetly in the great garden of the world that all the flowers were in love with him. They wore their gaudiest colors and exhaled their choicest perfumes to attract his attention. But the proud nightingale cared for none of them. He felt rather that his songs were wasted on these common things of the fields and gardens. The more he thought of it, the more positive he became that any flower worthy of his beautiful music must have in it some of his own aristocratic blood. So one evening he pricked his chest with his bill, and the first drop that fell to earth became a rosebush covered with radiant red roses.

Another more generally favored version exhibits the nightingale in a more sympathetic light. All roses were white until the nightingale was so overwhelmed by their charm that, in an ecstasy of love, he pressed a rose to his breast so that the sharp thorns pierced him and the blood flowing down dyed the white blossom of the rose, red—"the roses' color and the heart's own dye."

> "And rose, of thee this kindness I implore:
> As thy thanksgiving that thou art so fair,
> Upon the nightingale some pity take,
> And grant his prayer."

The quickest change of all from white to red was described by those tale-tellers who recount that roses were born of the tears shed by the broken-hearted Venus as she wept over the slain Adonis. Like her tears they were pearly white; but as she turned away:

> "Her naked foot a rude thorn tore,
> From sting of briar it bled,
> And where the blood ran evermore
> It dyed the roses red."

A less sanguinary Grecian tale claims that roses were responsible for their own incarnadining. Robert Herrick's lines

> "Roses at first were white,
> Till they co'd not agree

13

                    Whether my Sappho's breast
                    Or they more white sho'd be"

are based on this legend. The roses were disputing among themselves as
to which was the most beautiful. The more audacious claimed that the
title should be theirs because not even Sappho's breast was purer in color.
Such boasting made the more retiring blush for their daring sisters' egoism,
and since then there have always been some blushing roses.

As with the origin of roses so with their color, the classical myths assigned the honor not only to different gods but sometimes the same incident to either of two gods. Thus it is either Cupid or Bacchus who spilled
wine on roses and made them red. Each tale is kept in character, Bacchus
being in his cups when he accidentally spilled the wine that reddened the
petals; but Cupid, dancing blithely in a garden, mischievously dashed a
goblet of wine over the blossoms and they became a ruby red, a scene
poetically described by Herrick:

                    "As Cupid danced among
                    The gods, he down the nectar flung,
                    Which on the white rose being shed,
                    Made it, forever after, red."

Another legend has the rose borrowing its hue from the complexion
of a woman. This is one of the shortest, simplest, and most charming tales
of the incarnadining of the rose. Eve was so taken with the beauty of the
roses growing in the Garden of Eden that she kissed one,

                    "When blush the most beautiful its petals stains,
                    And ever after, red the rose remains."

The German rose legends as well as the German rose proverbs are almost countless. In ancient times, the flower was dedicated to Freyja, the
northern Venus, but with the advent of Christianity it became the *Marienroschen* of the Virgin Mary. The white rose in particular is her emblem.
A pretty story is told of how the Virgin laid her veil on a rosebush to dry.
So pervasive was her purity that the roses beneath the veil turned white;
and thereafter that bush and its descendants bore none but white blossoms.

The creation of the thorns characteristic of the flower has been an act
in itself. According to the ancient Hebrew *Book of the Bee* the rose had
no thorns before the fall of man. Basil, one of the early Christian fathers,
pictures their acquisition as a gradual process of more and more thorns
as men became more and more corrupt, until even the memory was almost
lost of that state of innocence when in the Garden of Eden there were, as

imagined by Milton in his *Paradise Lost,* "Flowers of all hue, and without thorn the rose."

Another traditional association of rose thorns with evil is the legend narrated by Lizzie Deas in her *Flower Favorites, Their Legends, Symbolism, and Significance,* published in 1898. In the Schleswig area of north-western Germany is the belief that when Satan fell from grace, he spent much thought on devising a method for regaining entrance into heaven, not by self-reform, but by subterfuge. He finally conceived the idea that the thorns of the briar rose could be used as a ladder by which he might climb up into the celestial regions. But God caught him trying and put a stop to any further upward growth of the rose briar by making it grow sideways instead. Satan, furious at being thus thwarted, wrenched the briars so that they pointed downward, even as they do today.

The Greeks, however, blamed an angered god for the stinging prickles of their favorite flower. Cupid, they said, had flown down to a rose garden on earth and jauntily alighted on a particularly attractive blossom, intending to kiss it. A bee, seeking honeyed nectar in its glowing heart, was irritated by this interruption and stung the intruding god on the lip. Indignant at this rude treatment, Cupid hastened back to Olympus asking his mother to punish the flower. To please the petulant boy, Venus gave him a quiver of arrows tipped with angry bees. He shot them gleefully into the rose garden, and to this day the stings of Cupid's darts may be seen as thorns on the roses.

These legends which deal with the creation of the rose, its colors, varieties, and the addition of thorns are only a few of the many accounts which have appeared in almost every country and century. The fact that they contain so little truth does not detract from their value or interest but rather increases it, as their number proves how great and constant was man's desire to explain what he believed to be one of earth's greatest miracles. Surely he must have felt deeply that this flower possessed a quality greater than those which appealed to the senses, something of a mystic nature which could only be accounted for by the invention of these and other rose legends.

II

ROMANCE

Whatsoe'er of beauty
Yearns and yet reposes,
Blush, and bosom, and sweet breath,
Took a shape in roses.

                               LEIGH HUNT

By REARRANGING the letters of the word *rose* according to the rules of the cabala we get Eros, the god of love. This seems significant in that the rose has always been called the flower of romance, the choice of lovers in every century.

Commencing with the legends of the early Hindus and Greeks, the rose and her human companion, woman, have been inseparable. This close association is interestingly accounted for by the fact that no other flower furnishes the same possibilities of comparison. The lily, which ranks second to the rose in popularity, can only be compared to a limited number of women, while another popular flower, the violet, is used solely to describe the color of eyes. Other flowers figure to a still lesser degree. The rose, however, offers ample scope for the poet's imagination. Take for instance Arthur O'Shaughnessy's lines which could be written of any fair lady:

> "Along the garden ways just now
> I heard the flowers speak;
> The white rose told me of your brow,
> The red rose of your cheek."

Aside from such romantic comparison, the style of which reached a height of popularity in the nineteenth century, there are other equally romantic uses of the flower. Hundreds of years ago there was a charm made with rose water that the Persian women claimed would bring back an erring husband. Another quite different example is the symbolic Order of the Rose which evolved in the heyday of English knighthood. Again, in the

Victorian era, the flower appeared in the tussie-mussie, an ornamental bouquet which a shy lover used to convey the message of love he dared not speak. These and other traditions parallel Webster's definition of the word *romance*: tales of love and adventure, the unusual, the picturesque, and the fanciful.

Research into the earliest uses of the rose takes us back to ancient Egypt and to the magician Myrithis, renowned for her practice of white magic. When her tomb was opened, it was found to contain a mass of dry rose petals, withered blooms and buds, wreaths, and garlands. The Egyptian concept of the afterworld was a practical one—hence these tools of Myrithis' trade were placed with her, in case she might find need of them! Myrithis' ceremonial robe was also found in her tomb. This silken mantle, woven in one piece, was bright pink embroidered with five-petaled roses. When discovered, it was still unfaded and in good condition.

It should be noted that the rose was never associated with black magic, or witchcraft, yet there was never a love philter designed to enchant a reluctant maiden or rekindle a husband's flame that did not contain rose water or rose oil, or some part of this sacred flower of Venus, the goddess of love.

The early Egyptians were not too familiar with the rose until the dynasty of the Ptolemys. Then from 300 B.C. evidences of the flower become more and more frequent. The Pharaohs had their palace rose gardens, and in the tombs of that period and later, the symbolic flower was often placed with the body, as in the case of Myrithis. By the era of Cleopatra, it would seem that roses had practically replaced the Oriental lotus as a ceremonial flower in that country.

Cleopatra contributed much to the popularization of the rose—in high circles, at least. The flower had become a fad and an obsession, and the lavish use of roses at court required the cultivation of enormous gardens. In this way the Egyptians became the rose-supplying nation of the Mediterranean and shipped roses as far as Rome, although no one has yet discovered the secret of how the flowers were kept fresh during that long voyage.

When Cleopatra received Mark Antony, she spared no expense in entertaining him royally. On one occasion, we read of the banqueting hall in which were placed twelve couches, each of which would hold three guests. The walls were covered with purple tapestry interwoven with gold. All the vases were gold, admirably executed, and ornamented with precious stones. On the floor of the hall, and covered by a very fine net, were strewn rose petals to a depth of eighteen inches, perhaps as an added demonstration of her wealth and certainly of her depraved sensuality.

After the loss of the battle of Actium, Antony, not wishing to survive his defeat and fall into the hands of Augustus, killed himself, requesting that Cleopatra scatter perfume on his tomb and cover it with roses.

Other noted figures indulging in romantic rose dissipations have been recorded in history. Verres, the greatest extortioner of his time, and whose name is remembered for the cruelties committed during his three years as governor of Sicily, was reproached by Cicero for his effeminacy and licentiousness: "When spring commenced, that reason was not announced to him by the return of Zephyr, nor by the appearance of any heavenly sign; it was not until he had seen the roses bloom that spring was visible to his voluptuous eye." In the voyages, which he made across the province, he was accustomed, after the example of the kings of Bithynia, to be carried in a litter borne by eight men, in which he reposed upon soft cushions of transparent material filled with the roses of Malta, having in his hand a net of the finest linen equally full of these flowers "whose fragrance incessantly gratified his eager nostrils."

Heliogabalus, celebrated for his indulgence in luxury and vice of every kind, had roses crushed with the kernels of the pine in order to increase their perfume. He also caused roses to be scattered over the couches, the halls, and even the porticos of the palace. Alma Tadema painted a picture of Heliogabalus overwhelming his guests with an avalanche of roses showered from a balcony above them.

When Nero honored the house of a Roman noble with his imperial presence at dinner, the host put himself to the enormous expense of filling his fountains with rose water. In addition, roses and rose leaves were scattered on the ground, and on the cushions upon which the guests lay. As if this were not enough, garlands of roses were placed on their brows and in wreaths around their necks. The *couleur de rose* pervaded the dinner itself, and a rose pudding challenged the appetites of the participants. To further encourage the digestion—or indigestion—rose wine was served.

After wearing, eating, and sleeping on roses, it is not to be wondered at that an occasional unhappy, and by this time quite unromantic, ancient grew sick. Nevertheless, whatever ailed him, the rose was made in some fashion or other to enter into the remedy for his recovery—usually in the form of a draught. If the patient died, as in time he naturally would, it might be truly said he ". . . died of a rose in aromatic pain."

Although this ridiculously lavish use of the rose was never repeated in history on quite such a scale, lesser examples have appeared in different countries in each succeeding century. Bishop Heber narrates that in India he was shown the ruins of the palace of Ghazipur and the deep trench which had been built around an octagonal platform of blue, red, and white mosaic pavement. This trench, he was told, was filled with rose water when the nawab and his friends were feasting there.

Also figuring in our story is the Taj Mahal, supreme achievement of Mohammedan art, built at Agra in 1632 by Shah Jehan for his favorite

Above: Illustration from "The Romance of the Rose," a thirteenth-century French allegory of the art of love. Three thousand copies of this manuscript were made in longhand writing, making it the original best seller. Right: Cleopatra, as painted by Henry Peters Gray (1819-1877). The Egyptian queen entertained Anthony in her palace, the floors on one occasion being covered with rose petals to a depth of eighteen inches. Below: The Taj Mahal, showing the pool upon which rose petals were strewn at night and skimmed off before Mumtaz Mahal bathed.

Nijinsky in his most famous role, "Spectre de la Rose," first performed with the Diaghilev ballet in Paris.

Rose, "First Love"

(Armstrong Nurseries

wife. The large pool in front of this magnificent edifice, reflecting the marble dome and minarets, was covered at night with rose petals. In the morning these were skimmed off before Mumtaz Mahal bathed.

In the original love story of Tristan and Iseult, the potion entrusted to Brangoene by Iseult's mother and to be given to Mark and Iseult on their wedding night, "a love potion of such power and magic that did any two drink thereof they must needs without will of their own, love each other above all things from that day forward," is thought to have contained essence of roses. An artist carried out this thought in the scene of Tristan and Iseult at the fountain, on the walls of the Castle Rhäzuns. Tristan stands at the left and Iseult at the right, attended by Brangoene who holds a garland of roses.

When King Mark discovered the secret of the fatal potion, he bore the dead lovers back with him to Tintagel and laid them in marble tombs on either side of the chapel wherein the kings of his line lay buried. By the tomb of Tristan he bade his followers plant a rose tree, and by that of Iseult a vine, and the two reached toward each other across the chapel and wove branches and root so closely together that no man thereafter might separate them.

Several Flemish tapestries portray the romantic "Ceremony of the Rose." The background of these tapestries is striped with the colors of King Charles II, alternating red, white, and green. His emblem, the rose, is harmoniously worked into the pattern. The figures of the courtiers suggest homage being paid to the king with roses, tokens of their tribute, presented at an annual parliamentary ceremony.

The Empress Josephine of France also contributes a colorful page to our history. In addition to her interest in the rose garden at Malmaison and in the rose poets and painters of her reign, she made unique personal use of the flower. Whenever possible, she carried a rose in her hand. She did this not only for the enjoyment of its beauty and fragrance, but for another very practical reason. Although her eyes were wonderful and her smile engaging, her teeth were notoriously poor and she cleverly used the flower as camouflage.

There is an entertaining story involving the Archduchess Marie. When, after replacing Empress Josephine in the favors of Napoleon, she set forth to Paris to marry the emperor, her last overnight stop was at Provins. Here the enthusiastic population plied the poor girl with so many rose sweets that she was sick all night. Marie was perhaps one bride who didn't choose to carry a bouquet of roses.

Few romantic rose stories come to us from Scotland, but the poet Robert Burns, like his English contemporaries, did make constant references to the flower—first by way of comparison in the immortal lines:

> "O my luve's like a red, red rose
> That's newly sprung in June:"

from "A Red, Red Rose," and then as the subject of poems such as "A Rose-Bud in My Early Walk," and "Yon Rosy Brier."

In England, the Order of the Rose originated sometime during the famous age of chivalry, and the leaves or petals of the rose embroidered on the sleeves of knights were highly symbolic. Three, for instance, represented not only the Holy Trinity but also the whole of life, the beginning, middle, and end. With a rose of crimson splendor in full evidence, knights went forth to "deeds of derring-do." The emblem of the rose came to stand for gentleness allied with courage and the promise of beauty's reward for valor.

"A Military Triumph at Brussels, Anno 1549," recorded in Holme's *The Academy of Armory* gives us a vivid picture of the romance and perils of early knighthood. "First there was a faind fortresse, with trenches, Baracadoes, and other furniture of defense erected; on the roofe whereof a sword of gold was set, adorned with precious stones, this castle was Invironed with water, like to an Iland; and Impossible it was to mount the walls, but by stairs exceeding steep." Upon the water, a ship of gold rode at anchor, with "sailes of silk and gold, with all other things, nothing being wanted to make Lustraous and beautifull."

On the first gate a roaring lion was painted, representing the gate of terror. Nearby was a turret which no man could approach without passing along a perilous passage kept by the Knight of the Red Griffin, a second passage kept by the Knight of the Black Eagle, and a third, next to the "Iland," kept by the Knight of the Golden Lion.

The owner of this "dismall castle" was the Enchanter Noraboc who, through the art of magic, had taken many noble personages and worthy knights unawares and now held them captive behind walls of darkness. A petition was presented to the emperor against Noraboc, "and for as much as it hath bine prophesied that the destruction of this castle is destined to the most virtuous and fortunate Prince living under the Sun . . . the excellent Prince of Spaine . . . they humbly desire that he with his knights may attempt the enterprise."

The petition being granted, the story then tells of attempts to overthrow the black knights stationed within the castle. On the first day, the Knight of Many Colors, the Knight of the Horne, the Knight of the White Moyle "which though they did all well behave themselves," lost to the evil forces of Noraboc. On the second day, the Feathered Knight became prisoner with several "Flemings, Spaniards and Knights of Hungaria." Yet again on the third day, the Knight of the Red Shield, the Golden Knight, the Knight of the Sun, the Knight of the Moon, the Knight of Death, and the stalwart *Knight of the Rose* failed to break Noraboc's spell.

Then came the appointed Prince of Spain with his Knights. "Their attire was scarlet cloth of gold and garded about with lace of gold: the caparisons of their horses were the same. All their saddles, petrels, croopers, and girths were of scarlett silke mixed with golde, so was their scaberds, and all the feathers in their crests were white and scarlett."

After furious combat, the Prince of Spain "gained the place where the fatall sword was: whereof having layd hold, he flourished over his head and forthwith mighty clouds of darkness vanished: soe as every man might see all places of the castle." The spell thus broken, the Prince touched the walls with the enchanted sword whereupon "Immediatly they fell down."

Noraboc, with a Turkish cap on his head, came forth and "Kneeling downe on his knees desired the Prince's pardon, and therewith set at liberty all the Knights he held in prison."

Flourishing from the twelfth to the fourteenth century, were the romantic troubadours. Undoubtedly connected with some mystical religion, while externally posing as wandering poets and composers of ballads of a highly cultivated type, they chose the rose as an emblem of Christ and universal love. Originally in southern France, northern Spain, and Italy, the troubadours counted such notable figures as Giulhelm IX, Count of Poitiers, and Richard I of England as among their aristocracy.

Besides its varied appearance on land, the rose was not forgotten at sea. In the early days of sailing vessels, many sailors, on long or tedious voyages, brought its romantic image to life with cord. This design they called the Rose Knot and it is the predominating motif in much of their ornamental rope work. In spite of more intricate designs and ornaments such as the Turk's Head, Star, or the amusingly named Whale's Eye or Monkey's Fist, it is the Rose Knot which blossoms eternally on their elaborate picture frames of knotted cord. An example of this historic art is shown in chapter IX, page 140.

Elizabeth I of England, like her immediate predecessors, made considerable use of this flower. Her *white* rose was embroidered on the banner that flew wherever the queen slept. Some cynics say that the intention was that it should represent her somewhat dubious virginity. Whatever the interpretation in this case, the royal standard was and still is hoisted wherever a reigning sovereign resides, be it only for a night. After Elizabeth's death the rose, which, following the Wars of the Roses had become an emblem of the House of Tudor, was carved upon the lid of her coffin, immortalizing the queen, last of this sovereign clan.

Many of the Elizabethan poets wrote of the rose. Shakespeare, in particular, brought the romantic flower to life in almost every play. In *Hamlet*, for instance, we find:

> "Such an act . . . takes off the rose
> From the fair forehead of an innocent love
> And sets a blister there."

Love's Labor's Lost contains:

> "Fair ladies masked are roses in their bud."

And *Romeo and Juliet* speaks of

> "This bud of love, by summer's ripening breath."

Among his sonnets it would be hard to find more beautiful lines than those of "Sonnet LIV":

> "O how much more doth beauty beauteous seem
> By that sweet ornament which truth doth give!
> The rose looks fair, but fairer we it deem
> For that sweet odour, which doth in it live.
> The canker-blooms have full as deep a dye
> As the perfumed tincture of the roses,
> Hang on such thorns, and play as wantonly
> When summer's breath their masked buds discloses:
> But—for their virtue only is their show—
> They live unwoo'd and unrespected fade,
> Die to themselves. Sweet roses do not so;
> Of their sweet deaths are sweetest odours made.
>   And so of you, beauteous and lovely youth,
>   When that shall fade, my verse distils your truth."

In the same century, Ben Jonson wrote "To Celia":

> "I sent thee late a rosy wreath,
>   Not so much honoring thee
> As giving it a hope that there
>   It could not wither'd be;
> But thou thereon didst only breathe,
>   And sent'st it back to me;
> Since when it grows, and smells, I swear,
>   Not of itself but thee!"

Early reference to the rose was made on our own shores. In the Capitol at Washington is Wier's picture of the Embarkation of the Pilgrims which shows the beautiful face of Rose Standish, wife of Captain Miles Standish. The following lines have been written of her:

> "Til in this late-found world, the pilgrim's home,
>   It fixed its root, our lovely Plymouth Rose.

> "Death found it there, and cut the slender stem;
>   It fell to earth; yet still it lives, it glows;
> For Christ has set it in his diadem,
>   And changed to fadeless Amaranth our Rose."

William Penn brought back eighteen roses from London, recording the event in his diary. He also wrote a *Book of Physic*, preserved by the Pennsylvania Historical Society, for the medical care of the settlers in Penn's Woods, in which he gives many recipes and formulas that use the rose in one way or another. If the following ailment and remedy is not exactly romantic, Penn's language is: "To comfort ye brains, and for ye palsie, and for ye giddiness of the head. Take a handful of rose flowers, cloves, mace, nutmeg, all in a powder, quilt in a little bag and sprinkle with rose water, mixed with malmsey wine, and lay it in ye nod of ye neck."

A touching little story revolves around General Sherman. When stationed at Monterey, Sherman fell in love with a Spanish girl of noble birth. His love was reciprocated and when he was ordered away, the Spanish maiden gave him a rose. He returned it, asking her to plant it. And she replied, "If you love me, it will grow." There is, we are told, a charming picture of the Spanish lady in her old age, standing under the General Sherman rosebush, true to her romance. The rose had grown, but the general had not returned.

Romantic themes in connection with the rose have filled countless books. In France, during the first half of the thirteenth century, a poet, Guillaume de Lorris, wrote the first part of *Roman de la Rose*. This long poem, almost 23,000 classic lines, presents an elaborate allegory of the Art of Love. Believe it or not, three thousand copies were made in longhand of this original best seller. (See page 19.)

The young man in the poem, allegorized as a Dreamer, enters a garden of roses on a May morning. The garden is ruled over by the God of Love, and for those who wish to become faithful vassals, there are definite regulations to be observed. The subject must avoid discourtesy, dress neatly, and keep his love secret. If he observes these rules faithfully, he will be admitted to the heaven of his lady's consent. The style of the narrative is somewhat similar to Bunyan's *Pilgrim's Progress*, and might well have been called "Lover's Progress."

The second part of the Romance was written in the latter half of the thirteenth century by Jean de Meun and represents the same characters, but in an altogether different light. This author is interested in life as a whole, not purely the subject of love, but he generally directs his satire against women. His barbed pen comes close at times to the spirit of the urban and unsaintly Roman, Ovid, who wrote the *Art of Love*.

Jean de Meun, obviously had fun with:

> "To win the Rosebud make it seem
> That love Platonic is your dream."

An English version of this poem is attributed to Chaucer. Although the first seventeen hundred lines may be original, the remainder is considered by some authorities to be a mere translation. However, *The Romance of the Rose* did have a decided effect on Chaucer's writing, producing in him the queer combination of a realist under the spell of the ever increasing rose cult. A setting for the fragrant flower is described in these Chaucerian lines:

> "I saugh a Gardin right anoon
> Ful long and brood and everydel
> Enclose it was and walled wel
> With hye walles embatailled."

Then, despite further quaint phraseology and spelling, he brings the Rose to life:

> "The savour of the Roses swete
> Me smote right to the herte rote."

26

Perhaps the most famous rose book in music form is Strauss's romantic opera *Der Rosenkavalier*, often called *The Cavalier of the Rose* or *The Rose Bearer*. For those who may not be familiar with the story, its setting is Vienna in the reign of Maria Theresa where, according to custom, the bridegroom must send his bride a silver rose before the ceremony. Octavian, scion of a distinguished Viennese family, already infatuated with the bride, Sophie, is, as chance would have it, chosen by the bridegroom as Rose Bearer.

Octavian is truly a dazzling figure, dressed in white and silver, and this meeting sets off a chain of new and very positive reactions. Each is deeply struck by the beauty of the other and to each comes the same thought, "Never have I lived 'til today. And may this heavenly vision last to all eternity!" Ecstasy attains its musical culmination when Sophie inhales the fragrance of the Silver Rose upon which drops of Persian attar have been temptingly sprinkled.

"A rose of paradise, not of earth, it is," she sings. "It is like a greeting from heaven; the perfume seems to tug at my heart." Throughout the score is the refrain of the Silver Rose motif.

Another famous literary and musical creation is *Le Spectre de la Rose*. This theme was suggested during the Diaghilev Company's first visit to Paris. It is an adaptation of Gautier's little poem, the evocation of the spirit of a rose given to a young girl at a ball.

> "I am the specter of the rose
> You wore last night at the ball."

The ballet was set to Weber's well-known piece, "L'Invitation à la Valse," and was first produced at the Theatre de Monte Carlo in 1911. Nijinsky danced in the original production, to the wild acclaim of those present. This particular ballet always made a deep impression on the dancer himself. (See page 20.)

When Romola (Nijinsky's future wife) met and fell in love with the dancer, her infatuation was no new phenomenon—such things were a daily occurrence, especially since *Le Spectre de la Rose*. Young girls had even gone so far as to steal rose petals from his ballet costume.

An interesting little story is told about the stage setting for *Le Spectre*. One day when Nijinsky was driving with Diaghilev, they passed the Grande Maison de Blanc, where they saw the furnishings for a young girl's bedroom, white tulle portieres and a bed with a tulle canopy and a delicate rose-bud design.

"This is the very thing we want. This bed, with its hangings and delicate rose-bud design, just echoes the theme."

Immediately Diaghilev went in and bought it and had it sent to the theater. But from the huge auditorium the delicate rose-buds could not be seen and after the first night the furnishings were discarded.

The selection of names for roses is another link in the romantic chain. The Greeks, for example, did not name their roses for mortals but always chose such mythological names as Adonis, Bouquet of Venus, Beautiful Juno, Nymph or Temple of Apollo. This practice may have been due to the fact that the Greeks believed unquestionably that "the Gods created roses."

Centuries later in France during the reign of Napoleon, when a definite recurrence of rose interest and stimulation took place, it was the custom to name roses for court favorites. Heading the list were the Grand Napoleon, followed in rapid succession by a long line of mesdames, marquis, dukes, and duchesses. In England, roses were named for lords and ladies.

Although the chrysanthemum happens to be the Chinese Queen of Flowers, roses, like peonies are almost as popular. Their apt naming of a flower by likening it to some object, circumstance, personal attribute, or other plant is poetic as well as fanciful. *Yu-go-tain-tsing* (After Rain— Clear Shining) is a beautiful, flesh-white, sweet-scented, climbing rose that grows well in Nanking. The Crimson Rambler is an old Chinese rose known as *Shi Tz-mei* (Ten Sisters). From a list of rose names in a Chinese collection of horticultural writings, the following translations have been made:

> Early Dawn, Wind, and Fading Moon
> Tiny Jade Shoulders
> Drunk Green Lotus
> Precious-Scented Ivory
> Green Butterfly
> Seven Precious Petals
> Three Rays of Dawn

The occasional likening of rose varieties to intoxicated persons is just another example of the Chinese genius for apt illustration. The roses referred to are of the flaming pink and red varieties. Some names, however, are very difficult to translate. For example, *Chi Lung Han Chu* means "a fiery red dragon holding a red pearl in its gaping jaws," and one can easily picture an open red rose with a center ball of folded petals.

In the Western world it has become the fashion to name many roses for impersonal qualities or abstractions with, of course, a few well-deserved exceptions. The latter represent a varied assortment of outstanding individuals in all types of fields. The former group contains names like Radiance, which suggests so perfectly its cameo-pink flowers. Enchantment has a delicate, elusive fragrance, whereas Magic Red is heart-warming, and Eternal Youth is the clearest of pinks.

One of the recent All American Winners is the Rubaiyat. A rose lovely enough to bring to mind these lines from Omar Khayyam:

> "And then and then came Spring, and Rose in hand
> My thread-bare Penitence apieces tore."

Certainly one of the most picturesque uses of the rose in all history was the floral tribute Henry VIII paid his first wife and then later, his second wife. In the eighth year of his reign, King Henry kept Christmas in honor of Katherine, the first queen. In the hall of his manor at Greenwich there was set a "garden artificie," called the "Garden of Esperance." Towered at every corner, and railed with gilt, the banks set with flowers of gold and silver with green leaves, this garden centered around a pillar of gold set with precious stones.

But Katherine's "garden artificie" seemed but a poor thing in comparison to King Henry's display at the coronation of Anne Boleyn, his second wife. For her no pageant was too extravagant, no honor too great. Descriptions by eye-witnesses tell of a glory of color and music. There was "a costly and marvelously cunning pageant" on the water. Everywhere was seen the Queen's device. On foists, which were lightly built ships, were "mounts bearing a white faulcon crowned upon a roote of golde environed with white roses and red, which was the Queen's device, about which sat virgins singing and playing melodiously."

No further accounts were given of rose displays for Henry VIII's other wives. However, these gestures for Katherine and Anne Boleyn were perhaps the epitome of rose romance in this or any other period of history.

A *Discourse on the Virtues of the Rose from Champier's "Rosa Gallica"*
(*Jodocus Badius, Paris,* 1514).

III

ART

The Powers whose name and shape no living creature knows
Have pulled the Immortal Rose . . .

                                                W. B. YEATS

FLOWERS, and particularly the rose, have been used by artists through the ages to express their ideals of beauty as well as the highest conceptions of religious feeling in art. Roses especially lend themselves to artistic endeavor not only because of their exquisite beauty but because of their symbolic meaning. Botticelli, who handled symbols with a depth of sentiment unknown to art before his time, made flowers truly significant. In his "Coronation of the Virgin" the air is literally filled with roses falling from heaven, symbols of the love of God.

The greater part of the early representation of the rose in art appeared in sculptured or carved decorations on churches and in paintings of sacred subjects. To explain the branch of Christian symbolism expressed by flowers requires a thorough knowledge of the development of Christian theology and the varying force with which different doctrines appeared in different centuries. However, it is plain to all that the use of flowers in these sacred paintings does show the conventions employed by the masters to illustrate the Divine Mysteries. By their genius, great artists have the power to make the intangible visible, but lesser ones must make their intentions clearer by the use of symbols. In the early thirteenth century, for example, an artist unable to show by the announcing angel's attitude that his message was one of peace and good will, placed in his hand a branch of olive. In time these definite emblems passed into what might be called the heraldry of the church and are popular to this day. These symbols have become the allegorical representations of Christian principles in material form.

One of the most outstanding examples of the use of the rose in sculpture is found in the decorations of the little chapel of Santa Maria della

Rosa in the Italian city of Lucca. Dedicated originally to St. Paul, it had fallen into disuse. Then in the fourteenth century a fresco was discovered beneath the creepers that covered the walls. These designs proved to be extremely ancient. They represented the Virgin with the Child, the former holding three roses in her hand. In 1309 the Bishop of Lucca conceded to the Universita de'Mercanti the power to erect on this spot a church dedicated to the Virgin of the Rose and to the Apostles Peter and Paul. The present exquisite, gemlike little building was begun. The outside, ornamented with lovely arabesques of roses in low relief, was executed in 1333. At one angle is a statue of the Virgin with a rose in her hand. This was possibly done by Giovanni Pisano. In the sacristy are the arms of the confraternity, figuring Mary surrounded by an oval nimbus and supported by two bushes which carry thirteen roses, forming a crown from which rise patriarchs and prophets.

D'Orbessan, in his work on the rose, states that in the Church of St. Luzanne, at Rome, is a mosaic of the time of Charlemagne. The prince is represented in a square mantle. He is on his knees and St. Peter is placing in his hands a standard covered with roses.

A quantity of roses are also represented among the large, almost life-size figures in the Church of St. Catalina in Cadiz. Here the Virgin is represented à la Watteau, with a beribboned crook and a rose-wreathed hat. This unusual painting, which features pink and white, appears extremely gay and dainty in a corner of the austere whitewashed chapel. A similar group, less frivolous in detail, is in the Church of the Holy Trinity at Cordova. This is quite a variation from the usual heavy baroque expression of the Spanish artist.

Sculptured roses cover the northern portal of the Cathedral at Upsala in Sweden. In other churches the imitations of the rose appear in stained-glass windows. Some of these can be found in English and European cathedrals such as Canterbury, Cologne, Milan, Rheims, and St. Denis. These paintings on glass are beautifully soft as seen from the interior of a church. In the rich, glowing light of sunset, the roses thus painted seem to possess all the freshness and beauty of the real flower.

The revelers in the *Book of Wisdom* cried: "Let us crown ourselves with rosebuds." So in the heavenly mansions where life is supposed to be a perpetual feast, unfading roses crown the elect. On canvas, wreaths of roses are the symbol of heavenly joy and are worn alike by angels and human souls who have entered this bliss. In the "Paradise" of Simone Martini (Saint Maria Novella, Florence), St. Peter with his key has opened the gate of heaven and two angels standing by are waiting to crown each soul with roses. More particularly, those souls are crowned who in their earthly life rejoice in their faith even when overwhelmed with troubles. Symbol of holy joy, for example, is the crown of roses which St. Cecilia wears. The legend concerning this patron saint of musicians is recorded in chapter X.

St. Dorothea is beloved in almost all Christian countries. On canvas she is usually painted with both apples and roses, symbols of the good works of the Christian life and of the holy joys even in the hour of death. She is very popular in the Low Countries and in Germany. There is a charming triptych at Palermo, the best picture Sicily possesses, attributed usually to Mabuse. On one wing, St. Dorothea is depicted seated on the ground with her lap full of red and white roses. It is a quaint, compact little figure, not a slender Italian maiden supported by angelic visions. She is the sturdy Flemish type who, having with clear brain calculated the cost, sets herself with stoicism to endure the pain which will be rewarded by the martyr's crown of unfading roses.

In the vision of St. Francis, so often painted by Spanish artists, the falling roses again represent divine love. But in Murillo's painting in the Prado, Madrid, the *putti* are energetically pelting the saint with blossoms.

An entire book could be written about the illustrations of saints and roses. Many of these flowers appear in simple form, held in the hand or in a basket, in the tunic or lap, or as a crown. The more unusual uses are St. Vincent dying on a bed of roses; St. Angelus with roses and lilies issuing from his mouth; and St. Francis with roses springing from his blood.

It has been said reproachfully of northern artists that many of them preferred gold, jewels, and rich embroideries for their Virgins rather than the more ephemeral loveliness of flowers. But this may have been in the nature of a tribute, just as the Wise Men brought rich treasures, not flowers, to the Infant Jesus. It may have been that these artists felt that as the Mother, the greatest of whose seven sorrows had not yet come, she should not carry the rose crown which symbolized joy, even though it were heavenly joy. These various conjectures must remain forever unanswered but we do know that in time religious sentiment demanded representation of Christ's Mother as risen to glory with all sorrow past, the Church eventually deciding to depict her as the woman clothed with the sun, a crown of twelve stars upon her head. Even in this conception, she is sometimes surrounded with roses.

The following are descriptions of some of the many paintings where the rose appears with the Virgin. A classic example is the "Queen of Heaven," one of twelve panels of the great altar piece painted by Hubert and Jan van Eyck and erected in the Church of St. Bavon in Ghent in May 1432. In this painting, the flower symbolism is very notable in the crown of the Madonna. The roses, three in number, denote the divine love of the Holy Trinity. Since these are placed singly, though in a crown, they hold also some measure of heavenly joy. In those pictures of the early

Florentine school in which she holds a small red or white rose, she is known as the "Madonna del Fiore." And so, as "Our Lady of the Flower," she has been named patroness of the city of Florence.

The roses of paradise must not be confused with the rose hedge or trellis so often placed behind the Virgin by the early German schools. These hedges indicate the *Hortus Conclusus* and identify the Virgin with the bride of the Canticles by recalling the verse, "A garden enclosed is my sister, my spouse." Very often there is merely a trellis covered with roses, and the thorns are carefully drawn, illustrating the verse, "As a lily among thorns, so is my love among the daughters." But in spite of the thorns, the general significance of these roses is joy and delight.

At the beginning of the eighteenth century there was an odd fancy to represent the Virgin as *La Divina Pastora* feeding her sheep with roses. The original picture (Prado, Madrid) was by Alfonso da Tobar. In the nineteenth century, Dante Gabriel Rossetti in "Girlhood of Mary the Virgin" used the flower symbols. One of the details of this picture is a rose in a transparent vase on the balustrade, which is interpreted to be the rose of divine love cojoined with the symbol of transcendent purity.

An equal number of sacred paintings give the Christ Child His share of roses, too. At the Palazzo Pitti there is a canvas that depicts angels playfully sprinkling rose petals over the Infant Christ in a rose-trellised garden. "Adoration" by Botticelli shows the Holy Child lying on a bed of flowers with a background of quantities of freely growing roses, drawn apparently from memory. These roses signify the divine love that impelled the Saviour of the World to be born as a human child. Another painting of the Christ Child in Cadiz has the background filled with blood-red roses, symbol of the Passion which is to come. In the "Adoration" of Neri di Bicci in Florence, the Holy Child lies surrounded by lilies and red and pale roses.

In Spain, where the Christian faith was stern, faith and suffering were more closely allied than faith and joy. In a picture by Francisco de Zurburan in the Museo Provincial in Seville, their Christ is not smiling, but is rather a sad-faced Child who wounds Himself with the rose twigs which He twists into a crown. The rose thorn tears His flesh but the roses lie beside Him and around His feet.

In the later life of Christ, the rose is also used as a symbol. The crown of thorns with which jesting soldiers crowned Him was in itself an emblem, or at least a parody of an emperor's festal rose crown. In northern art the crown of thorns remains always unchanged, a symbol of Christ's suffering. But in at least one Italian Pieta, the dry prickles around the dead Christ's brow have bloomed with delicate white briar roses, an exquisite figure of love's triumph over pain.

This perfect flower was a natural accompaniment for angels and their paradise. In Signorelli's "Paradies" the angels not only carry roses in their looped draperies, but scatter them down upon the redeemed souls beneath. Also, in the celestial meadow of Hubert van Eyck's "Adoration of the Lamb," Ghent Cathedral, we find bushes covered with roses. There are roses, too, on trellises, and roses woven into swinging garlands in that most alluring of all painted paradises set forth by Benozzo Gozzoli upon the walls of the Palazzo Riccardi, Florence. In Ruskin's description of the picture, "roses and pomegranates, their leaves drawn to the last rib and vein, twine themselves in fair and perfect order about delicate trellises." It is a "Painted Paradise" after the heart of a Medici, in which no monotony, no boredom need be apprehended, for the place is filled with gay and witty folk and the most heavenly angels imaginable.

The sacred symbolic use of the rose engendered many designs on other objects. In the Louvre there is on display a Persian dish from Rhages, thirteenth century, and an ivory plaque with a rosebush between two erect figures of warriors. A silk carpet of the sixteenth century depicts a rose garden with various animals in the enclosure. In Persian art roses are so conventionalized that they often resemble zinnias.

In the Palace of Delhi in India, the fountain pipes were carved with images of roses. The flower is also sculptured in the center of each face of a Corinthian capital. A similar design is frequently seen in iron banisters and has been chiseled on the pavement in front of certain Old World mansions.

Rose emblems have been carved on countless coffins. Two noteworthy examples are Queen Elizabeth's, already mentioned, and Victor Hugo's. In cemeteries the flower is not only carved on tombstones but appears in the iron grill work of fences and gates. Pleasing evidence of this in America can be seen in the Edgartown Cemetery on Martha's Vineyard, Massachusetts. The composition of these early individual fences or gates is made up of at least three elements chosen by the buyer to represent his own taste and symbolism. This particular one contains a combination of the rose vines, willow, and lambs.

Rose designs often as lovely as any painted on canvas were also used on china. Appropriately named, Thomas Rose did many of these designs on Lowestoft china. The flower also appears on many of the finest of William Cookworthy's Plymouth and Bristol porcelain. Wedgwood and Spode found it among their most popular motifs, and there are countless examples of its decorative use, particularly in the golden age of porcelain. Eighteenth century figurines from the manufactures of Meissen, Nymphenburg, Capo di Monte, Chelsea, Derby, Worcester, and others featured it as the most sought after ornament of the century. The Chinese used the flower too, though in second place to the peony and spring blossoms. However, they are responsible for the famous Rose Medallion, thought to be over one thousand years old.

Although Baron Stiegel did not make much use of the rose design in his American glassmaking, there is one drug or cordial bottle, privately owned, with a varicolored enameled decoration of a rose and bird. The rose is many petaled and the bird resembles the nightingale. Other manufacturers of glass produced Rose in the Snow, Hundred Leafed Rose and the Rosette Pinwheel. Etched designs of the rose on glass have appeared throughout the centuries, and, in contemporary ware, the motif still keeps recurring.

Early bed coverlets also brought the charm and colors of the rose indoors. The patterns for these designs bore the alluring names of Rosy Walk, Rose in Bloom, Pansies and Roses in the Wilderness. For quilting pieces there was the Rose of Sharon, World's Rose, Rosebud, Cherokee Rose, and dozens of others that occupied the attention of our grandmothers and great-grandmothers at their busy quilting bees.

An old lacquered box found in a cupboard of a New England home disclosed a lovely cut-paper design. It was a valentine in exceedingly delicate and appropriate pattern mounted on bright paper. Its form suggested these lines:

> "The dextrous scissors ready to produce
> The flying squirrel or the long neck'd goose,
> Or dancing girls with hands together join'd,
> Or tall spruce trees with wreaths of roses twin'd."

The "spruce trees with wreaths of roses" was especially marvelous. It proved the design a derivative of the English Maypole and encircling wreath. No other flower was reproduced more in valentine art than the rose. The great makers of the nineteenth century like Addenbrooke, Mansell, A. Park, Rimmel, and Mullord, used it ad infinitum with appropriate verses to enchant Victorian lovers.

Illustrations in books have contributed their share, no less than prose and verses, to the immortalization of the rose. A typical volume, featuring Anacreon's verses, contains a charming illustration of five cherubs entwining a lyre with roses. Lines like these could not help but inspire the depiction of our favorite flower:

> "The Gods beheld this brilliant birth
> And hail'd the Rose—the boon of earth!
> With nectar drops, a ruby tide
> The sweetly orient buds they dyed
> And bade them bloom, the flowers divine."

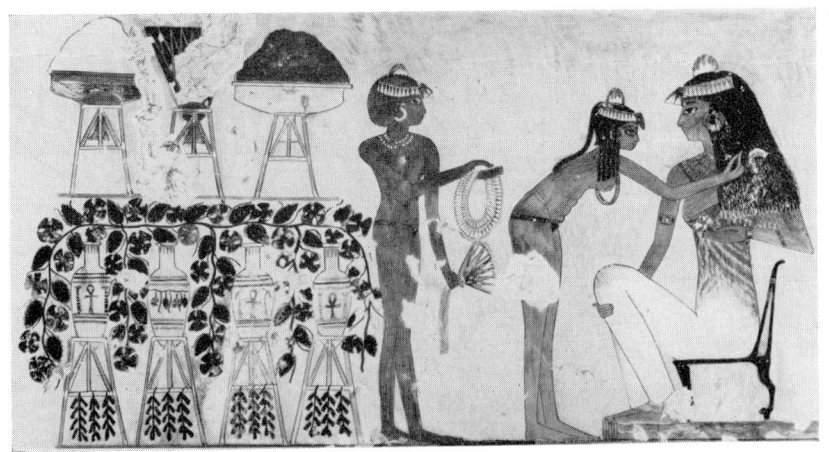

Above: One of the earliest examples of the rose in art, found on the tomb of Tuthmosis IV (1420-1411 B.C.) in Egypt. Below: "Courtiers of the Rose." Franco-Flemish fifteenth-century tapestry.

(Metropolitan Museum of Art)

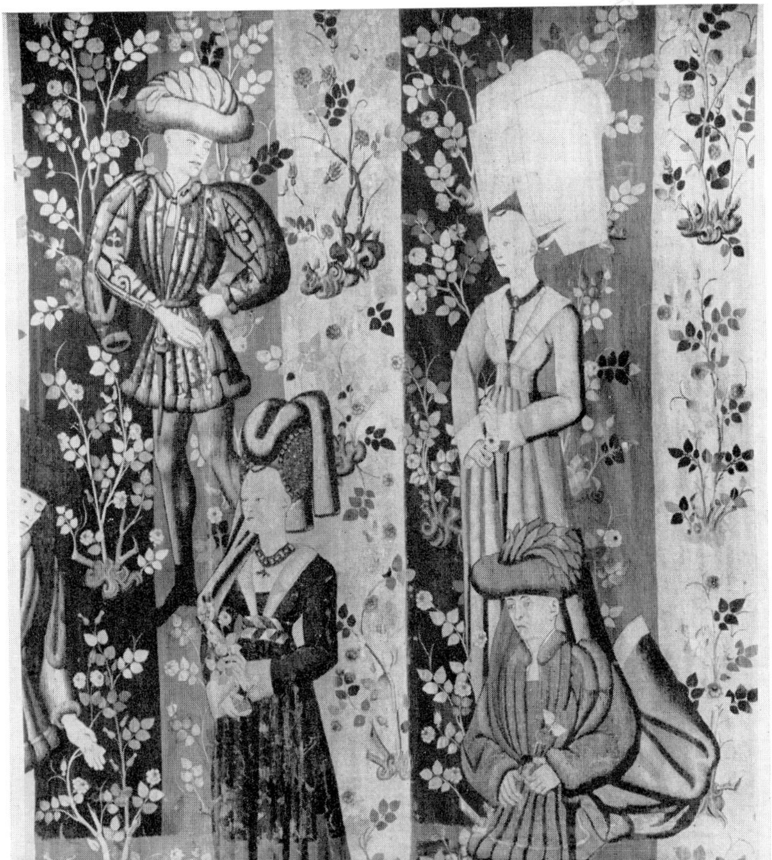

A beautiful seventeenth-century German chest in gilded iron, with rose designs. Below: Centifolia rose, often referred to as the "rose des peintres" and reproduced in many master paintings, especially the seventeenth- and eighteenth-century Dutch flower pieces.

"Madonna and Child in the Rose Garden" by Stefano da Zevio, the Italian painter who lived in Verona during the first half of the fifteenth century.

"Spring" by the French artist François Boucher (1703-1770). This painting with an abundance of roses reflects the great popularity of the flower in eighteenth-century Europe. The rose was the most favored decoration in paintings and murals and on porcelain figures and costumes of the period.

A typical late-eighteenth-century illustration, depicting a moss rose (Rosa muscosa). Published by W. Curtis in London (1788).

The exquisite frontispiece illustration by Mary Lawrance from her book, "A Collection of Roses from Nature," published in 1799, and including ninety of her color plates. A diminutive rose was named after this famous English artist—Rosa Lawranciana (Rosa chinensis minima).

41

Empress Josephine by V. G. Dubray (1813-1891) in the museum at Versailles. Famous, among other things, for her rose garden at Malmaison, also as the patroness of Redouté and other painters and poets, Napoleon's consort is here shown carrying her favorite flower, as was her usual custom.

Provins rose by Pierre Joseph Redouté (1759-1840). One of the greatest flower artists of all time, Redouté produced the monumental work "Les Roses." He was the favorite artist of the Empress Josephine (opposite) and a contemporary of Audubon, whom he met in Paris, and whose work he admired.

43

An attractive composition of roses and Victorian prints by Jean Austin, photographed by F. M. Demarest.

Detail from a muslin flounce with roses embroidered in silk. Made in France about 1770.

Rose Tallyho.

A *charming water color by an unknown nine-teenth-century artist.*

Valentine design featuring the rose, made by Joseph Addenbrooke around 1850. The border is perforated lace. The rose was used more than any other flower in Victorian valentines.

*Handmade needlepoint rug with rose motifs. Be-
low: Modern engraved glass plate "The Rose,"
designed by Don Vier for Steuben Glass.*

Rose design diamond and emerald clip made in Russia around 1790.

Below: Gold pin with white diamond "dew drops," by Maubossin of Paris.

(A La Vielle Russie)

(Fleur Cowles)

Left: The John Cook Medal of the American Rose Society.

A contemporary Scalamandre textile, making use
of the rose design repeated many times in the
background of Botticelli's painting, "Coronation
of the Virgin." A small detail from the Renaissance painting is shown in the insert—the original
is in the Uffizi Gallery, Florence.

(Jones & Irwin)

Above: A detail from Twelve Oaks Rose Vine wallpaper pattern originally used in the film sets of "Gone with the Wind." The motif was taken from a nineteenth-century design.

Right: Montici intarsia, designed by Richard Blow and made in present-day Florence.

Many early hymnals show flowers illuminated in resplendent colors. In the *Sacrum Book of Hours,* by Philippe Pigouchet, published in 1501, the huge rose held by the Virgin definitely proves her title of "Rosa Mystica." Another hymnal contains an illustration of fifty pink roses representing Aves and five red roses representing Paternosters and Glorias from the fifteenth century *Hours of the Virgin.** This manuscript was written and illuminated on vellum in northern France (Bourges) by Jean Colombe, the rosary dating from the founding of the first Confraternity of the Rosary at Cologne in 1475 by a Dominican, Jacob Sprenger.

Woodcuts from the fifteenth century contain similar composition but lack the pleasing brilliancy of the illuminated page. In the library of the Hispanic Society in New York is the volume, *Contemplaciones sobre el Rosario* by Caspar Gorricio de Novaria, friend of Columbus. He belonged to the Carthusian Order at Santa Maria de las Cuevas outside Seville. In the woodcut of the "Legend of the Knight of Cologne," the roses in the border have been printed in red. The knight is kneeling and from his lips issues a chain of roses which the Christ Child, sitting on the knee of the Virgin above the knight, is encircling into a rosary. Another woodcut shows the Virgin standing in the center of a chain of conventionalized roses. In her arms is the Christ Child holding a rose in His left hand.

A manuscript of the *Le Roman de la Rose* is also worth noting. It shows the lover and his rose tree in this semi-religious moralized allegory. The manuscript is on vellum and was illuminated in Paris toward the middle of the fourteenth century. A popular edition of Chaucer's *Romance of the Rose* contains the famous Kelmscott Press border, designed and executed by William Morris, the English designer and romantic figure of the nineteenth century. A copy of this work, printed on vellum, is at the Morgan Library in New York. The rose design has a pleasing rhythm of blossom and leaf, but the background is somewhat confusing. It lacks the simplicity of the rose sculpture, as it was termed, of the engraver who designed the notable rose border for the *New Psalter of the Virgin Mary.* This border was printed in 1492 at the monastery at Zuenna. The border of the first page of the second part of this Psalter is a wood engraving of a splendid scrollwork of rose branches, buds, and blossoms of bold and almost architectural device. It was cut on oblong blocks so it could be used in variously shaped places. This work has more freedom and, in some indefinable way, more character than the later much redoubled rose of the Morris design, although if the background of the latter is removed there is disclosed a startling similarity to the early woodcut.

Various artists in different centuries and countries have used the rose in either natural form or conventionalized design to illustrate canto XXXI in "Paradise Regained" of Dante's *Divine Comedy.* William Blake, late

* See page 150.

eighteenth century English mystic, in particular made such an illustration.*
It is a rough, shadowy sketch of a huge many-petaled rose. Half lost in
its petals, the Bible, Homer, and several female figures are distinguishable.
Three at the top are especially clear, and behind them are various planets.
The picture, while requiring considerably more interpretation, suggests
much of the mysticism of these lines:

> "On this wise then, in form of a white Rose
> Was shown to me the holy armament."

Longfellow, a great student of Dante, draws a similar pen picture of
the rose in "Michael Angelo." Of the Colosseum he writes:

> "Behold
> How wonderful it is! The queen of flowers,
> The marble rose of Rome! Its petals torn
> By wind and rain of thrice five hundred years;
> Its mossy sheath half rent away, and sold
> To ornament our palaces and churches,
> Or to be trodden under feet of man
> Upon the Tiber's bank; yet what remains
> Still opening its fair bosom to the Sun
> And to the constellations that at night
> Hang poised above it like a swarm of bees."

Artists who studied and illustrated the rose as a flower, aside from any
known symbolism, or for merely decorative purposes, are many. Perhaps
the earliest known painting of this type is in a cave—the House of Frescoes,
at Knossos, on the Island of Crete—and dates back to about the sixteenth
century before Christ. These early Cretans were pre-Greek, a small dark
people who worshiped the snake goddess and the Minotaur. In this painting, done with an unfamiliar pigment, the blossoms are conventionalized.
Oddly enough, they have six petals instead of five. They are reddish rose
color with yellow dots in the center to represent the stamens.

Thirty-two or more centuries later, artists in England and France, due
to the great renaissance of the rose at that time, spent years of their lives
on what might be called portraits of the rose. Pierre Joseph Redouté,
Mary Lawrance, and in the United States, Paul de Longpre, are perhaps
the best known rose artists.

Redouté has been spoken of as the "Raphael of Flowers" and in particular, the "Raphael of the Rose." Early in life he became acquainted
with the flower paintings of Jan van Huysum. Later he collaborated with
L'Heritier de Brutell, the botanist, who called him to London in order
to draw the plants he had collected there. On Redouté's return to Paris,
he was made *dessinateur du cabinet* of Marie Antoinette, and in 1805,
flower painter to Empress Josephine. The perfection of engraving in color

* See page 200.

54

WHAN I had smelled
the savour swote,
No wille hadde I, fro
thens yit go,
But somdel neer it
wente I tho,
To take it; but myn
hond, for drede,
Ne dorste I to the
rose bede.
For thistels sharpe, of many maneres,
Netles, thornes, and hoked breres;
Ful muche they distourbled me,
For sore I dradde to harmed be.
The God of Love, with bowe bent, The God
That al day set hadde his talent   of Love
To pursuen and to spyen me,
Was stonding by a fige-tree.
And whan he sawe how that I
Had chosen so ententifly
The botoun, more unto my pay
Than any other that I say,
He took an arowe ful sharply whet,
And in his bowe whan it was set,
He streight up to his ere drough
The stronge bowe, that was so tough,
And shet at me so wonder smerte,
That through myn eye unto myn herte

The takel smoot, and depe it wente.
And therwithal such cold me hente,
That, under clothes warme and softe,
Sith that day I have chevered ofte.
WHAN I was hurt thus in that
stounde,
I fel doun plat unto the grounde.
Myn herte failed and feynted ay,
And long tyme ther as wone I
lay.
But whan I com out of swoning,
And hadde wit, and my feling,
I was al maat, and wende ful wel
Of blood have loren a ful gret del.
But certes, the arowe that in me stood
Of me ne drew no drope of blood,
For why I found my wounde al dreye.
WHAN took I with myn hondis tweye
The arowe, and ful fast out it plight,
And in the pulling sore I sight.
SO at the last the shaft of tree
I drough out, with the fethers three.
But yet the hoked heed, ywis,
The whiche Beautee callid is,   Beautee
Gan so depe in myn herte passe,
That I it mighte nought arace;
But in myn herte stille it stood,
Al bledde I not a drope of blood.

Decoration with the famous Kelmscott border for Chaucer's
"Romance of the Rose."

Woodcut from the book "Contemplaciones" by Gorricio de Novaria, a
friend of Christopher Columbus (1495).

was of vital interest to him, and his classic volume, *Les Roses*, attests to the success of his project.

Mary Lawrance's *A Collection of Roses from Nature* contains ninety color plates in her still celebrated book. The frontispiece of this work is exquisite in detail, representing many varieties and colors of roses twined in a wreath. Sixteen of her color plates plus the frontispiece, making a total of seventeen, are reproduced in Francis E. Lester's *My Friend the Rose*. There is no symbolism in these paintings, no mysticism intended, but the fresh, clear beauty of each blossom brings the same enjoyment today as it did when first painted in England in the eighteenth century.

Paul de Longpre also loved the rose beyond all other flowers. Born in Lyons, France, he came to New York in 1855 after a Paris bank failure. As flower models in New York were expensive, he moved to California. His "Yard of White Roses" started him on a spectacular career, enabling him to build a magnificent Moorish Mission dwelling with gardens that eventually contained four thousand rosebushes. Most of his pictures were either straight rose subjects or roses combined with other flowers. In many of the bouquet type, the artist depicts great, velvet-winged bumble-bees poised airily above his superb roses. By a simple, but skillful treatment of line, highlight, and shadow, he often portrayed a clear drop of dew on a rose petal or leaf. His style is noted for three outstanding qualities: accuracy of drawing, purity, and marvelous handling of water color and flower arrangement.

In his workroom there was a grand piano always covered, except for the keyboard, with partly finished pictures. It has been said that his piano, painted in white or cream oil, was decorated with roses on the sides.

In addition to painting, Monsieur de Longpre composed a number of instrumental compositions. Here again, roses enter into the picture because many of the covers of the compositions were decorated with large, half-tone reproductions of his rose paintings.

The eighteenth century French painters, François Boucher and Jean Honoré Fragonard, should also be mentioned here. Although they were not rose artists in the same sense as Redouté, their realistic and abundant use of the flower in their paintings places them in a special category. Boucher, favorite of Mme. de Pompadour, never lost an opportunity to please his patron by painting her favorite flower, and Fragonard, one-time assistant to Boucher, also catered to the romantic tastes of the era. Young lovers dallying in rose-filled gardens, swinging, dancing and otherwise amorously employed among arbors or festoons of roses were daintily portrayed to satisfy the whims of the ladies at court.

Also notable for their rose and flower paintings are John Lindley, famous for his "White Rose," and Alfred Parsons, who made drawings for the comprehensive *The Genus Rosa* by Ellen Ann Willmot. This book was dedicated to Queen Alexandra of Great Britain, and gives us the rose of our Greek manuscript with all its developments and additions during ten centuries.

Ruskin in his *Modern Painters* attempts to explain the reason for the popularity of the rose throughout the ages, especially the red rose. "Perhaps few people have ever asked themselves why they admire the rose so much more than all other flowers," he wrote. "If they consider, they will find, first, that red is, in a delicately graduated state, the loveliest of all pure colors; and secondly, that in the rose there is no shadow except which is composed of color. All its shadows are fuller in color than its lights, owing to the translucency and reflective power of its leaves."

But no matter what may have been the reason for an artist's choice of the rose for design and inspiration, we are more than satisfied with the effects of his creations. In this generation, he has increasingly brought the beauty of the rose into our homes in every imaginable form, in fabrics, wallpapers, carpets, and decorative ornaments as well as in pictures and photography. Today, too, the rose often lends charm and radiant coloring to advertising and public decorations. In fact, once we become rose conscious, we will find more and more examples of its presence in our daily lives and appreciate with increasing pleasure the beauty of the flower as well as its symbolism which the Great Masters felt so keenly. The "Painted Paradise" has indeed come down to earth. No longer is it roses for the privileged few, but Roses for the Millions!

IV

CHARMS AND PORTENTS

Look how the world's poor people are amazed
At apparitions, signs, and prodigies.
                    SHAKESPEARE, "Venus and Adonis"

SUPERSTITIONS have prevailed in every civilization and in every culture, reflecting man's way of life. Handed down through generations as part of a folk heritage, their hold has faded before advancing scientific knowledge. Literally, superstition means the belief in something regardless of reason or knowledge. That this is dangerous goes without saying, and we owe science an additional debt of gratitude for the freedom it has brought from many useless fears, and at times even cruelties, based on blind belief in certain notions, the origins of which have long since been forgotten. Nevertheless, as always, there is more than one side to the case. Science does not take into account many psychological and religious factors, it deals with things seen, rather than things unseen, and can therefore be helpful to humanity only up to a certain point.

Rabelais said, "I know of a charm . . . but it will do me no good because I do not believe in it." There are others who have known of charms and did believe in them, and sometimes, perhaps only as a consequence of their belief, they worked. It is not our purpose here, however, to credit or discredit the validity of certain ancient superstitions connected with the rose, but rather to present some of the better known ones, impartially, as they have been handed down to us. As regards charms and portents, some of them are for more mundane purposes than others, as we shall see, and thus may be taken a good deal less seriously than superstitions of a deeply religious nature.

Reference was made earlier to a seductive rose potion reportedly used by Persian women of long ago. It would indeed be interesting to read a description by one of these ladies as to the effect it really did produce

59

upon the object of her affections, but unfortunately we must content ourselves with the formula, which was guarded less secretly. This formula called for an aromatic mixture of cloves, cinnamon, and cardamom placed in a large jar. (A bucket would probably be more convenient, but the word *jar* has no doubt a more romantic connotation.) Over this is read seven times backward the Yasin chapter of the Koran (or whatever other the sacred book of the suppliant's faith). Then the jar is filled with rose water and a shirt belonging to the wayward lover is immersed. To this mixture is added a paper inscribed with the name of the truant and four angels (but certainly not the so-called "angel" he may be chasing). The jar is next placed over a fire; and as soon as it begins to boil, the wanderer will be on his way home.

It has been said of the Persians that the rose had such appeal for them that they would gather before a bush in flower, "spread their rugs, sip sherbet, play a lute or a guitar in the moonlight. Then all would serenade the lovely flower with an ode from Hafiz and depart."

Faith admittedly was one of the factors in another fanciful Persian belief. On a certain charmed day, the rose is supposed to have a heart of real gold; but only the fortunate and the faithful can find this magic blossom.

Like the Persians and their neighbors, most other nationalities have handed down in folk tales, love charms and fetishes centering around the rose. The queen of flowers was also used by the Greeks as an ingredient of a love philter, while northern Europeans carried with them rose apples or rose hips as an amulet that would keep their lovers true so long as the charms were worn.

Roses have been used in many ceremonies concerning the divination of coming events. The rose of Jericho, which the Germans often called the Weinachtsrose from the once popular novel of that name by the Swiss author David Hesz, conferred the power of foreseeing the events of the coming year if it was steeped in water at Christmas time.

Roses, according to a custom in *The Queer, the Quaint, the Quizzical,* written by F. H. Stauffer and published in 1882, have revealed to young girls their future husbands: "Upon midsummer eve, go into the garden backwards without speaking a word. Gather a rose, place it in a clean sheet of paper and don't look at it until Christmas (it will be as fresh as in June). At Christmas wear it stuck in your bosom, and the man who plucks it out will be the future true love and husband." This has some logic to it, for the fellow bold enough to do so would surely have some such intentions toward her.

The verses of "The Cottage Girl" quoted by John Brand in *Observations on Popular Antiquities* published in London in 1813, told of a similar custom:

"The Moss-rose that, at fall of dew,
  (Ere Eve its duskier curtain drew)
  Was freshly gathered from its stem,
  She values as the ruby gem;
  And, guarded from the piercing air,
  With all an anxious lover's care,
  She bids it, for her shepherd's sake,
  Await the new-year's frolic wake—
  When faded, in its altered hue
  She reads—the rustic is untrue!
  But, if its leaves the crimson paint,
  Her sickening hopes no longer faint,
  The Rose upon her bosom worn,
  She meets him at the peep of morn,
  And, lo! her lips with kisses prest,
  He plucks it from her panting breast."

This midsummer gathering of roses as indices of faithfulness and chastity is but one of the many forms to test lovers or mates by means of the flower. In one tale, three roses fall as a sign of unfaithfulness; and in another an adulteress craftily pretends to faint when her husband strikes

61

her with a rose; only the pure presumably would be so sensitive. Perhaps the most delightful of such stories, told with humor and wit, is *The Wright's Chaste Wife*, or a "Fable of a wryght that was maryde to a pore wydows dowtre/the whyche wydow havyng noo good to geve with her/ gave as for a precyous Johelle to hym a Rose garlond/the whyche she affermyd would never fade while she kept truly her wedlock." This merry tale was written by Adam of Cobham in 1462.

The garland he described:

> "It was made
> Of flourys most of honoure
> Of roses whyte that will not fade,
> Whych floure alle Ynglond [England] doth glade."

And the "wydow" carefully explains to the "wryght" that he may carry the garland with him in his travels, plying his trade around the country-side and have no fear of being duped by his wife at home alone for

> "Wete thou wele withoutyn fable
> Alle the whyle thy wyfe is stable
> The chaplette wolle holde hewe;
> And yf thy wyfe use putry
> Or tolle eny man to lye her by,
> Then wolle yt change hewe,
> And by the garlonde thou may see
> Fekylle or fals yf that sche be,
> Or elles yf sche be true."

Keeping faith in another sense, that of truthfulness, was tested by the use of a rose in the Italian forms of the Bluebeard stories, one of the al-most universal patterns of folk tales. In these tales, Bluebeard gives each of his wives in turn the keys to the rooms of the palace. One room he forbids each wife to enter, sealing the command with the presentation of a freshly picked rose. Later, when the wives deny in turn that they dis-obeyed him, he knows that they have looked into the forbidden room because the rose has faded. When the youngest sister's turn comes and the customary injunction is repeated against opening the door, she has the wit to remove the rose from her dress before peeping into the room. When Bluebeard returns and sees the rose fresh and fair, he cannot but believe that she has obeyed him fully. Thus they live happily ever after.

Another Italian superstition is a typical example of the rose as an evil omen. It is considered extremely unlucky to present anyone with a full-blown rose, for the petals will surely fall and that will mean that the recipient will lose a relative within a year.

A variant of this superstition is found in the British Isles. If petals fall from a red or a pink rose as one plucks it, misfortune awaits the picker in the very near future. The corollary to this belief, however, adds one of the comparatively few good omens: if the petals fall from a white rose as it is picked, the person's guardian angel is praying for him.

Because of the legendary association of red roses with the Agony of Christ, red roses reputedly having sprung from the crown of thorns, a full-blown red rose in almost every European country has at some time been regarded as an exceedingly evil omen. Should one see its petals fall, this meant sudden death. Thus the tale is repeated again and again in Ireland of how "a husky Irish lad saw a red rose fly past his window, dropping its petals as it crossed the pane. Knowing his end was near, he ran with all speed to the village to find the priest, and was killed by a runaway horse before he arrived there."

Another folk tale tells of the short-lived joy of a boy who went with his mother to gather sticks in the forest near the Schalksburg Castle of the Hohenzollerns. The mother suddenly realizing that her son had wandered from view started to search for him. Just then the son reappeared with a wild rose in his hand, claiming that it had been given to him by a radiantly beautiful lady dressed in white. The mother was puzzled, for she had seen no one in the forest, but, relieved that her son was safe, she did not scold him for wandering off. She told him that whether or not the rose was given him or he found it, he must put it in water when they went home. Here, the rose remained fresh for three days, then started to wither and fade. And the boy withered and faded even as the rose. Three days later both were dead.

In Germany and England the sudden and unexpected blossoming of a white rosebush, as in the autumn, used to be considered a presage of death. "When Roses and Violets flourish in Autumn, it is an evil sign of an insuing Plague the year following, or some pestiferous disease." A milder omen is that of the dog rose, or *Rosa canina*, also called the canker rose from the grub, the canker, which eats its young buds; a profusion of dog rose hips is a promise of a hard winter to come.

Although the use of roses as a funeral flower was almost universal, in Westphalia and Thuringia to throw a rose into an open grave was to invite a slow wasting away and ultimate death. Because of this same idea no doubt the rose flowering on a tree by a grave represented the spirit of the dead person on whose burial plot it was planted. Thus, according to the Norse tradition, over the grave of a maiden three white roses will grow which none except her lover may gather. The folklore of Sweden reveals a belief that if two lovers are buried in the same grave a rose will grow from the mouth of each.

Perhaps the best known example of this belief is immortalized in the ballad about William and Margaret:

> "Margaret was buryed in the lower chancel
> And William in the higher;
> Out of her breast there sprang a rose
> And out of his a briar.

> "They grew till they grew up to the church top,
> And then they could grow no higher;
> And there they tied a true lover's knot
> Which made all the people admire."

A symbolic rose version of the grave-tree belief is also found in Oscar Wilde's famous poem of the burial of a murderer in a prison yard:

> "Out of his mouth a red, red rose!
> Out of his heart a white!
> For who can say by what strange way,
> Christ brings His will to light."

A slightly different symbolic use of a rose as the abode of a spirit is found in Russia. This fairy tale tells of an evil enchantress who lived as a spirit of a blue rose tree in a blue forest and met her death at the hands of Prince Ivan. This legendary hero found out by trickery the spirit abode of the wicked witch who had been casting spells and keeping the populace in torment. Prince Ivan uproots the rose tree whereupon the enchantress straightway sickens. He carries the rose tree to the evildoer's house and finds her on the point of death. He throws the rose tree into the cellar in which she kept her tortured victims, crying, "Behold her death!" At once the whole building shakes violently "and becomes an island, on which are the people who had been sitting in hell and who offer thanks to Prince Ivan."

In the Middle Ages when the superstitious endeavored to reconcile their pagan heritage to their comparatively new Christian religion they made every operation of nature emblematical of something connected with the Christian faith. Thus it was said that the summer roses always began to fade on St. Mary Magdalen's day (July 22) because roses were dedicated to her.

As with most superstitions and folk beliefs, the same reasoning that is used to explain the prevalence of the rose as an evil omen is found in reverse, making the flower a good luck charm. The red rose is a symbol of evil because of its sanguinary origin at the time of the Crucifixion; and contrariwise, witches and devils are supposed to hate and fear the wild or briar rose because the blood of the Lord touched it. In Germany even natural phenomena were considered influenced by roses, for the sweetbriar was believed to be able to drive away lightning.

The good luck uses of roses as talismans and charms antedate Christianity. Thus the German belief that the petals thrown into the fire and burnt brought good fortune to the householder was also found among the ancient Greeks. In certain parts of the Continent, however, only naturally fallen petals thus burned were capable of exorcising devils and breaking spells.

Midsummer Eve was generally regarded as a period when imagination could run riot, "a very midsummer madness," in the words of Shakespeare. On this night people gathered the rose, St. John's wort, vevain, trefoil, and rue, all of which were supposed to have magical properties.

In many parts of Europe the flower wreaths thrown across the Midsummer Eve fires were used throughout the year to purify and protect homes and farm buildings from evil. On St. George's Day the Transylvanians uprooted rosebushes, setting them in the doorways of their houses as protection against witches. On the same day the Bulgarians performed elaborate rituals to protect their cattle from all forms of the evil eye and witchcraft. An essential part of the ceremony was the offering of salt to each cow by the housewife early in the morning. To get at the salt the cow was forced to step over smoldering coals on which various kinds of rose petals were burning. The rose-petal smoke wreathing around the animal cast a spell that made all demons and witches powerless to harm it for a whole year.

In the volume *Taboo and the Perils of the Soul* of *The Golden Bough,* James George Frazer tells how among the Thompson Indians of British Columbia, widows and widowers after the death of the spouse had to pass through a patch of rosebushes four times. This was probably done to rid themselves of the ghost, who might be supposed to stick on a thorn. For a year thereafter the bereaved had to sleep on a bed made of fir boughs on which sticks of rosebushes were laid. As added protection many such mourners wore on their persons pieces of rosebushes and juniper wrapped in a piece of buckskin.

A completely feminine superstitious application of a rose is that which uses the rose of Jericho, or Resurrection rose, as an emblem and symbol of safe childbirth. It is thus used in Italy, where the belief was probably transmitted by traders or Crusaders returning from the Holy Land, for, according to F. H. Stauffer, the usage was common in Jerusalem. Here, it is said, women about to give birth place an unopened rose in water at the beginning of their labor in the hope that its blooming may be the welcome signal of their deliverance.

A more fanciful association of the rose with childbirth is mentioned in some old tales where conception occurs from eating a rose leaf. One of these happenings is written up in the *Cunto de li Cunti* or *Pentamerone* of Giambattista Basile, the oldest and richest of all collections of popular tales. The book, like *The Decameron* and *The Canterbury Tales*, is a round robin of stories within a frame story. In this instance they are told to amuse a prince's moody wife who had never laughed until she witnessed an accidental collison between an old hag and one of the castle's pages and overheard the stream of colorful invectives the old woman used. Inspired by this incident, the prince gathers together a group of harridans and beldams to tell stories that will amuse his wife. The eighth diversion of the second day, which is related by "bleary-eyed Paola" is the story of the Baron of Selvascura who had an unmarried younger sister, Lilla, who used to play in a garden with other girls of her own age. One day finding a lovely rosebush in full bloom they devised a game in which the one who could jump over it without touching a single leaf would win a prize. Lilla was the last to try, all the others having failed. She leaped clear over the bush, but the breeze she stirred loosened one single leaf which fell to the ground. Unwilling to lose the prize and knowing that no one else had seen the petal fall, she popped it into her mouth and hurriedly swallowing it, claimed the prize.

Three days later she found herself pregnant, and ran in bewilderment to her fairy friends who told her that the rose petal was the cause. Lilla succeeded in hiding her condition from her family and associates, and in a miraculously short time gave birth to a lovely girl child which she named Lisa. From the birth of Lisa on, the story resembles that of the Grimms' "Briar Rose," even to the happy ending.

In the Tyrol the rose gall which, when mixed with bear's grease, was a cure for baldness, could produce an unnatural sleep if rubbed on the head of a sleeping person. Nothing could waken the slumberer except the removal of the gall, which would have to be done by the original applier for apparently the salve left no visible deposit by which it could be identified.

And in France when a maiden wanted rosy cheeks it was believed that all she had to do was prick her finger with a thorn from a red rosebush. One of the drops of blood oozing from the wound was then buried beneath a rosebush. This accomplished, all the maiden had to do was wait patiently for the change in her complexion to take place.

Roses have been the "open sesame" not only for such miraculous improvements in complexions, but have replaced the usual cowslip or forget-me-not in Germany as the opener of locked treasures in fairy castles.

For mortal applications such as closing wounds and stopping hemorrhages, rose leaves were applied with the accompanying incantation: "Abek, Wabek, Fabek; in Christ's garden stand three roses. One for the good God, the other for God's blood, the third for the angel Gabriel.

Blood, I pray you, cease to flow." Fuller treatment of the medicinal uses of the rose is given in the chapter on drugs and cures; although many of them appear to today's scientifically minded people as superstitions, at that time they represented the art of medicine as it was then understood.

A wondrous rose with both magical and medicinal properties was the *Gul-i Bakawali,* or the "Rose of Bakawali." The story of this flower was originally written in Persia by Shaybeh Izza Mlah of Bengal in the year of the Hirja 1124, or A.D. 1712. It is a long story of the type in which a number of brothers set out in quest of some wonderful and much-desired object, the youngest being always successful with supernatural aid.

In this instance, a young Indian prince sets out to find the Rose of Bakawali; the only cure, as foretold by the astrologers, for his father's blindness.

After many strange adventures, the prince finds the fairy garden in which the Rose of Bakawali is enshrined. The garden has "ground of gold . . . the walls which surrounded it were studded with the rubies of Badakshan and the carnelians of Yaman. . . . Through parterres of emeralds flowed streams of rose water in beds of topaz. . . . That garden! If a drop of its dew were to fall in the ocean, it would make the fishes exhale the perfume of roses. . . . An outer hall of the palace, made of ruby and jasper, inlaid with a pond full of purest rose water. Its sides were studded with the most precious stones, and in the middle of it bloomed a lovely flower, delicate to view and most pleasing in fragrance. . . . The Rose of Bakawali." Needless to say, at the end of the story the cure is effected and everybody lives happily ever after.

Other folk tales parallel and antedate by centuries the well-known story of the princess and the pea. The characters in these stories must have been more sensitive than either the princess who could feel the pea through layers of mattresses, or Verrus who, according to Cicero, probably suffered sleeplessness from a crumpled rose leaf in his bed of roses, for in one of these tales the young heroine actually gets a blister on her back from sleeping on crumpled leaves. In another, so sensitive is the princess that she is injured by falling rose leaves. This sensitivity, was, of course, possible only for those of royal lineage and was a revelation of that lineage despite attempts at disguise. In other tales, roses falling as an unidentified or masquerading personage enters a room or a garden reveal his or her aristocratic heritage.

Christian legends of supernatural happenings involving roses are so numerous and so fraught with symbolism that they are dealt with separately in the chapter on Martyrs and Miracles. Perhaps the strangest of all records of the bewildering uses of the rose is to be found in *The Boke of Secretes of Albertus Magnus of the Vertues of Herbes, Stones and Certaine Beastes.* Nothing is actually known of the author of this portentous volume, for certainly the writer was not the famed Albertus Magnus, Bishop of Ratisbon, one of the greatest thinkers of his age. Besides the many wondrous recipes, including one for reviving drowning flies and bees, is this strange entry for the use of powder of roses: "If the aforesayde poulder be put in a lamp and after be kindled, all men shall appear blacke as the deuiel [devil]."

These selected charms and portents have been carefully documented in various centuries and countries. Each adds further proof of the great power the rose has always held over the mind and imagination of man.

V

FRAGRANCE

The rose looks fair, but fairer we it deem
For that sweet odour which doth in it live.
SHAKESPEARE, "Sonnet LIV"

AMONG those notables who have been carried away by the scent of the rose was Rudyard Kipling. In "The Rose of Eden" he vowed that:

> "There is never a daughter of the earth but once, ere the
> tale of her days is done,
> She will know the scent of the Eden Rose, just once be-
> neath the sun.
> And whatever else she may win or lose, enduring or do,
> or dare,
> She will never forget the enchantment it gave to the
> common air;
> For the world may give her content or joy, fame, sorrow
> or sacrifice,
> But the hour that brought the scent of the rose, she
> lived it in Paradise."

To others the scent of the rose has been something to be analyzed, intellectually as well as emotionally. Herodotus, the Greek historian often called the father of history, was probably the first to differentiate between the odors of various roses. In his *History* he recorded that the sixty-leaved rose had a finer scent than any other kind. Modern botanists question his accuracy and believe he meant the hundred-leaved rose, or *Rosa centifolia*. This rose, often called the "flower of Persia," has a scent like that of the old-fashioned Jacqueminot rose, its fragrance remaining in the dry petals long after the flower has fallen to pieces. It grows throughout Persia in great profusion and is carefully watched and picked by the householders to obtain the maximum scent for making rose water.

The first modern attempt to classify rose perfumes was published in *The Gardener's Monthly and Horticulturist* in Philadelphia in 1886. The article, "Varieties of Perfume in the Rose," had little actual scientific basis. Later, in 1889, Blondel catalogued roses into ten categories according to their fragrance. Although his grouping is still widely accepted, Dr. Hampton has more recently reduced the number of classes to six.

"1. Old rose scent, or 'damask scent,' found mostly in pink roses.

2. The tea group, which includes tea roses, Golden Dawn, and the Dijon group.

3. Fruit scent, including the Permet group and Golden Emblem.

4. Musk scent, the English field rose, or *Rosa arvensis*, and the Jersey Beauty.

5. Spicy-scented roses.

6. Individual scents: the distinctive smell of the wild dog rose; the violet scent of the *Rosa Banksia*; and the [direct quote] slightly disagreeable scent of the Mrs. Edward Powell (which has been compared to beer)."

Not only do the flowers, but in certain varieties the leaves have an aroma. Sometimes the two scents are distinctly different; in others only the leaves have an odor. Pliny, in the chapter on roses in his *Natural History,* was the first to have noted and recorded that the leaves of the *Rosa rubiginosa* have a distinct and pleasant odor resembling that of cinnamon.

The accidental discovery or the actual invention of perfumery did not occur until far along in the history of the cultivation of the rose for its decorative uses. Until then the fragrance of the rose was available only so long as there were fresh flowers to be had. But even after the art of distillation had been discovered there were some rose enthusiasts who held the sentiment expressed in *Othello*, preferring the scent together with the beauty of the living flower:

> "When I have pluck'd the rose,
> I cannot give it vital growth again,
> It needs must wither; I'll smell it on the tree."

Only the minority, however, have had such aesthetic scruples, for no perfume has been so consistently popular as that of the rose. Nor has anyone been able to displace the true attar, or otto, of roses with a pure synthetic, this despite constant research conducted by the perfume industry. There is no artificial "attar" of outstanding merit marketed that does not contain a substantial amount of the actual essential oil of roses.

The use of perfumes did not wait upon the more modern discovery either of the process of distillation or the separation of the essential oil of the rose, from which time the history of the rose in perfumery dates.

The ancients discovered that by steeping the flowers in liquids and oils, which absorbed the scent of the petals, they could make delicious perfumes. Thus the rose water in which Cleopatra bathed could more accurately be described as a tincture of roses.

An even earlier discovery was the form of scent known as incense—substances which give off a perfume when burned. Actually the word, *perfume*, means "through smoke." Incense is found in all primitive forms of worship, from the altars of Zoroaster and Confucius to the temples of Memphis and Jerusalem. In the earliest editions of the Old Testament, ingredients are sometimes listed for making incense to be offered to Jehovah by the high priests. And in Proverbs (27:9) is found approval of a less religious use of perfume: "Ointment and perfume rejoice the heart: so doth the sweetness of a man's friend by hearty counsel." Not only was incense burned profusely, but the oil of the lamps and even the wax tapers were scented. St. Matilda embodies in her *Book of Spiritual Grace* three perfumes symbolical of divine love. The first in sweetness and desirability is that of rose water that has been distilled from the most beautiful rose of all, the heart of Christ.

The floral scents of the ancient Egyptians were probably prepared in the same manner as those used by the Romans and Greeks, of whose methods more complete records exist. Theophrastus, the Greek father of botany, said that the perfumes currently popular were made from roses, white lilies, and violets, "some from stalks and some from roots." He gave a recipe for making rose perfume by first steeping the flowers in sweet wine. Ginger grass, aspalathos, and sweet flag were then mixed with the roses, and a large quantity of salt added, presumably to strengthen the aroma or to extract more completely the odorous substances of the petals. This salt treatment was peculiar to the making of rose perfumes and Theophrastus found it exceedingly wasteful, "twenty-three gallons of salt being put to eight and a half gallons of perfume." Theophrastus also advised his compatriots that "the lightest perfumes are rose, kypros, and lily, which seem best suited for men."

His opinion apparently was a departure from the ancient usages recorded by Homer seven centuries earlier, for it is a very feminine goddess, Cupid's mother, described in the *Iliad*, who breathes of this perfume when she visits Achilles:

> "Celestial Venus hovered o'er his head
> And roseate unguents heavenly fragrance shed."

Whether or not his contemporaries followed Theophrastus' advice is not known, but the Greeks' use of perfume continued to be as lavish as it had been approximately two hundred years before when Solon was moved to issue a law to prohibit its sale in an attempt to curb popular excesses. The law, however, was honored more in the breach than in the observance, for the populace, continuing to set great store by their perfumed oils and unguents, scented their persons and their homes the year round with midsummer fragrance.

The Romans considered scent-making one of the fine arts; and in Rome the multitude of perfumers' shops occupied nearly a quarter of the town. Even so their output was nowhere near sufficient to meet the enormous demand, and merchants of Arabia and India gained a hundred million sesterces from the Empire out of the perfume trade.

At least one Roman use of scent would seem to have been lavished on men when they were least in a state to enjoy it: slaves of rich Romans burned rose petals in the bedrooms while their masters slept. A certain Persian satrap, had he thought of it, would probably have had his slumbers likewise attended. It is a matter of record that when the Jewish scholar Raba, a renowned ancient haggadist, journeyed to present him with a gift, he found the satrap sitting up to his neck in rose water and waited upon by beautiful odalisks. Accepting the gift, the satrap asked the scholar, "Have ye aught like this in Paradise?"

Another Jewish legend is of a macabre nature. Rabbi Low, the famous cabalist of Prague and the favorite of Emperor Rudolph II, is said to have died of the perfume of the rose, the form of which Death took, knowing he could not gain access to the sage in any other way.

It was the Jewish physician Aben-Zohar of Seville, Spain, who is credited by Gmelin in his history of distilled waters with the first manufacture. Aben-Zohar reputedly used distilled water for diseases of the eye. Others reserve the honor for the original distillation of rose water for either of two Arabians: Rhazes, a physician living early in the tenth century; or Avicenna, the Mohammedan chemist and philosopher who lived from 980 to 1037. Another authority, Ernest John Parry, in his *Cyclopedia of Perfumery*, favors the Near East as the birthplace of rose waters. He points to the vast quantities traditionally manufactured in Persia and exported to China, India, Egypt, Spain, and Morocco. The principal seat of the industry was at Dschur, now called Firuzabad, located between Shiraz and the coast, where the perfume manufacture still flourishes. According to Ibn Khaldun, the tribute of thirty thousand bottles of rose water paid to the treasury of Bagdad by Faristan during the reign of Caliph Mamoun was distilled locally.

The prodigious output of rose water attests to the large demand. A tale is told that when Saladin retook the ancient city of Jerusalem from the Crusaders in 1187, he refused to enter the famous Mosque of Omar, which had been converted into a Christian church by the invaders, until its walls and every object in it had been purified with rose water brought from Damascus. Five hundred camels were scarely sufficient to bring the load from that city to Jerusalem. Almost three hundred years later Mohamet II emulated Saladin when he captured Constantinople in 1453 and similarly bathed the Mosque of St. Sophia.

This theory of the Eastern origin of distillation credits the Arabs with the introduction of the process into Europe. Apparently the knowledge of distillation was slow in crossing the Pyrenees, for the first recorded distillation of rose water in France was not until the thirteenth century by Armand de Villeneuve. At about the same time Johannes Actuaris in *De Methode Medendi* also acknowledged the industry in Europe.

The discovery of the essential oil of the rose lagged many centuries after the conception of distillation. It is difficult to determine exactly the year or even the decade of the isolation of this floral essence. As with so many milestones of human progress, many men reached it at approximately the same time in attempting to improve on methods and customs already existing.

Langles in his *Recherches sur la decouverte de L'essence des Roses*, published in 1804, determined the date of the discovery in the Near East to have been the year 1612. Despite exhaustive research, he could find no literary references to it in works preceding that date. Hafiz, he points out, often refers to *gulab* (rose water) but makes no mention of the *athr* (essence); similarly in Sadi's *Gulistan*, among the many references to the rose there is none regarding its essential oil.

The first description of attar in Persian literature appears in the *Tarykh montekheb lubab*, a history of the great moguls from 1525 through 1667, written by Mohammed Achem. In the chapter grandiloquently entitled, "The Marriage of the Princess Nour-Djihan with the Habitant of Paradise, the Divine Djihan-Guyr: Inventions and Discoveries of the Queen of the World," is given a detailed account of the marriage fete at which every sensual extravagance was indulged in. The princess had a canal constructed in the flower garden, and through it was made to flow sweet-scented rose water. As the divine Djihan-Guyr walked with his bride beside the canal, they noticed an oily liquid floating on the surface of the rose water. When this was collected by the slaves, it was recognized by the whole court as the most delicate of all perfumes.

In another chapter of this same work the occasion on which this essential oil received its name is described. At the commencement of the perfumed feast of the new year, the mother of Nour-Djihan, having presented to the prince some essence of rose water which she had prepared, the prince attached to it his illustrious name, A'thr Djihan-Guyr.

The romantic appeal and popularity of this and other stories have overshadowed the much more prosaically reported European discoveries, some of which apparently antedated these accidental findings. In 1582 Geronimo Rossi published in Ravenna the *De Distillatione Liber*, in which

73

he stated that eight years previously, in 1574, he had noted that under proper conditions one could separate an extremely odorous oily substance from the surface of rose water. The sale of a small quantity of this essential oil is recorded by Permet at the end of the same century. Apparently the medical employment of this highly scented extract at first overshadowed its use as perfume: "Besides the water which one can obtain from roses, one can extract an odorous, inflammable spirit, most useful for fortifying and rejoicing the heart and the stomach."

Probably it is this lack of romantic emphasis on the part of the Europeans in contrast to the Eastern stress on the poetic and sentimental, combined with the ease of growing roses in profusion in such countries as Persia and Syria, that has helped to make the East appear the spiritual home of perfumes. Only in one Eastern country has the ancient art of perfumery lapsed. Whatever knowledge they have had in the past, the Chinese today produce fewer scents than any other Eastern people. C. F. Leyel points out in *The Magic of Herbs* that their marvelously scented flowers are never distilled for perfume, though some of their finest teas are scented with a rose called *Tsing-moi-gui-hwa*.

No Western religion has ever emulated the sensual pleasure accorded the Mohammedan paradise where the very houris are made of pure musk and every known and imagined perfume keeps the senses in a state of ecstatic delirium. Mohammed told his faithful followers, "When I was taken up into heaven, some of my sweat fell on earth, and from it sprang the rose, and whoever would smell my scent, let him smell the rose."

Appropriately, Taif, the suburb of Mecca, and birthplace of Mohammed, has been turned into an oasis of flowers. Doughty, at the end of his long sojourn in the Arabian desert was almost overwhelmed by its scented air: "We met some trains of loaded camels marching upward to et-Tayif: and out went others which descended before us to the Holy City. The most of these carried sacks . . . oh, blissful sweetness! in the pure night air . . . of rose blossoms; whose precious odours are distilled by the Indian apothecaries in Mecca. This is the 'atar,' which is dispersed by the multitude of pilgrims throughout the Mohammedan world."

Perhaps the most delightful of the Persian stories concerning the fragrance of the rose are those in which objects have by their proximity to the queen of flowers acquired some of her appeal. One of these tells how Sadi, the great Persian poet, saw at his feet a half-dead leaf which exhaled a delightful fragrance. "You that exhale so sweet an odor," said he, "are you the rose?" "No," the leaf replied, "I am not the rose, But I have lived near her, hence comes the sweetness I possess."

Sadi wrote into *Gulistan* a similar incident that revolves not around a leaf but the saponaceous clay used throughout the ancient world before the invention of soap.

74

" 'Twas in the bath, a piece of perfumed clay
   Came from my loved one's hand to mine, one day.
   Art thou, then, musk or ambergris, I said;
   That by thy scent my soul is ravished?
   Not so, it answered, worthless on earth was I,
   But long I kept the roses company;
   Thus near, its perfect fragrance to me came,
   Else I'm but earth, the worthless and the same."

Scientific distillation of the essence, despite the Nour-Djihan story, is believed to have been introduced from Persia through Bassorah and from Arabia into India—first to the town of Kananj on the Ganges, although the industry is no longer there, and then to Ghazipur, where it still thrives. Distilleries are also found at Amritsar, but their large output is sold in the bazaars and consumed locally. Cashmere, however, is a large exporter of attar, which is generally extracted from either the musk or damask rose.

Despite the introduction of considerable modern machinery, one can still see in Cashmere the time-honored method of extraction of rose essence. Petals are placed in a wooden vessel with pure water and exposed to the heat of the sun for several days. Gradually oil particles rise to the surface. These are scooped up with absorbent cotton from which the oil is expressed into bottles that are then carefully sealed.

Attar of roses has approximately the consistency of butter and is never found as a liquid except in the very warmest weather. Its color varies: it is generally green, sometimes lemon or rose color, and occasionally brownish. The differences are partly inherent in the varieties of roses used, and are also dependent upon the type of manufacture, and the state of maturity of the roses.

Pure attar has always been extremely expensive; shortly after its discovery it was valued at five times its weight in gold. But pure attar is comparatively rare in commerce, it being estimated that five thousand parts in weight of rose petals produce one part of essential oil.

The process of making attar was probably brought to eastern Europe at about the same time that it was carried into France from the North African coast. No facts appear to be available, though one record states that the essence was distilled on the island of Chios and in Smyrna "at an early date." According to a tradition still current in Bulgaria, the industry was brought to Kazanlik from Tunis about 1680 by a Turk.

Bulgaria today is one of the greatest sources of attar. The industry is particularly concentrated in the region which was originally known as Roumelin. The harvest season of from twenty to thirty days begins in May with a national festival. The gaily costumed pickers gather the flowers before they have been exposed to the sun, and take them to the stills.

These stills are truncated cones of sheet copper, a little over three feet in height. Their middle diameter is about two and a half feet, and the neck is about ten inches across. The mushroom-shaped head about a foot in height is connected by a pipe to the condensing tubes that pass through a wooden tub through which cold water is kept constantly running. A charge of about twenty-five pounds of flowers is thrown into the still with from sixteen to eighteen gallons of water. When about two gallons of liquid has distilled over, the still is opened, the old flowers are taken out and a fresh charge put in with sufficient water to bring the quantity up to the original amount. The process is then repeated.

The distillates are mixed and redistilled, and the attar is allowed to form on the surface of the last distillate. It is then separated from it by a small conical funnel which allows the water to drain away.

The odors of the various distillations are very different, and another scent is obtained if steam stills are used rather than naked flames. Extraordinary differences in both amount of attar obtainable and in scent are found in the same variety of roses grown in different districts. Probably the first to notice this phenomenon was Pliny, who held that roses had more profuse perfume when grown in dry soil.

In the fabulous perfume industry centering around Grasse in France, the hundred-leaved rose, until recently, was used exclusively. Known also as the Rose de Mai, it yields an exquisite perfume, but the care it requires in cultivation and the small crop of flowers it produces have been considered drawbacks. Gradually other varieties have come into their own, including the Ulrich Brunner rose, a magnificent cherry-red hybrid perpetual, which is very decorative and has a sweet odor not quite so powerful as that of the Rose de Mai. Louis Van Houtte, another hybrid perpetual, and Marie Van Houtte, a tea rose of charming, creamy yellow with a bright rose edge, both have a high yield of exquisitely perfumed attar, their aroma being compared to a bouquet of mixed roses.

The craze for perfume in the French court under the influence of Mme. de Pompadour earned for it the title of *La Cour Perfumée*. La Pompadour herself used a different scent each day. One of these was the rose.

The rivalry between perfumers was keen. The French perfumer was declared to be an absurd fraud by Charles Lillie, author of *The British Perfumer*. Lillie's book, published in 1822, is a collection of choice recipes and observations made during an extensive practice of thirty years, by which "any Lady or Gentleman may prepare their own articles of the best quality, whether of Perfumery, Snuffs, or Colours." His choicest recipe for rose perfume for "hair-powder" calls for nothing less than "two pecks of fresh and very dry damask rose leaves" and the instructions following would have taken four days to compound.

Lillie's volume abounds in directions for making scents for every conceivable purpose from soap to snuff, and his pride and sensibilities must

Rose Taffeta.

"Perfume," by François Boucher (1703-1770).

Rose Vogue.

have been greatly offended by the advice of his contemporary, Beau Brummell, "that no man of fashion should use perfume, but should instead send his linen to be washed on Hampstead Heath."

Many of these instructions or recipes date back to Elizabethan days. Sweet candles were burned in the bedroom, sweet cakes were thrown on fires, scented cosmetics were kept in equally odorous coffers, rose water was used for the complexion and for washing the hands after meals, and aromatic lozenges taken to sweeten the breath. Queen Elizabeth's favorite footwear was made of scented Spanish leather, steeped and cured in a mixture of oils including oil of roses. And the fragrance of one's person or clothing could be renewed throughout the day by a few drops of scent carried in jeweled casting bottles. Recipes abounded for renewing the odor of sweet powder bags and pomanders.

> ". . . the bob of gold
> Which a pomander ball doth hold
> This to her side she doth attach
> With gold crochet or French Pennache."

And this "bob of gold" often had a number of cores, each for a different scent. For all of these fragrant uses, the perfume of the rose was the favorite.

The odor of a fine perfume has been compared to a chord in music rich in suggestive overtones; the chief constituents of the perfume corresponding to the notes of the chord, the subsidiary odors giving quality and richness to the whole. Septimus Piesse, the outstanding exponent of the musical interpretation of odors, developed a scale of fifty scents, each odor corresponding to a seminote in the musical scale, and called it the odophone. A false odor was as inharmonious as a false note. Sharp smells were represented by high notes, heavier ones by low notes. The perfect balance of the rose scent placed it at middle C.

The appeal of the fragrance of the rose has never been reserved, however, for such aesthetes as Piesse. Its appeal has been universal. And as the sense of smell has been called the sense of imagination, the subtle fragrance of the rose can conjure up memories of things past:

> "Long, long be my heart with such memories filled
> Like the vase in which roses have once been distilled,
> You may break, you may shatter the vase if you will,
> But the scent of the rose will hang around it still."

Eleanor Sinclair Rohde sums up this rose fragrance with these words in *The Scented Garden:* "The scent of the summer flowers are rich and joyous, and sweetest of all scents are the scents of old roses. The scent of the *rosa centifolia* is the beauty of life itself."

79

VI

ROSE CURES, COSMETICS, AND COOKERY

It is not my purpose to make my book a Confectionarie, a Sugar Baker's Furnace, a Gentlewoman's Preserving Pan, nor yet an Apothocaries Shop or Dispensatorie.

JOHN GERARD, "Great Herball" 1556

S. B. PARSONS, in *The Rose, Its History, Poetry, Culture, and Classification,* published in 1856, offers what he considers scientific justification for the medicinal use of the rose. A chemical analysis of the petals of the Provins Rose shows them to contain "vegetable matter and essential oil, gallic acid, coloring matter, albumen, tannin, some salts with a base of potash or chalk, silex, and oxyde of iron." The taste of the dried Provins petals is astringent and bitter. Parsons concludes that their use as a tonic is scientifically sound. "A small dose [of the dried petals] in powders strengthens the stomach and assists digestion," while "a conserve of any variety [of fresh rose petals] is excellent in cases of colds or catarrh."

Parsons' choice of the petals of the Provins Rose for analysis was undoubtedly no accident, rather was it based on the then current belief that of all roses the Provins Rose was the best for medicinal usage. It was largely because of this belief, and not solely from civic pride, that the citizens of Provins petitioned the French government in 1807 to encourage the cultivation of this particular species by ordering its preferential use in all public hospitals and military dispensaries.

During World War II when the supply of citrus fruits had been cut off, some of this rose lore proved valuable to British chemists. After exhaustive tests they determined that rose hips have a vitamin C content 400 per cent greater than that of oranges. Following this discovery the British government instituted a campaign during the autumn of 1941 that led to one of the greatest medicinal uses of the rose in modern times. In

Scotland alone, women and Boy Scouts collected approximately two hundred tons of the bitter red fruit of the dog rose, the commonest hedge rose in the British Isles. It has been estimated that this harvest represented 134,000,000 individual hips, which were converted into syrup. Rose hip powder had had some earlier distribution on the Continent, but neither the proportion of its manufacture nor its nutritional value could be compared to the British undertaking.

The use of rose hips instead of petals was a distinct departure from tradition. Bartholomeaus Anglicus, the only Englishman to write a treatise on herbs during the Middle Ages, described in great detail the varying characteristics of the hips of both wild and cultivated roses, concluding that any and all of them were "not ful good to ete for roughnesse that is hyd wythin. And greuyth [grieveth] wythin his throte that ete thereof." But apparently Bartholomeaus, considered one of the greatest thinkers of his age, was mistaken about the painful aftereffects of eating hips. Alice Morse Earle records no such unpleasant aftermath. She writes in *Sun Dials and Roses of Yesterday* (1902) that when she was a child, "we always nibbled the hips of wild roses and eglantine, but had a firm notion that other rose-hips were poisonous."

Although the use of roses as medicine has all but disappeared except in a few countries such as Persia and India, the cosmetic use of the flower and its by-products is still popular. What lady has not at some time used glycerine and rose water as a lotion or beauty creams of which rose water is a principal ingredient? The most universally used and most popular of beauty creams—cold cream—was invented by the Greek physician, Galen, a little more than a century after the birth of Christ. The recipe he developed still forms the basis for the following, currently used beauty preparation: "Melt four ounces of white wax in a pound of rose oil. Stir in a little cold water very gradually to give it a clear and opaque whiteness. Wash this mixture in rose water, and add small quantities of rose water and rose vinegar to make it the right consistency."

Galen's selection of the rose for his recipe may have been linked with the mythological legend of Milto which was popular in his day. Milto, a beautiful young maiden, was in the habit of taking a garland of roses every morning to the temple of Venus as an offering to her favorite goddess. Then one day a disfiguring tumor began to appear on her face, rapidly destroying her beauty. Medical science knowing of nothing that would cure such an affliction, the girl had no choice but to resign herself to her unhappy fate. However, one night, it is said, the grateful Venus appeared in a dream to her faithful worshiper and told her to anoint her face with the leaves of the roses she had placed on the altar. Hurrying to the temple the following morning, Milto eagerly took up some of the roses and crushed the leaves against her face as she had been bidden,

Rosa Hollandica Siue Bataua (Gerardes Herball).

whereupon the tumor miraculously started to subside. Later, when it had completely disappeared, according to the legend, Milto was more beautiful than ever.

What have proved to be cures for some people, however, have brought harm to others, for it is possible to be allergic to roses, just as it is to other plants (and certain animals). Medical knowledge of the exact nature of allergies is recent, but the complaint is old. Marie de Medici would not look at a painting or a carving of a rose, and the Chevalier de Guise took every opportunity to express his loathing of the most popular flower of his day. Lady Heneage, one of the maids of honor to Elizabeth I was made ill by the scent of roses; and writing in the seventeenth century, Dr. Ladelius mentions a man who had the choice of remaining a recluse during the rose season or suffering a violent and perpetual cold in the head.

In one of his wittiest moments, Oscar Wilde said there was only one thing that he could not resist—temptation! Even so, it is doubtful if many would want to emulate the allergic scarabee—often represented on ancient gems as an emblem of luxurious enervation and self-indulgent destruction. Unable to resist their fatal attraction, the beetle chooses to die among rose blossoms, the heady smell of which supposedly causes its destruction. All of us may wish this fate to the scarabee's distant cousin, the Japanese beetle, but nature seems to have decreed the reverse, as in the case of most ordinary mortals.

In the *Arabian Nights,* the Caliph of Bagdad had seven palaces, the seventh and most sumptuous being the Palace of Eternal and Unsatiating Delights. Here an appeal was made to every one of the senses with so lavish a display of color, sound, and fragrance as to beggar description. At the feasts, there was served, among other dainties, a rose-petal jam, the honeyed sweetness of which was supposed to have a secret power that held captive anyone who ate it. This same confection is manufactured today by the Syrians and is considered a taste thrill for the epicure, though no magical properties are claimed for it.

Burton, in his notes on this same classic, points out that although common water sprinkled on the face was a good cure for fainting among the commonalty, nothing short of rose water must be used on the faces of the nobility and gentry. Burton also recounts, with some feeling, that upon occasion he was obliged "to drink tea made in complement with rose water and did not enjoy it."

More potent drinks than tea have been rose-flavored. In *Gulistan,* the famed collection of Persian wisdom named after the equally famed gardens, we are told of a secret process for making rose wine, so strong that "a glass could make the sternest monarch merciful or make the sickliest mortal slumber amid his pains." The effects of the *rosa solis,* a smooth, oily rose liqueur of Elizabethan days, were less sedative. A moderate amount would "wash molligrubs out of a moody brain"; an immoderate amount, by Pepys' account, caused at least one imbiber to jump from a high second-story window from sheer exuberance—"the desperatest frolic I did ever see."

Not recorded for posterity are the effects produced by drinking one of the most popular liquors of ancient Greece—a concoction of the juice of the Corinth grape, rose water, and fragrant, heady spices—but we can well imagine it might occasionally have thrown a monkey wrench into one or more of those platonic discussions!

Following out the principle, expressed fifteen hundred years later by John Heywood in his *Proverbes*,

> "I pray thee let me and my fellow have
> A haire of the dog that bit us last night,"

roses, particularly dried rose petals steeped in wine, were supposed to have the peculiar virtue of curing hangovers or, as it was more politely put, of "dissipating the fumes of wine." This same "straining of the drye roses sod in wine is good for the headach, for the eyes, the ears, and ye gummes." For other headaches, Athenaeus recommends merely the wearing of a crown of roses to alleviate the pain and also, apparently, for its general uplifting effect. At least this presents us with a more romantic picture than a precariously balanced bag of ice, though experimentation alone can prove which is the more efficacious!

Frequent references to the rose are found in manuscripts and books surviving through the centuries, either in their original form or through translations. The earliest known book to appear during the Middle Ages on gardening and medicines of plant origin was written by Walafrid Strabo (807–849), abbot of Reichenau.

Walafrid was famous both as a botanist and physician, also as a biographer of Charlemagne. His *Hortulus* consists of twenty-seven poems, each of which is a description of a plant grown in his own garden. His favorite flowers were roses and lilies, the latter running a close second to the rose which, he considered, "in virtue and scent surpasses all other herbs, and may rightly be called the flower of flowers." For most of the flora noted he also offers remedies to be made from them, carefully noting their comparative value. The most effective nostrums, and his preferences, were horehound tea for internal use and oil of roses for external applications.

During the Renaissance, the start of the transition from medieval to modern times, the rose continued to grow in significance and the multiplicity of its use. Gerard in his famous herbals (published in the latter half of the sixteenth century) listed among the "virtues of red roses" that they "strengthen the heart and helpe the trembling thereof" as well as invigorating "the liver, kidneys, and other weak intrails." The time-honored use of roses as an eye ointment winds up his commendation: "the nailes or white ends of the petals of the flowers are good for watering eies." Red roses may also be used to "stanch the blood in any part of the body."

According to Askham, whose *Herbal* appeared in 1550, dried roses were as effective as the fresh blooms. "Also drye roses put to the nose to smelle do comforte the braine and the harte and quencheth spirites."

Another characteristic use of the rose was succinctly expressed in Parson Herbert's rhyme:

> "What is fairer than a rose,
> What is sweeter, but it purgeth."

These lines evidently made sport of the popularity and profusion of recipes exploiting the laxative qualities of the flower. The form in which the blossoms were ingested was immaterial; for example, *The Treasuris of Hidden Secrets*, published in 1637, claims almost the same properties for either the rose vinegars or conserves for which recipes are given. Vinegar of roses is to be made by a lengthy process of adding quantities of fresh blossoms to a crockful of vinegar. "Moreover you may make your vinegar with wine, white, red or claret, but the red rose is astringent, and the white is laxative."

"Also the Damask Rose is not so great a binder as the Red Rose, and the white looseth most of all."

Nostradamus, the learned doctor and astrologist whose prophecies recently had a renewed, if temporary, vogue, was reported in his time to have used crushed rose petals to combat one of the recurrent outbreaks of the black plague. The petals were pressed into pellets and placed on the tongues of sufferers. Strangely enough witnesses claimed that the patients so treated recovered.

During the frequent medieval epidemics, which swept through a community or nation, roses were more often used as a safeguard against infection, rather than as a specific cure. People were urged to make smoky fires of aromatic woods, herbs, roses, and other flowers to purify the air in their homes. As protection against infection in public places, pomanders, first described by Pliny, had a great surge of popularity, which survived in their modish use as perfumers long after the belief in their protective properties had died.

Like pomanders, goa stones were carried in elaborate silver or gold cases as safeguards against infection. Only the extremely wealthy, however, could afford this aromatic prophylactic, for goa stones were made by grinding precious gems into a powder to which was added enough rose water to make a paste from which the "stones" or pellets were then formed.

From very early times sweet bags were hung on the arms of chairs as well as in closets and linen chests. Not only were they prized for their perfume, but they were considered an aid to slumber. In Ram's *Little Dodoen* of 1606 we find this pleasant suggestion: "Take dried Rose leaves, keep them in a glass which will keep them sweet and take powder of mynte, powder of cloves in a grosse powder, and putte the same to the Rose leaves: thanne putte all these togyther in a bagge and take that to bedde wyth you and it will cause you to sleepe and it is good to smell unto at other tymes."

The preparation of rose petals for sweet bags was much the same as for potpourri, a fashion which lasts to this day. For those wishing to make it, an excellent present day recipe is as follows:

"Remove petals from open flowers and dry them on sheets of paper. Sprinkle with salt. Add a few other fragrant blossoms such as garden pinks or heliotropes, a few herbs, such as rosemary or marjoram. Add a sprinkling of balsam needles and a bit more salt. When all are thoroughly dried, measure out two quarts (rose petals should always predominate) and place in a crockery jar with the following:

¼ oz. cloves	⅛ oz. crushed coriander
¼ oz. mace	⅛ oz. cardoman seeds (powdered)
¼ oz. cinnamon	gum benzoin
¼ oz. allspice	1 oz. violet sachet"

Stir occasionally during a period of two or three weeks and keep the jar lightly covered in between times. Then place your potpourri in a glass jar for enjoyment in the living room, or in bowls where they will give a delicate scent throughout the winter months.

The high value placed on the properties of another ancient rose medicine is revealed in its name—*arcanum regium*—and was referred to as "drinkable gold" by Roderigo a Fonseca. A veritable aristocrat of elixirs, the method of its making was unfortunately kept secret. It was considered an indication of the high regard in which Queen Elizabeth held Emperor Rudolph II that she presented him with a quantity of it.

The old Roman use of roses as a cure for overindulgence reappeared with additions in the writings of Paracelsus, the sixteenth century Swiss philosopher and physician. "Flowers that are of a burning color like the rose are apt to heal inflammations; those which bear the color of a face heated by wine, as the rose does, obviate drunkenness."

Perhaps the most extravagant claims made during the seventeenth century for the therapeutic value of the flower are to be found in Hagedorn's *Cynosbatologia* and in the hardly credible Rosenberg's *Rhodologia*, a book of about 250 octavo pages published in 1631. No less than thirty-three fatal diseases are listed as being curable by nostrums made particularly

Rose potpourri vase. Meissen, c. 1747.

A fitting setting for dainty recipes is this table arrangement by Patricia Easterbrook Roberts, featuring red and white roses in the centerpiece.

(Collection, Dr. S. Ducret, Zurich)

(Armstrong Nurseries)

Left: Sutter's Gold rose.

(Armstrong Nurseries

Spellbound flowers. Natural roses treated with a special formula to last indefinitely are arranged here in a shadow box picture frame. The new process of preservation has recently been developed by Alma Doody.

In recent years the art of flower arranging has come into its own. It provides a test of skill for the lady of the house and a welcome change from her duties in the kitchen. This charming arrangement by Agnes C. Hamblen features Margot Koster, Ramond Bach, and Mrs. Sam McGredy roses.

Opposite page: Rose Pinkie. A study of the rose named after the famous painting by Sir Thomas Lawrence (1769-1830), a reproduction of which is shown in the background.

Rose Mission Bells in a fashionable arrangement with driftwood.

An all-rose table arrangement featuring Briarcliff roses, Lenox Rhodura pattern china, and Damask Rose Heirloom silver.

from the climbing rose. Rosenberg praises the rose as the universal panacea for the ills of the flesh, maintaining that at least every third proved remedy is compounded wholly or in part of these flowers. And Pomet, in his renowned *Historie des Drogues*, goes Rosenberg one better by unconditionally declaring that "so many diseases are healed with roses that without them medicine would not be as advanced as it is."

One doubts, however, that the most effective ingredient, or the one that held the greatest appeal for the patient was always the rose, especially after reading the following recipe for palsy drops to be made from "lavender, rosemary, saffron, borage, musk roses, cowslips, lilies of the valley, orange blossoms, and *liberal* quantities of . . . French brandy!"

Throughout the pages of old medical books are hints and recipes for the use of the rose in the kitchen. The vogue for rose conserve is attested by the multiplicity of recipes available for this concoction, but with little emphasis on its medicinal value. A *Queen's Delight*, the cookbook published in 1695, describes ways of preparing both cooked and uncooked conserves. One of the recipes for "conserve of roses boiled" instructs you to take "a quart of red Rose water, a quart of fair water, boil in the water a pound of red Rose leaves, the white cut off, the leaves must be boiled very tender; then take three pounds of sugar, and put to it a pound at a time, and let it boil a little between every pound, and so put it up in your pots." This recipe has been tried out recently, using smaller quantities, and with excellent results.

For "conserve of roses unboiled" another old recipe calls for "a pound of red Rose-leaves, the white cut off, stamp them very fine, take a pound of sugar and beat it with the roses, and put it in a pot and cover it with leather. Set in a cool place." No indication is given whether this preparation must age before use or whether setting it in a cool place is simply a preservative measure of a period that lacked mechanical refrigeration.

Pickled rosebuds were much in demand as a condiment at this time, and rose water, made in abundance in rose stills owned by every household of means, was used to flavor even meat and fish.

The extremes to which roses were sometimes utilized is exemplified by a recipe concocted by a cook who evidently desired too much of a good thing. The formula calls for forty bushels of Damask roses, to which, when prepared, are to be added some tincture of roses, a quantity of syrup of roses as well as honey, rose troches, and a special rose cordial brewed from new sweetbriar roses. Just what this fanciful mixture tasted like, has never been recorded by any gourmet, and probably never will be.

As unlikely to appear on a modern table are the "potted roses" prepared for a king of Italy. In the words of the royal cook: "I first pound some of the most fragrant roses in a mortar; then I take the brains of birds and pigs, well boiled and stripped of every particle of meat. I then add some yolks of eggs, some oil, a little cordial, some pepper and some wine. After having beaten and mixed it well together I throw it in a new pot and place it over a slow but steady fire." After due time the pot was uncovered and "the most delicious fragrance issued forth, overcoming the guests with delight."

If such exotic fare as "potted roses" has little appeal to the modern appetite, it must be remembered that even the confectionaries of the seventeenth century would be strange to today's taste although a fondness for them could undoubtedly be acquired. The *Accomplisht Cook* contains recipes for such sweets as "jemelloes," which were made of sugar, caraway seeds, and rose water. They were considered to be excellent for banquets. "Muskechives" or "kissing comfits" were more elaborately prepared from sugar, gum-dragon, musk, civet, orris powder, and rose water. Laid on a flat surface to harden, they were cut into lozengers with an "iging-iron."

Rose-petal jams, jellies, and marmalades, cakes made with rose water, and sugar delicately flavored with roses graced the table of fashionable Victorian hostesses even as they had the tables of previous centuries. Rose-petal sandwiches were teatime favorites, dark red roses on thinly cut and buttered brown bread being considered the choicest.

But the vogue for such fragrant fare did not last long after the turn of the present century. The swift-paced lives of today, dominated by an increasing quantity of mass-produced commodities, have unfortunately lost, except in rare instances, the leisure, the opportunity, and the flair for such dainty experiments. Roses are no longer sold by the bushel, and increasing millions live in environments lacking any facilities for either a "ferned grot" or a "rose plot." Even in such a comparatively unindustrial-ized nation as China, increasingly few remember or observe during these war-ridden times, the rose customs so charmingly described by Tun Li-Ch'en in *Annual Customs and Festivals in Peking*. In the "Fourth Month" were served rose cakes made from roses, sugar, and fine flour. Or those with a less pronounced sweet tooth might choose instead to have a sour prune drink or soup "made from sour prunes boiled with sugar, to which rose blossoms and olives are added, and which is cooled with ice water until it chills the teeth."

A popular custom which has come down to us through the years is the ceremony of tea drinking. Rose blossom tea, with its dainty flowery overtone, like Jasmine tea, was originally intended for honored guests. Ming Rose Blossom tea, still made and distributed in this country, has for a long time delighted the epicure because of its hauntingly delicate bouquet. Made from succulent tea leaves of the earliest pickings, it is cured and carefully blended, then combined with the fragrant rose petals and fired. It has the charming appearance of a potpourri.

VII

CUSTOMS AND FASHIONS

When roses in the garden grew
And not in ribbons on a shoe;
Now ribbon roses take such place
That garden roses want their grace.
                    FRIAR BACON, "Prophecy," 1604

THE USE of the rose for costume decoration in all countries and centuries is such common knowledge that we need only concern ourselves with one or two more unusual examples.

Enormous "ribbon roses" were the fashion of Shakespeare's day, and we see them in many full-length portraits of that period. In their creation, both the botanical color and characteristic number of petals were carefully considered. Thus the wearer of "two provincial roses in his razed shoes" in *Hamlet* sported rosettes in the shape and tone of the Provins roses. In many of the original Shakespearean folios, the playwright is also shown with his shoes decorated in this manner. In others he wears a hat ornamented with several huge ribbon rose creations.

Another fashion we can trace back to sixteenth century England was the mode of wearing roses behind the ear. It is possible, however, that this custom came from Spain. Some authorities hold that it was a faddish way of illustrating that the wearer heard all and told nothing. Queen Elizabeth is shown in a few portraits, also on one of the coins of her reign, wearing a rose behind her ear. If the fanciful interpretation is true, it likely gave birth to the expression "keep it under your hat."

The origin of the term *sub rosa*, as a synonym for secrecy and silence is obscure and disputed. Both the Romans and Greeks considered it a symbol of silence. The unknown author of *Rosa Flos Veneris* explained that "the rose is the flower of Venus; and Love, in order that his sweet dishonesties be hidden, dedicated the gift of his mother to Harpocrates, the god of silence. Hence the host hangs the rose over his table, that his

93

guests may know that what is said beneath its bloom will be regarded as secret." Other authorities contend that the use of the rose on graves made it the symbol of secrecy and concealment.

Teutonic legend on the other hand credits the origin of *sub rosa* differently. The rose was the flower of Freyja, the northern counterpart of Venus, and as such was often carved and sculptured on ceilings. When wine and mead had loosened tongues to indiscreet speech, the symbol reminded the revelers that their words were spoken "under the rose" or under the protection of Freyja, and were therefore not to be bandied about.

There are also those who claim that this term stemmed from the English Wars of the Roses. At that time two taverns near the Houses of Parliament, displayed signs featuring the white and red rose, respectively. Each tavern was frequented by the adherents of the one or the other faction whose emblem was shown outside. Many political conferences were held in these taverns and measures requiring great secrecy were discussed. The participants in referring to their conversations said they had taken place "under the rose."

In 1526 roses were hung over confessionals or carved on stone or wooden benches as an indication of the confidential and secret nature of the act of confession. In many of the city council chambers on the Continent, the rose was suspended over the door as an emblem of reticence. A time-honored variant of this is still to be found in London where at the meeting of aldermen and sheriffs deciding the election of the Lord Mayor of the city, the ornate and symbolical sword of the city is laid on a bed of roses at the beginning of the proceedings to show that all transactions are *sub rosa*, or secret.

This conspiratory use of the queen of flowers has been but one small part of the large floral vocabulary. Roman lovers sent their favorites huge baskets of the first spring roses, as visible interpreters of their expression of endearment—*mea rosa*. The hieroglyphics of ancient Egyptians abound in floral symbols, and it was probably from them that the Greeks, and then the Romans, learned this figurative language which spread throughout Asia Minor.

> "In Eastern lands they talk in flowers,
>   And they tell in a garland their loves and cares . . .
> The rose is a sign of joy and love."

Almost two milleniums later, shy lovers of the Victorian era found in the tussie-mussie, mentioned earlier in the book, a means of conveying their messages. The rose symbolism in it meant "may you be pleased,

94

and your sorrow mine." The old-fashioned tussie-mussie was a compact cluster of flowers. The center blossom was the keynote and conveyed the desired sentiment and dominant fragrance. The intended message was emphasized by the surrounding leaves and flowers.

The rose code, as it might be called, was no casual achievement and it often required much study to interpret the true meaning of a bouquet. An Austrian rose at the center of a bouquet, for instance, breathed the tender message, "Thou art all that is lovely," while a yellow rose in the same position—harbinger of smelling salts—disillusioningly signified "decrease of love on better acquaintance."

The modifications of this flowery language were almost limitless. If a flower were given reversed, its original significance was understood to have been contradicted and the opposite meaning implied. For example, a rosebud divested of its thorns but retaining its leaves revealed that the sender no longer feared the outcome of his chaste pursuit, but hoped for a happy ending, thorns being symbols of fear and leaves the symbol of hope. Stripped of both leaves and thorns, the bud expressed a melancholy state, indeed: "There is nothing to hope or fear."

Roses have also formed part of the marriage customs of many lands. Brides and grooms were as rose-festooned as Hymen, the god of marriage. According to Mishnaic tradition the rose, like the myrtle, formed part of the bridal couple's garlands as they walked down their scented and flower-strewn way. Medieval women, on becoming brides of mortal men, or brides of Christ by symbolically taking the veil, wore chaplets of roses. In France, women on their wedding morning threw petals from their rose wreaths into a pool or stream with the words "*Rose de ma jeunesse ne quitte pas ma vieillesse*" (rose of my youth do not forsake me in my old age). And in the Tyrol a man proclaimed his engagement by wearing a rose.

Perhaps the most picturesque of rose marriage customs is the ancient Armenian one in which a rose leaf is placed on each of the bride's palms the night before the wedding. Her hands are then covered with henna and carefully bandaged. The next morning when the bandages are removed, her hands are colored an orange-red except for the imprints of rose petals on both palms. After an elaborate marriage ceremony, the health of the couple must be drunk in rose syrup no matter what other foods and liquors are served.

Rose water played its part in marriage customs, too. In *Amoenitates* Kampfer wrote of his travels in the Near East: "Distilled rose water is freely carried all over India and the provinces of Persia, itself. It is deemed as an article of luxury at marriage feasts and reunions of friends. It is boiled with cinnamon and white sugar, and is drunk as an alternative to *kahwa*. Rose water is used to sprinkle on the guests as a sign of wel-

95

come." It is this custom of sprinkling with rose water that is alluded to in Byron's "The Bride of Abydos":

> "She snatched the urn wherein was mixed
> The Persian Atar-gul's perfume,
> And sprinkled all its odours o'er
> The pictured roof and marbled floor."

The association of roses and graves has lent itself to the varying philosophies of many centuries and nations. The flower the Greeks claimed was bleached white by the tears of mourners has been found in an Egyptian tomb excavated in 1882 and sealed perhaps in A.D. 2. The garlands, rosebuds, and rose petals found in other Egyptian burial places have been identified as the *rosa sancta*, which for centuries was known as the "rose of the tombs." This species still grows in parts of Ethiopia.

Five hundred years prior to the first discovered funereal use of roses by the Egyptians, the Greeks associated the flower with man's transition. Anacreon, who is generally thought of as a poet who wrote of love, and conviviality in general, gave birth to the early Greek belief that the fragrance of roses on graves signified the purification of the dead:

> "When pain afflicts and sickness grieves,
> Its roses' juice the drooping heart relieves;
> And after death its odors shed
> A pleasing fragrance o'er the dead."

The Greeks, as did the Romans, left legacies to have their tombs planted with rosebushes and decorated with the cut blossoms. Romans not rich enough to provide funds either for maintaining gardens or for supplying garlands of roses, had their grave markers inscribed with pleas to passers-by to scatter roses on their tombs.

The Christians took this pagan custom and adapted it to their own philosophies. Jerome, one of the early Christian fathers, wrote: "The ancients scattered roses over the urns of the deceased, and in their wills ordered that these flowers should adorn their graves. . . . These flowers were emblematic signs of grief. Our Christians . . . place a rose among the ornaments on the grave as the image of life." The history of "The Fair Rosamund," known also to posterity as Rosa Mundi,* is an interesting one. The inamorata of Henry II of England, Rosamund finally met her death at the hands of Eleanor of Aquitaine, jealous wife of the king, and was buried at Godstowe. Her tomb, decked with roses, was later removed

---

* The rose named after her stems from *Rosa gallica*, the French or garden rose figuring in stained glass windows of the Gothic cathedrals.

outside the abbey by order of St. Hugh, Bishop of Lincoln, lest Christian religion grow in contempt and to the end that, through example of her, other women, being made afraid, may beware. The Latin inscription on the gravestone was translated by Stowe:

> "The rose of the world, but not the cleane flower,
> Is now here graven; to whom beauty was lent.
> In this grave fulle darke now is her boure
> That by her life was sweet and redolent;
> But now that she is from this life blent,
> Though she were sweete, now foully doth she stinke,
> A minor good for all men that on her think."

King John endowed Godstowe with a yearly income that the nuns there might "releeve by their prayers the soules of his father, King Henrie and of Lady Rosamund there interred."

The custom of decorating graves with roses was so prevalent in Germany that the cemetery was often called the rose garden. Here, as elsewhere, roses were not only grown but were engraved on the tombstones as representative symbols of the souls of the dead. Throughout Wales white roses are planted on the graves of the young and unmarried. In Scotland, roses are generally found growing in burial plots, especially on children's graves.

Many renowned men have carried on this traditional custom of decoration, echoing Omar Khayyam's plea:

> "So bury me by some sweet Garden-Side.
> That ev'n my buried Ashes such a Snare
> Of perfume shall fling up into the Air,
> As not a True Believer passing by
> But shall be overtaken unaware."

A rose tree from the tomb of Omar Khayyam was moved to the grave of his translator, Edward FitzGerald, who caught the essential spirit and beauty of Khayyam's verses, making them among the most widely read and quoted poetry in the English language. Father Tabb, in his own little book of poems, explained the symbolic significance of the legacy of this rose in a couplet:

> "Alike from alien lips one music flows
> To flush the Orient Rose."

Bertel Thorwaldsen, the noted sculptor, by his written request, was buried under a bed of roses in the courtyard of his museum in Copenhagen, and when the immortal Victor Hugo, who had always hoped to die in the season of roses, passed away on May 22, 1885, his friends heaped roses on his coffin and arranged for the carving of roses at the base of his tomb. Many other personal examples of this elegiac use of the rose could be cited, nor was the practice confined to the occident. The Chinese plant the flower on their graves, as do the Turks, though the latter reserve either the flower or its graven image to indicate the resting place of virgins.

One of the most charming descriptions of a fanciful rite comes from the pen of William Blake:

"I was walking alone in my garden; there was a stillness among the branches and flowers, and more than a common sweetness in the air; I heard a low and pleasant sound, and I knew not whence it came. At last I saw the broad leaf of a flower move, and underneath I saw a procession of creatures, of the size and colour of green and grey grasshoppers, bearing a body laid out on a rose-leaf, which they buried with songs, and then disappeared. It was a fairy funeral."

After sufficient time had elapsed to permit the divorce in people's minds of the association between garlands and crowns of roses with the conviviality and debauchery of the Romans, these lay traditions, like all folk customs, found new favor in churches. On the day of Fête-Dieu, the Roman Catholics in southern France and other parts of Europe scattered rose petals in the air during the solemn procession. In Dominican churches the last roses of summer were blessed on the first or Rosary Sunday in October and distributed among the worshipers. Young girls at the Orphanage of Beyrout received their first communion with wreaths of white roses on their heads, starting a widespread custom.

So prevalent was the dedication of roses to the Virgin and the decoration of her statues with roseate wreaths, that many authorities consider the custom to be the origin of rosaries. The usage itself stemmed from the older tradition of offering crowns or chaplets of roses to distinguished persons, and was in turn transformed into one of offering wreaths, not of material roses, but of prayers and praises. Catholic legends tell of such transformation as a miraculous and sudden one, but rosaries are not a device unique to the Catholic Church. It is possible that rose pods or hips strung together were first employed for counting the aves as they were repeated. This particular fruit may have been chosen either because of its convenient shape and size or because of the sacred symbolism of the flower from which it is harvested. In China the rosaries of the Buddhists are similarly made from the fruit of a tree, the hard kernel of which is beautifully adapted to the purpose. For some of the first rosaries, the rose flowers, themselves, or petals may have been used, for the fabrication of rose pearls can still be found in the East.

Flowers also played an important part in the history of the church in

Above right: The medieval custom of manning a mimic castle with fair ladies who bombarded their suitors with roses is described on page 103. This illustration from a fourteenth-century French ivory casket depicts a similar assault on the castle of love from "The Legend of Aristotle, the Fountain of Youth." Above: The fashion of garlands as a dress ornamentation is typified by this eighteenth-century painting from a portrait by Jean Honoré Fragonard (1732-1806).

(*Metropolitan Museum of Art*)

The custom of carrying American Beauty roses at the Ivy Day processional at Smith College in Northampton, Massachusetts, is still followed. This photograph showing turn-of-the-century gowns was taken in 1902.

Photographed fifty years later, this illustration shows a mid-twentieth-century hat featuring the ever fashionable rose. It was designed by Laddie Northridge, New York.

England. There was a *gardenia sacristae* at Winchester as early as the ninth century, and the church of Eton College was bequeathed such a garden by Henry VI. At many great functions held in the churches, the priests were crowned with garlands: "this was especially the custom at St. Paul's in London. On June 30, 1405, when Bishop Roger de Walden was installed there, he and the canons of the Cathedral walked in solemn procession wearing garlands of red roses." Wearing of such *coronae sacredotales* was prevalent up to the time of the Reformation.

A very colorful ceremony of the Christian church is found in Armenia. The festival of Transfiguration Sunday is popularly called *Vartavar*, which literally translated means the "flaming, or burning, of the rose." The celebration is preceded by a night of bonfires, similar to the midsummer fires dedicated to St. John or St. Peter throughout central Europe. The name *Vartavar* is probably an allusion to some forgotten rite in which roses were burnt or else thrown across the flame as in Europe. The traditions of the celebration can be traced back to pagan festivals. One of these was the midsummer feast in honor of Anakit, the goddess of chastity. The central act of her festival was the offering of a dove and a rose to her golden image. Later on, with the advent of Christianity, the temple of Anakit was replaced by the Cathedral of Etchmiadzin, customarily decorated with masses and garlands of roses.

During the ecclesiastical procession of the festival of Anakit the priests scatter rose water over the congregation, and throughout the ceremony the people themselves drench each other with the same fragrance. This unique custom is a survival of an old water festival which antedated Christianity and was connected with an indigenous legend of a deluge which covered the earth. Under Christian instruction the deluge became the flood of Biblical history, the universal baptism with which God cleansed His sinful earth; and the sprinkling with rose water is emblematic of it.

The origin of another church custom among Catholics, now obscure, was that of presenting a golden rose to an illustrious person or group of people conspicuous for loyalty to the Holy See. Some authorities claim that it displaced the ceremony of bestowing the golden keys of St. Peter's confessional. Constantine the Great, the first Roman emperor to become a Christian, was also the first known person to make use of a golden rose. He had one, weighing a hundred and fifty pounds, placed on the tomb of St. Peter in Rome. However, his gesture seems to have been an individual one, for the golden rose does not appear until approximately seven hundred years later.

In 1049 the presentation of the golden rose as it is known today was instituted by Pope Leo IX, although, in 1051, he himself spoke of it as an ancient custom. To him it may have been a variant of the familiar feudal custom of the presentation by serfs to their lords and masters of a real rose as a symbol of their fealty or as a token of the payment of annual rent to the landowners. During each year of his pontificate, Pope Leo exacted a golden rose from the Monastery of the Holy Cross in Alsace as a sign of the religious order's submission to his undisputed authority. It was presented to him at elaborate ceremonies on Laetare Sunday.

The blessing of this flower of pure gold, set with costly gems, was not coeval with its beginning. The first pope thus to bless it was Innocent IV, whose pontificate was from 1245 to 1254. The consecration added even greater solemnity to the ceremonies celebrated on the fourth or Laetare Sunday of Lent, often referred to as "Rose Sunday." The earliest examples of the golden rose were modeled after the single, or five-petaled, flower, and often comprised more than one blossom. In this case the topmost flower was shaped into a cup which the pope filled with balsam and musk during the rite of blessing the ornament. This sacred vessel was then carried in solemn procession to the sacristy of the pope's private chapel. On Laetare Sunday, rose-colored vestments, also altar, throne, and chapel draperies (signs of joy and hope) are substituted for penitential purple during the solemn function. This ancient ceremony has changed but little through the centuries. Sometimes the same rose may be used for years at the annual ceremony before it is finally given to some distinguished recipient as a token of special esteem.

Both the form and the symbolism of the golden rose gradually changed. The ornamentation came to represent the frailty of human life, while the indestructibility of the metal from which it was contrived stood for the immortality of the soul. Then as popes and church authorities refined and expounded its significance, the rose finally symbolized the risen Christ and the living Church. The Church on this Laetare Sunday bids her children look beyond the fasting and penitence of the Lenten season to the risen Christ, and the shining splendor of the golden rose shows Christ in His kingly majesty, heralded by the prophets as "the flower of the field and the lily of the valley." Its incensed fragrance represents the sweet odor of Christ which should be diffused widely by His faithful followers, and the thorns and red tint tell of His passion. According to Isaiah: "Why then is thy apparel red, and thy garments like theirs that tread in the winepress?" An example of this symbolic rose is shown on page 198.

Roses have appeared throughout the ages in many nonecclesiastic awards. In France, the winners of the poetry competitions known as "floral games," received a golden rose and a marigold of silver.

Then, of course, there is the example of the French Rosati, or Society of the Rose, the Anacreontic organization, founded in Arras in 1778, and composed of men of education and culture who loved nature. The requirements for membership included the writing of verse and song in honor of the rose which had to be accepted by all the members. Robespierre, the Terror, was a member of this society.

Another old French institution was the Tribute of Roses. When the peers of France met in parliamentary session, a designated nobleman decorated all the chambers with roses. Then before the sitting opened the nobleman who had been awarded this prized position distributed a crown of roses to each member of parliament. As one can easily imagine, it was not long before a heated Gallic discussion as to whose turn next it was to perform the honor led to a fatal quarrel, and the ceremony was abandoned thenceforth.

The custom of selecting the "rose girl of Salency" was established by St. Medard, Bishop of Noyon in the sixth century. At the festival known as the *Fête de la Rosiers*, which is held every third year, a prize of a chaplet of roses and a purse filled with gold francs is given to a girl selected for her outstanding virtue. The standards for the selection are rigid: not only must the girl be irreproachable, but also her family and relatives "even unto the fourth generation."

A prize for virtue of another sort was to be found in Switzerland. If a man accused of crime was able to justify himself and prove his innocence the same day on which he was accused, he was liberated and given a white rose called the "rose of innocence," by a young and beautiful girl, especially chosen to bestow this emblem of acquittal.

Extensive use of roses in public was made by the Greeks who encircled the statues of Venus, Hebe, and Flora, as well as Hymen, the god of marriage, and Comus, the god of pleasure, with garlands of freshly picked blooms. At the festivals of Hymen at Athens, the youths of both sexes were also crowned with the same flowers as they mingled in dances representing the innocence of primeval times.

Another medieval custom originated in Treviso, Italy. A mimic castle, hung with rich carpets and silks, was erected and "manned" by the girls of the city. Their weapons consisted of roses, rose water, and other equally delicate missiles. The young blades of the town, similarly "armed," attacked the fortress to win their "queens." In the twelfth century the emperor Barbarossa took part in one of these parties and declared himself to have been delighted with the sport.

Many local midsummer festivals, featured the "crown of roses." At Grammont, Belgium, the midsummer bonfire was ignited on St. Peter's Eve, and the festival of "crowning" was held the following Sunday. The young folk elected a king and queen of roses from among the dancers in the flower-wreathed streets. At a signal the wreaths fell on the chosen pair, who then had to entertain their fellows at a feast.

Fynes Moryson, the noted traveler who lived from 1556–1617, wrote that "the Germans . . . commonly weare garlands of Roses (which they call Crantzes). . . . For they keep Roses all Winter in little pots of earth, whereof they open one every Saturday night, and distribute the Roses among the women of the house, to the very kitchen maids; others keep them all in one pot, and weekelly take as many Roses as they neede, and cover the rest, keeping them fresh till next Summer. And the common sort mingle gilded nutmegs with the Roses, and make garlands thereof. Only women weare these Garlands in Winter, but in Summer time, men of the better sort weare them within doors, and men of the common sort weare them going abroade."

Not all of the rose customs have necessarily resulted in a happy ending. On one occasion, though hard to conceive, a number of Nero's guests were actually smothered when an avalanche of rose petals were thrown from the balconies above. And an incredible punishment based on a rose custom was recorded by Pliny. Because the wearing of festive rose garlands was forbidden in Rome at times of national calamities, Lucius Fluvius, a banker, by order of the Senate, was imprisoned for the duration of the Second Punic War, a period of sixteen years. This sentence was given because he had dared look from his gallery on the Forum while wearing a crown of roses!

VIII

ROSE GARDENS OF THE WORLD

A garden is a lovesome thing, God wot!
Rose plot,
Fringed pool,
Fern'd grot.

THOMAS BROWN

THIS WAS the thought of Thomas Brown in the middle of the nineteenth century. But he was not the first person to praise a rose garden, or the miniature "rose plot." Centuries before these lines were printed, the prophet Esdras described heaven as: "Seven mighty mountains, whereupon there grow roses and lilies."

This rose garden of heaven staggers the imagination. Sandro Botticelli and the school of Italian painters in the fifteenth and sixteenth centuries scaled the size down to enclosed gardens of roses or "gardens of adoration." One of these, "The Enclosed Garden of the Virgin" by Stefano da Zevio is at the Royal Museum at Verona. The painting shows the Virgin sitting in a garden enclosed by trellised roses with St. Catherine, the only other human occupant, weaving a crown of these flowers. Another lovely Garden of Adoration, ascribed to Botticini, is that of the Infant Christ in a rose trellised garden where angels playfully sprinkle rose petals over Him. "They worship here always alone, though there is no gate to the garden; the angels have relinquished high heaven for these delights; for the scent of these roses which they pluck." (Robert de la Condamine, *The Upper Garden.*)

These visionary or picture gardens were not unimportant, for they lent inspiration and design to many real rose gardens of the world. The latter may be divided into three general groups: first, public or test gardens; second, private; and third, natural or nature's rose gardens. There is no distinct line of separation between these classifications. The so-called private gardens are often open to the public and test gardens cater im-

Herbarius Latinus. 1486. An early illustration of a rose bush.

partially to both private and public interests. Although the test garden is most valuable to rose growers, it also furnishes rare delight to the rose-loving public as well.

Of the first group, L'Hay in Paris is voted the most famous municipal rose garden in the world. Its inception came from a chance remark made to Jules Gravereaux, the owner of Le Bon Marché, a large department store in Paris. It was during the rose season while on a business visit to Domaine de Cartigny, the estate of a cotton manufacturer, that Gravereaux remarked:

"I wish I owned a rosary like this!"

"If I had your fortune," his host replied, "I would retire from business and devote my life to the rose."

Those last words must have echoed and re-echoed constantly in the mind of Gravereaux until a few years later he bought an estate in Paris. Here, in truth, he dedicated his life to the rose and his efforts met with great success. Not only is Roseraie de L'Hay the most important rosary but also the most beautiful from the standpoint of architecture and design.

The artistic layout and completeness of this collection of species, combining both historical and modern roses, have never been duplicated. Miniature gardens, each featuring a different kind of rose, blend into a uniform pattern, culminating in a court of honor and theater of the rose. The entire effect is a rose-filled tapestry interspersed at intervals with gleaming marble statues.

Close by, there is a museum that contains rose paintings and records of the roses of France. Also, rose manuscripts that record rose development ever since the French began to write of this flower, are housed in the library.

Proposition d'un arbre généalogique de la Rose

(Reproduction d'un document d'études de la Roseraie de l'Haÿ)

LÉGENDE :

1° **Arbre généalogique :**

1ʳᵉ ZONE. Les Ancêtres de la Rose.

2ᵉ ZONE. Dispersion de la Rose sur la Terre.

Rosiers à organes imparfaits.
- 1. Rosiers vêtus.
- 2. Rosiers inermes.
- 3. Rosiers aiguillonnés,
- 4. Rosiers à feuillage vernissé.
- 5. Rosiers à organes perfectionnés.

3ᵉ ZONE. Les Roses améliorées par l'homme. Roses hybrides

2° **Aire géographique :**

Les hachures indiquent les parties du monde où les Roses, probablement venues du Plateau Central de l'Asie, se sont répandues, et croissent de nos jours à l'état sauvage.

107

L'Hay is not a test garden, and no contests are ever held there. However, M. Gravereaux made it a point to acquire all the new roses developed each year until in 1902 it was officially recorded that his collection totaled 5,545 bush and 514 climbing varieties. After his death in 1906 the family decided to limit the yearly acquisitions to varieties rewarded at the important contests and test gardens. This brought the number up to eight thousand in 1937, with over fifty thousand plants in the gardens.

Another famous French rose garden was created by Empress Josephine at Malmaison. This contained every known rose of her day, totaling about 250 varieties. The garden suffered after her death, but in 1910 it was publicly restored and is once more very much as it was during her lifetime.

Josephine might well be called the fairy godmother of roses. She stimulated research and experiments in rose hybridizing with grants from her own private funds, and during the Napoleonic wars, captured ships were searched for plants and seeds for her garden. Choicest varieties that could be obtained from Holland, Belgium, and Germany gave an increased impulse to the cultivation of roses in the vicinity of Paris. When Dr. Delile, Director of the Botanical Garden at Montpellier, accompanied Napoleon on the expedition to Egypt, he was particularly interested in two new roses found there, *rosa alba*, and *rosa centifolia*, which he brought back with him to Paris, probably for Josephine.

The passion of the empress for roses did not end with the creation of a magnificent garden and the cultivation of new stock. She surrounded herself with specialist artists and writers, among whom was Redouté. Through her marshaling of great and serious-minded men in the service of the rose, Josephine, with her little army, accomplished greater lasting good for the world at large than did Napoleon with his armies of fighting men. The emperor's own love of flowers, however, is reflected in his well-known statement: "Wherever flowers cannot be reared, there man cannot live!" His last night as emperor of France, before he embarked for Elba, was spent in the rose garden at Malmaison, alone.

The great Bagatelle Rose Gardens are also famous in France, and so is the rosary at Lyons, where the Rhone and Saône rivers meet. This magnificent forestlike park *de la Tête d'Or* (Of the Golden Head) is a modern rosary, staging the yearly contest for the most beautiful rose of France.

The foundations of the modern English garden roses were laid in France, yet the flower has always been the national emblem of England, and probably in no other country is it universally so beautiful or more loved. As one English authority over a hundred years ago said: "the rose attains a larger size in England [than in France], from the comparative moderation and humidity in the climate; and the blossom of any

La condufion du rommant
e it quelwne voiczeylamant

Medieval rose gar-
den, from an early
manuscript in the
British Museum. Be-
low: The Mary
Margaret McBride
rose.

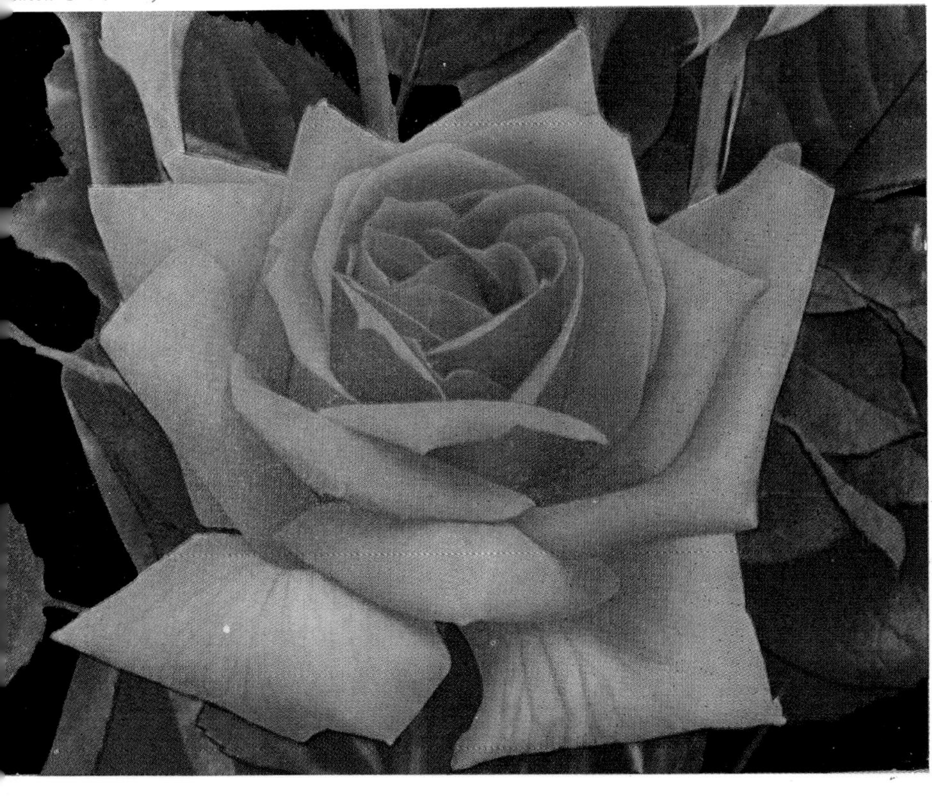

Above: The Aventine trial rose garden next to the Palace of the Caesars in Rome. *Below:* Pergolas in the famous Roseraie de l'Hay, near Paris.

Above: Queen Mary's rose garden at Regents Park, London. Below: The Orangerie at the head of the Bagatelle Municipal Rose Gardens of Paris.

Above: Acres of roses near Tyler, Texas. A typical scene from spring through autumn in the fields of rose growers. Below: At Tombstone, Arizona, the Lady Banksia rose tree, claimed to be the largest in the world. It was planted over half a century ago by a young bride from Scotland.

A beautiful vista in the Oakland Municipal Rose Garden, California. The steps are lined with hedges of Japanese Rosa Wichuraiana.

(Photo: Eric M. Sanford)

Above: An arbor view at the famous Hershey Rose Garden, Hershey, Pennsylvania. Left: The home of Benjamin Franklin's mother at Nantucket, Massachusetts, with walls covered with climbing roses.

(Photo: Gottscho-Schleisner)

Yellow and white rose garden at Jackson and Perkins Nursery, Newark, New York.

115

individual kind of rose remains a longer time expanded in our cloudy atmosphere, than under the intense heat and light of a Continental sun, unobscured by clouds or mists." Even the French had to admit that the rose, in these days at least, attained its highest perfection in the British Isles.

It is no wonder, therefore, that the number of rose gardens to be found in England is prodigious. We find formal rose gardens laid out in the spacious gardens of the "stately homes," in the gardens of castles, palaces, and ducal estates. At the famous Royal Botanic Gardens of Kew, just outside London, the public is permitted a glimpse of some of the finest specimens. But everywhere through the length and breadth of the land, the traveler sees the less pretentious gardens surrounding smaller country homes, the quaint cottage gardens, the walled gardens—and the high spot of all of them in June is a colorful display of roses.

Everyone loves gardens, but all gardeners do not like the work necessary to keep them beautiful. In Persia, the saying goes: "Does not Allah choose if the roses bloom or not, while the gardeners sleep or are engaged at the side door with official or unofficial fruit buyers?" Perhaps this is why there are few large rose gardens in Persia, but many lovely small ones. Be that as it may, the important factor of the Persian garden is its privacy, for it is here the Persian host receives his guests. A mud wall surrounds it, whether it is geometrically oblong or square. There are rose trees within and a tank of water, for water in a pool would disappear overnight. The patches of flowers are set out in designs influenced perhaps by the national industry of carpet-making. In a short time this garden space is a mass of color. In most countries of the West, one searches for new rosebuds among the leaves; in a Persian garden, a search must be made for leaves among the profligate profusion of roses.

Hafiz wrote eloquently of the rose gardens of Shiraz. To him the little *Ruknabad* (streamlet) was a perennial spring; a rose garden an earthly paradise. His tomb is not far from the Koran Gate, in the center of the Shiraz gardens which also inspired many of his songs. The rose garden of Masalla where he eventually spent most of his life in retirement may have suggested the larger garden in the love poem containing the following lines:

> "In the rose garden of the world, one rose
> For me's enough."

Here, too, these other lines were definitely written:

> "The rose's hundred thousand laughters ring
> the garden through."

117

Opposite page: Wild roses by the sea at Little Boar's Head, New Hampshire. (Photo: Eric M. Sanford, in "New Hampshire Profiles.")

In Spain the rose plot is very similar to the Persian rose garden. And no private garden is too small to be without at least one little *glorieta*, or arbor of roses, that shades the crossing of a side path. The word *glorieta* means tiny paradise or private glory and it is a refuge from the sun by day and often the dining place of the family on a hot summer night.

In Italy, the love of the rose dates back to the days of the Roman Emperors. We have already read how roses were shipped from Egypt to Rome, and of Nero's great passion for the flower. Again, at the time of the Renaissance, over a thousand years later, there are several references to the cultivation of the flower in the formal gardens of the nobility. There is a lyric by Lorenzo de Medici (1449–1492) inspired by his rose garden in Florence:

> "Into a little close of mine I went
> > One morning when the sun with his fresh light
> > Was rising all refulgent and unshent.
> Rose-trees are planted there in order bright.
> > Whereto I turned charmed eyes, and long did stay,
> > Taking my fill of that new-found delight.
> Red and white roses bloomed upon the spray;
> > One opened, leaf by leaf, to greet the morn,
> Shyly, at first, then in sweet disarray;
> Another, yet a youngling, newly born,
> > Scarce struggled from the bud, and there were some
> > Whose petals closed them from the air forlorn;
> Another fell, and showered the grass with bloom;
> > Thus I behold the roses dawn and die,
> > And one short hour their loveliness consume." *

The Villa d'Este, one of the most beautiful gardens in Italy, is so famous for its fountains that flowers here play a less important part. But an example of lovely roses in this country may be found in the garden of the Hotel San Dominico located on a cliff overlooking the blue sea. This hotel was the convent of the Dominican fathers, and the original old courtyard, cypress trees, and roses produce an unforgettable picture of peace and serenity.

The most recent rose garden in Italy, and certainly the most beautiful, is on the Aventine, one of the Seven Hills of Rome. On one side of a quiet street are the trial gardens, and on the other a general collection of

* Translated by J. A. Symonds.

all kinds. The only competition affecting the beautiful display is the glorious setting. The garden slopes eastward; underneath is the hollow where the Circus Maximus lies, the largest of the Roman amphitheaters, while opposite and directly facing the rose gardens are the ruins of the Palace of the Caesars. Visible is the imperial box from which the emperor watched the games in the circus below.

In Germany, the essence of the story of Sleeping Beauty (*Dornroeschen*) is the victory of spring over winter which is won in the rose garden. It was here that the driving out of winter took place, a traditional belief of which we learn not only in folk songs but also in present-day customs. In the *Rose Garden Song*, this mystical cult is transferred into the sphere of heroes and troubadours, and blooming roses sometimes become burning wounds and sometimes kissing lips. Thus the rose assumes three symbols dear to the Germanic heart: the power of the sun in spring, the prize of honor in battle, and the bliss of fulfilled love. It is natural that this feeling for the rose should find expression in lovely rose gardens in Germany. At the fashionable resort of Baden-Baden in the Black Forest a rose festival is held every year, making use of several thousand species. Tourists from all over the world find relaxation and enjoyment in this colorful display augmented by music in the park.

A nursery in Switzerland deserves honorary mention because it provides one of the most spectacular examples of rose scenery in the world. On one side of the highway, about ten miles out of Geneva, is the famous lake with its expanse of clear water, backed by snow-clad Alps. The grandeur of Mont Blanc, although forty miles south of the lake, is plainly visible in clear weather because of the reflection of the sun on the glaciers. On the opposite side of the road is Heizmann's Nursery, terraced on the slope of the mountain. This veritable carpet of roses spread out against so breathtaking a setting is the personal choice of many as one of their "seven wonders of the world."

A scene not unlike this in many respects is conjured up by Sir Edwin Arnold in *The Light of Asia.* In the garden of the young Prince Siddārtha, which had for a backdrop the white ranks of the Himalayas, roses grew in such profusion that the gazelles and antelopes would feast on these flowers:

> "By winding ways of garden and of court
> The inner gate was reached, of marble wrought,
> White, with pink veins; the lintel lazuli,
> The threshold alabaster, and the doors
> Sandal-wood, cut in pictures panelling;
> Great-eyed gazelles in sunny alcoves browsed
> The blown red roses."

In many parts of China there are small and exquisite rose gardens. This comes as no surprise in a nation so devoted to the beauty of flowers. The Chinese housewife does not, like many a foreign sister, buy a magnificent bouquet of flowers for her table when guests are expected and then forget about them for the rest of the week. Practically every day the Chinese woman carries home a single carefully selected spray, or perhaps one perfect rose or other flower. This is chosen with infinite care, also according to her means or what is growing nearby, and is as necessary to the family table as the rice for dinner.

There are really no so-called private gardens in China. Most Chinese deem it a personal privilege to walk in and quietly enjoy the garden of a wealthier neighbor. The idea, for instance, that a rose garden should be shut away for private use only is seldom comprehended. Foreigners who have insisted on having private gardens have found it necessary in China to employ guards, one sure way of detracting from their own enjoyment in a country that traditionally accepts nature as a universal treasure.

Thousands of miles away are the Cape Gardens of Africa which are filled with the glory of the rose. It is claimed in this part of the world that nothing can compare with the rose for hedges, nor can it when they are able to thrive in such abundance. Whether it is a long line of crimson Jupiter's Lightning, a border of the old sweet-scented China, or a country road edged with White Macartney, it is always breathtakingly beautiful. The red Cramoisie is even finer than the pink China or the white Prince Charlie, perhaps because it blossoms almost all year in this climate.

These are only a few of the roses found in the hedgerows of the Cape Gardens, where roses have been growing for 250 years and more. It is of interest to rose lovers to know that many of the old-fashioned varieties seldom seen in other countries, having been removed to make way for the more glorious teas and hybrids, are still blossoming in Africa. Another favorite hedge rose in the Cape Gardens is the Breda. Whether it was named after the Dutch family is not known, but most probably it was brought to the Cape from Holland. It is a dumpy little flower with many petals, growing in thick clusters of dull carmine, such as you sometimes see in the paintings of the early Dutch Masters.

From the pages of the past come many interesting facts about monastery or medieval gardens and their rose plots. The religious establishments, especially the nunneries, taught the fair ladies how to plant and care for their gardens, for very practical reasons.

In the Middle Ages physicians were scarce, and women had to know how to patch and dose their gallant knights, who were constantly being injured in jousts, local wars and skirmishes, not to mention the Crusades. The plants the housewife grew were not merely potherbs but included many flowers, especially the rose which was used extensively in compounding medicines and in the distillation of flower water. Many of these roses the Crusaders themselves brought back from their pilgrimages, such as the Damask and Provence rose.

From their travels, the Crusaders formed a fresh concept of gardens and their possibilities. Accustomed as they were at home to little patches within castle walls, they were fascinated by the size and beauty of the gardens in the Levant. Upon their return they not only enlarged their own gardens but began to make better use of them. These enclosures became the setting for games and tournaments. Tents were put up under which they ate their meals. Later in the day, the knights played games on the flower-spangled turf while the ladies wove garlands.

It is pleasant to think of the great gardeners of those early days—of St. Radegonde, Queen of Clothair, who fled to Poitiers with her nuns and tended the roses and violets in the garden they made on the sunny slopes beneath the walls of the city; of the Merovingian Childebert's queen, in whose garden "the air was balmy with the perfume of roses of paradise"; and later, of the ninth century monk, Walafrid Strabo who, above all, loved his roses and lilies and "the glow of their sweet scent." "The rose," he said, "should be crowned with pearls of Arabis and Lydian gold."

In the early history of America, John Josselyn, a cheerful traveler, published a book in 1672 entitled *New England Rarities Discovered*. His flower list is the earliest known in the States and forms a fair picture of the gardens of the settlers. Among other flowers he mentions in quaint style:

> "Patience and
> English Roses very pleasantly."

And with "a rose looking in at the window," a sweetbriar, or English rose, these colonial dames might well find "Patience growing very pleasantly" in their hearts as in their gardens. These "rose plots" must have provided sanctuary to offset the thoughts of the savage Indian and the bitter cold winters.

There is pathos in the fact that in so stern and hard a life, there was time and place for any gardens at all. One can imagine how carefully little slips and cuttings, brought over in sailing ships, must have been guarded, and how much they must have meant to all concerned as they took root and blossomed on the new soil. One of these rosebushes planted by the first settlers still blossoms every June above the river in Kittery. It is strange to think that New England is no older than this tree of little red roses.

The story of roses and sailing ships, the story of roses and the East India Companies and their botanical garden in Calcutta and Singapore has yet to be written. How those weather-beaten plant hunters and hard-fisted old captains, with hearts as soft as their prized cargo, must have petted their plants and protected their seeds on those long, difficult voyages!

There are any number of semiprivate rose gardens today in the United States. One at Lake Mohonk, New York, is part of the Mohonk Estate and near the hotel which housed the members of the first Peace Conference in the United States. Then there is the Hershey Rose Garden at the Hershey Hotel in Hershey, Pennsylvania, where seven acres are allotted to the roses of the world, 32,750 plants of more than 750 varieties. The Biltmore Estate at Biltmore, North Carolina, owned by George W. Vanderbilt contains another lovely rose garden.

In many cities, the parks and botanical gardens feature rose gardens. San José, California, has a rose garden that covers five and a half acres and contains over ten thousand bushes. Another rose garden in San José was made from an abandoned eleven-acre orchard. From the entrance one looks across the garden to two great Chinese vases at the back, and over a hundred thousand roses surrounding a wide reflecting pool. Much attention has been paid to color, with copper shades around the pool itself, yellow next, and then red. One section of the garden is devoted to selected types of historical interest, including, of course, the beautiful York and Lancaster roses, old-fashioned musk roses, and many varieties of moss roses. Old Mexico is represented by pink Castilian roses which survive a long time without water. These are extremely fragrant, although not very handsome.

The Rose Garden at Topeka, Kansas, is said to be the second largest in the world, although many Chambers of Commerce would question this statement. However, it is recognized as being exceptionally beautiful and was the winner of a thousand-dollar prize offered by *Better Homes and Gardens*. It was created in 1929 as a memorial to the late Mr. E. F. Reinisch, superintendent for more than thirty years of the parks in that city. It comprises about nine acres, including the test gardens, and there are approximately 24,000 plants. All the gardens are flood-lighted so their beauty may be enjoyed by night as well as by day. There is only one sign to be found in the gardens, cut into a stone on one of the pillars at the main entrance. It reads: "The Honest Need No Watchman."

More recently a rose garden was built at Yaddo, in Saratoga, New York. Designed by Spencer Trask, and dedicated to his wife, Katrina, the author and poet, this garden is particularly outstanding for its picturesque topography. Great native pines over eight feet in diameter somberly guard the radiant roses. The garden vistas, walks, and connecting daffodil plantation and rock gardens cover over ten acres. After entering the colonnaded porch, the main garden stretches down the fine marble steps past statues of Diana and Paris, along paths of standard roses. Here a shallow fountain stands before the statue of Christalan, the figure created in Mrs. Trask's "Under King Constantine."

The first municipal display of roses in America was held at the rose garden in Elizabeth Park at Hartford, Connecticut, and one of the most recent test gardens is Dr. Mendel's in Coral Gables, Florida. In Portland, Oregon, the American Rose Society sponsors the International Rose-Test Garden. Much of the popularity of rose-growing in this country is due to the combined efforts and enthusiasm of this society and the smaller groups of rose enthusiasts throughout the United States.

The names of rose hybridizers, rosarians, and nurserymen in this century is legion. One such hybridizer lives in Barcelona, Spain. It is said of Pedro Dot that he "has put more beauty in the world than any other Spaniard who ever lived, Velasquez, Murillo, El Greco or Valdes Leal not excepted." Second, the late Dr. McFarland, a famous rosarian, was in a sense the godfather of the American Rose Society. The third example is the late Robert Pyle, nurseryman and president of the American Horticultural Council, who did so much to promote international interest and relations in regard to roses. His Star Rose Gardens at West Grove, Pennsylvania, have been visited by celebrities from all over the world. When Helen Keller, famed deaf and blind writer, visited his nursery, the roses gave her "vivid moments among so many flat ones." Roberta Lord wrote of this experience in "To Helen Keller":

> "Her senses could display the shadow of scent,
> She realized
> And fully could enjoy the different,
> Etheralized
> Half-tones of perfume most pass by nor try
> To savor.
> Alone to those who seek will Roses give
> That favor."

There is an increasing interest being shown in rose memorial gardens, especially Peace rose gardens, a number of which have been planted in the United States.

The Peace rose was born out of the agony of crucified France in World War II, and was first called *Gloria Dei* (glory of God). The originator of this rose is Francis Meilland and its first public appearance was in San Francisco at the VE day celebrations. The buds of this rose are golden yellow, the spiritual, healing color of the East, each petal edged with deep rose. With maturity the yellow petals fade into a cream color and the rose periphery diffuses into pink over the pistil part of the petals. The colors fade until a light, almost white, rose is formed before it finally drops.

In Jacksonville, Florida, a beautiful Peace Memorial Park has been planted with 200 symbolic Peace roses as a tribute to the American fighting men and an expression of hope for future peace. Although the park was organized by the Garden Club of Jacksonville the project was developed by a Gold Star Mother, Mrs. Wesley Coleman, on her return from Quebec where she saw the park of Belgian roses established there by war widows of World War I.

Another Peace Rose Garden is the setting for the new building of the Central Presbyterian Church of Abilene, Texas. It is a circular formal rose garden containing approximately a thousand Peace roses, divided into quadrants by four gravel walks converging in a central grassed island.

Lexie Dean Robertson wrote of this in his "Sonnet to a New Church and Its Garden":

> "I think God loves the garden of a church
> More than the highest mountain, or the span
> Of mighty rivers, or the deepest sea;"

Last but not least of the different kinds of rose gardens are the wild ones that encircle the globe without restriction.

Eskimos, as Boitard tells us in his interesting *Monographie de la Rose* adorn their hair and raiment of deer and sealskin with the beautiful blossoms of the *rosa nitida*, which grows abundantly under their stunted shrubs. In Iceland, where the vegetation is so sterile that the natives in some parts are compelled to feed their horses, sheep, and oxen on dried fish, we find the *rosa rubigimosa*, with its pale, solitary, cup-shaped flowers. In Lapland, blooming almost under the snows of that severe climate in the Arctic Circle, the natives, seeking mosses and lichens for their reindeer, find the brilliant and sweet-smelling *rosa majalis*. This particular wild rose is also found in Norway, Sweden and Denmark.

Wild roses are plentiful in northern lands but nowhere are they so abundant as in China. Everywhere, from sea level to mountain top in that ancient land, roses luxuriate so that the air in season is filled with their fragrance.

Widespread in the warmer parts of the United States is the Cherokee rose, and few who bask in the purity of its whiteness realize that it is merely a naturalized plant brought no one knows how or when from China, its original home. Often vast fields of these roses spread out like a velvety white and green carpet. It is recorded that when the *Mayflower* landed at Plymouth on a beautiful day in June, "the shore was fragrant like the smell of a rose garden and the happy children gathered strawberries and single wild roses."

IX

HISTORY AND HERALDRY

Then will I raise aloft the milk-white Rose
With whose sweet smell the air shall be perfumed.
SHAKESPEARE, "Henry VI"

ALTHOUGH more readily associated with idyllic settings and circumstances, roses have appeared on battlefields and have otherwise found their way into the pages of world history. Idealism was not absent when Roman emperors allowed certain generals to decorate their shields with rose emblems signifying honor and distinction, or when the flower signified the aristocratic principles of early knighthood. On the other hand, the red or white rose was used as a political emblem in the bloody civil war of fifteenth century England. In Bulgaria, too, the decisive battle of Shipka was fought in 1877, amid the rose gardens that had previously lent enchantment to thousands of acres on the slopes of the Balkans.

Each branch of what might be called the World's Great Rose Tree has blossomed gloriously or ingloriously, sometimes indifferently, in wars and crusades, in laws and ceremonies, or in connection with some person or family of national importance or distinction. In the history of France and England, particularly, these rose tendrils reached out colorfully into public ceremonies such as Browning's "Patriot" described:

> "It was roses, roses all the way,
>   with myrtle mixed in my path like mad."

In France we find an entertaining little story which took place when Henry IV was fifteen years old and his cousin, Charles IX, came to visit him at the court of Navarre. Although Charles was most adroit in archery, young Henry's first shot carried off the orange which served for a mark. According to the rules of the sport he, as victor, could shoot first in the next trial. When King Charles opposed him in this, Henry stepped back a little, drew his bow, and made as if to direct the arrow against the breast of his adversary. The monarch speedily took shelter behind the largest of his courtiers, requesting them to take away "that dangerous little cousin."

The following day Charles found an excuse for not appearing at the test. This time the Duc de Guise carried away the orange, which he split in two, and was thus entitled to the next turn. Prince Henry, perceiving a rose in the bosom of a young girl who was watching the proceedings, boldly seized it from her and placed it on the mark. The Duke shot and missed. Henry, succeeding him, placed an arrow in the middle of the flower and gallantly returned it to the pretty villager with the victorious arrow which had pierced it.

In England, Shakespeare wrote of the events of the Wars of the Roses in *Henry VI*. His narration of the quarrel in the temple garden between the Duke of York and the Duke of Somerset * gives us one version of how the civil wars between the houses of York and Lancaster came to be named. Finding their followers excited, the Duke of York suggests that they "shall in dumb significance proclaim their thoughts," adding:

> "Let him who is a true born gentleman
> And stands upon the honor of his birth,
> If he supposes I have pleaded truth,
> From off this briar pluck a white rose with me."

The Duke of Somerset replies:

> "Let him who is no coward nor no flatterer,
> But dares maintain the party of the truth,
> Pluck a red rose flower from this briar with me."

Not until the two houses were united by the marriage of Henry VII of Lancaster and Elizabeth of York did the nation obtain internal peace. The roses, thus blended, became the national flower emblazoned on her arms, and on the coin of the realm.

> "Let merry England proudly rear
> Her blended roses bought so dear."

It is natural that such romantic material leading up to the Wars of the Roses should produce a wide range and variety of stories. Parkinson,

---

* Who with the Queen, Margaret of Anjou, were in control of the weak Lancastrian King, Henry VI.

in his *Theatrum Botanicum* (1640), refers to an old tradition of a rose tree at Longleete which bore both white and red roses. "It is too lamentably knowne in this land, the civill warres betweene the houses of the two brethren, John of Gaunt, Duke of Lancaster, and Edmond of Langley, Duke of Yorke, the one making a red rose his cognizance for them and their followers, the other a white; but it is said that before this division, there was seene at Longleete a white rose tree to beare on the one side faire white Roses, and on the other side red, prognosticating as it were both the division and uniting of both their families."

Following the Wars of the Roses, when Henry Tudor came to the throne as Henry VII in 1485, he set about glorifying the ancient British hero, Arthur. This was done in order to conciliate all parties in England and also the Welsh, from whom he was descended. On the birth of his son to whom he gave the name Arthur, suggesting the king's return, Henry had the design of the Round Table placed on the wall of the great hall of Winchester Castle. The central rose of this table is the Tudor emblem, combining the white rose of York with the red rose of Lancaster. The radiating spokes are painted in the Tudor colors, green and white. A crudely painted figure of King Arthur fills one compartment; in the others are the names of the twenty-four knights. Around the rose runs a circular band, inscribed: "Thys is the rounde table of Kyng Arthur w [with] XX iiii of hys namyde knyghttes."

Other pages in English history tell of the payments of fines and rent in roses. Some overlords stipulated for a rose at Christmas and a snowball at Midsummer, which was tantamount to a tenancy terminable at will of grantor. In 1379 one freshly picked rose was a fine levied for a minor building violation, and in the present century, one red rose is presented to the Lord Mayor of London as yearly installment on this original fine.

Three large estates in Britain cost their tenants only one such flower per year. In the year 1576, for example, the Bishop of Ely leased Ely Place for a term of twenty-one years to Sir Christopher Hatton, Queen Elizabeth's handsome Lord Chancellor, for a red rose to be paid on Midsummer Day and in addition to this, ten loads of hay and ten pounds per annum. The bishop and his Episcopal successors reserved the right of walking in the gardens and were to receive twenty bushels of roses yearly.

The use of the rose in English history continued to be frequent and diversified. It occurred at the coronation of Elizabeth I, where roses "Appeared in effigy, her majesties grandsire, Henry Lancaster, in a great red rose; her majesties grandmother, Elizabeth of York, in a great white floure, and her majesties father, King Henry VIII of blessed memory, alsoe her majesties self in fayre red roses well stript with white, shewing thus her royal title through both contending lines."

Later, the Jacobites, supporters of the House of Stuart, wore a white rose to show their loyalty. An old Jacobite song, "Kenmure's on and Awa" tells of this:

> "Here's to him that's far awa, Willie!
> Here's to him that's far awa.
> And here's to the flow'r I loe best,
> The Rose that's like the sun."

The rose is not on many pages of United States history. However, the dramatically lovely American Beauty rose is the flower of the District of Columbia. The white Cherokee rose is claimed by the state of Georgia, while Iowa and New York accept the wild prairie rose. There are also a number of towns that have rose significance, such as Lancaster and York in Pennsylvania. These are known as the Red Rose City and the White Rose City, following the tradition established by the English Wars of the Roses. Red and white roses are planted along the Lincoln Highway outside these respective towns. The same idea is also carried out in sports as football and basketball teams are named Red Roses and White Roses.

One story which connects the rose with the history of the United States is that of Rosemont. In lower Laurens County, South Carolina, near the brow of a long gentle slope that falls away to the bank of the yellow Saluda River, lies a tangled, forest-pressed garden, Rosemont of the Cunninghams. Its silence, today, is eloquent with voices of yesterday. During the period of Robert Cunningham and his wife, Louisa, Rosemont knew its greatest glory. Of Louisa, Governor B. F. Perry of Sans Souci wrote, "She was not only beautiful herself, but she had a love and taste for the beautiful; her passion for flowers was unsurpassed."

This love was translated into reality by her creation of a fourteen-acre garden at Rosemont, surrounded by a stately grove and park of thirty acres. In front of the house was a formal flower garden bordered by English box. English roses formed the chief floral accent, giving meaning to the name of the estate. The daughter, Ann Pamela, a lifelong invalid from a fall in girlhood, found her chief joy in the acres of flowers encircling her home.

In the summer of 1853 she received a letter from her mother telling how she sailed down the Potomac one moonlight night. As they passed Mount Vernon, the ship's bell, as was the custom, tolled in honor of the tomb of Washington. Looking up at the mansion, white and lonely in the shadows, she brooded sorrowfully on the neglect and dilapidation of the spot. "How wonderful," the letter continued, "if the women of America could acquire this estate, restore it, and preserve it forever as a shrine of patriotism." As Ann Pamela read these words and looked at the beautiful garden of Rosemont, she was inspired by a sudden resolution, to the accomplishment of which she was to devote her frail life. With indomitable will she launched the undertaking. The orator, Edward Everett, sent her the proceeds of his lectures for an entire season. Washington Irving contributed five hundred dollars. The school children of America were organized to contribute ten cents each. At last she secured the necessary sum, quoted by certain historians as $200,000. Mount Vernon was purchased and at Rosemont, Ann Pamela Cunningham, as first regent of the association, signed the papers. A few years later when war divided the land, she appealed to leaders of both armies to spare the shrine of their common hero.

Few flowers bloom now at Rosemont due to a fire which burned the house and its priceless treasures. Only the hardy English roses have gone native, spreading their ghostly whiteness beyond the garden and defying for a time the advancing forest growth. This now is the rose garden by the Saluda River.

At the White House in Washington, the Bouquet Room looks out on a rose garden enclosed by privet. The bushes are healthy, with red and pink roses predominating.

A touching story coming from the Presidential mansion occurred after the death of Coolidge's son, Calvin. Every night the bed covers were turned back on the bed in his room upstairs, and every morning a fresh rosebud was placed upon the pillow, as if Calvin had merely gone off on a holiday trip and would soon return.

In 1946 a white rose was worn by each member of the House of Representatives to commemorate the sixty-fourth birthday of Franklin Delano Roosevelt. This gesture was not only a tribute to the man but also to the name Roosevelt, which means "field of roses." It was also the late President's wish to be buried at Hyde Park in the rose garden which is the most beautiful place on the estate.

There are four well-known military Orders of the Rose, the medals of which are strikingly beautiful. The Mexican medals of the Order of the Madonna of Guadalupe are encircled with delicate pink enameled roses. The Order of the Rose in Brazil also features a pale pink rose, while Finland's Order of the White Rose has a rose of that color outlined in gold on several different medals. The Imperial Order of the Yellow Rose in the United States uses a four-leaved gold rose, topped by a tiny crown and two eagles.

The Order of the Rose in Brazil was created by the Emperor Pedro I of Brazil, by decree of October 17, 1829. Especially established in honor of the emperor's consort, Princess Amelia of Leuchtenberg and Eischstoedt, it is flatteringly said to have been inspired both by her fresh cheeks and her favorite rose-patterned dress. Brazilians describe the order as a military and civil one "to which will be admitted those who are worthy, both nationals and foreigners" because of their services and fidelity to the Emperor and the Empire of Brazil.

The object of the Imperial Military Order of the Yellow Rose was to keep an authentic record of the ancestry of its members and to further historical research; the membership being all those, male and female, of royal lineage of Aryan race in any part of the world. Prior to 1805, an order of chivalry was formed in the United States known as the Imperial Order of the Yellow Rose and on the scroll appeared the following names: "Viscount de Fronsac, John Milledge, Augusta, Ga., late governor John Irvine Bulloch, Judge Archibald Stobo Bulloch of Savannah, Ga., Judge Noble Wymberley Jones, M.D., John Glen, Chief Justice of Ga., Major John Habersham, W. Harden and J. Maxwell, all of Georgia, and James De Veaux and John Rutledge of South Carolina."

This order was revised May 11, 1908, in Washington, D.C., the title "Military" being left out and the proviso added that "None but those of Royal descent shall hereafter be admitted into membership in the Order." After several meetings and consultations, a constitution was adopted and application for a charter was made, which was granted under the laws of the United States in the District of Columbia on June 15, 1908.

An old order of a different kind is the Knights of the Garter, or Order of St. George. This was established in England by Edward III about 1344. When chosen by the sovereign as one of the companions of this "most honorable order" the knight, according to an original transcription, had to swear to keep all the rules and "to defend and maintain, so much as in you lieth, the Right and Liberties of the Colledge of our Blessed Lady, and St. George the Martyr, wherein the Honorable Order of the Garter is founded."

The principal emblem of this rank is the Garter, on which the words, *Honi soit qui mal y pense*, are embroidered. Among other official trappings, all of which are traditionally worn by the knight on St. George's Day (still celebrated by the populace of England by the wearing of roses), is "about his neck and shoulders a collar of his order, being of pure gold, made of garters and knots and enamelled with roses, white in red; with the image of St. George richly garnished with precious stones pendant thereat." The present Queen of England is head of this order, certain of the rules, customs, and robes having been only slightly changed or modified since its inception.

Traditional crowns incorporating the rose emblem are listed and illustrated in Holme's *The Academy of Armory*. A duke's coronet of the "Blood Royal" "is railed into flowers de lis, with blown roses interposing, and both set on an equal height." A duke's crown, not of royal blood "hath the railing from the circle composed of four open blown roses, and as many small ones, or pearls set between." The crown of a marquess "is

The Order of the Garter—Chancellor's Badge.

a middle degree between a Duke and an Earl, and therefore the crown partakes of the flower [rose] from one and the Pearl from the other and both railed to an equal height." The "Marquesses Crown of France is made with three Pearls between each rose, and they not much exceed the middle of the roses."

Roses, some in heraldic designs, have often been used on postage stamps in England, the Netherlands, Switzerland, Austria, and other countries. Newfoundland has several stamps featuring roses with sheaves of wheat. Bulgaria also put out a recent Christmas stamp showing a child's head in profile with a full-blown rose in the child's hand. This use in Bulgaria of the rose is significant because of the extensive cultivation of the flower for the manufacture of perfume and attar.

The entire subject of heraldry is a fascinating one. Generally speaking, a badge, or cognizance, was a figure chosen by its owner either as openly significant of some exploit of honor by a member of his family, or as alluding to his name, estate, office, or calling. Each nobleman's badge was prominent in his dress, on sleeve or breast, and it also glittered on his standards. This badge was an open declaration of the wearer's personality; its chief object was to accomplish publicity.

A heraldic device or *imprese* had an inner meaning. It should not be "so obscure as to require a sphinx to interpret it," Sir William Drummond said, "but should be somewhat retired from the capacity of the vulgar."

The searcher after facts in regal heraldry finds an indelible record of the rose on many badges and devices, especially those of royal lineage. In a general sense, the appearance of the rose in heraldry could be interpreted as meaning mercy and justice. In full bloom, with a bud in the center and five points to imitate thorns, it is an emblem of beauty and nobility acquired with difficulty. But this did not always apply to family crests. For example, the Comte de Trignano's crest was a rose tree between two onions, the motto *Per Opposita* meaning "Through Things Opposite." Plutarch had made a somewhat similar statement centuries before the appearance of this crest with this explanation, "when planted among onions, the rose produces the sweetest flowers. So a good man shines most and is purified living in a wicked world." The cognizance of the Richmonds was a rose in the mouth of a fox. This English shield is in the public house called the Holland Arms, Kensington. The story behind the unusual design concerns the daughter of the Duke of Richmond (Lady Caroline Lennox) who ran away with Mr. Henry Fox (finally made Baron Holland of Foxley). So . . . the fox stole the rose and ran away with it!

A number of the rose mottoes on shields are familiar to students of heraldry. Here is a brief sampling with meanings appended:

> *Rosam ne rode,* "Do not speak ill of the rose."
> *Rosario,* "In a bed of roses."
> *Rosas coronot Spina,* "Roses are crowned with thorns."
> *Rosa sine spina,* "A Rose without the thorn."

These four, respectively, were the mottoes of the families of Ross, Harvey, Forbes, and Penrose.

Homer gives perhaps the first account of the heraldic use of the rose: "Roses adorned the shield of Achilles and the helm of Hector." The next record appears in papal heraldry where the rose, because of its religious significance, became the crest or seal of many of the Popes. Rose heraldry then spread in a greater or lesser degree to France, Germany, England, Ireland, and Scotland. In some instances, the selection of this flower was due to its symbolic meaning or to represent the surname Rose or Ross (a derivative of Roose for rose), Rosen, Rosset, or Roosevelt. Through intermarriage, however, the original form was often lost.

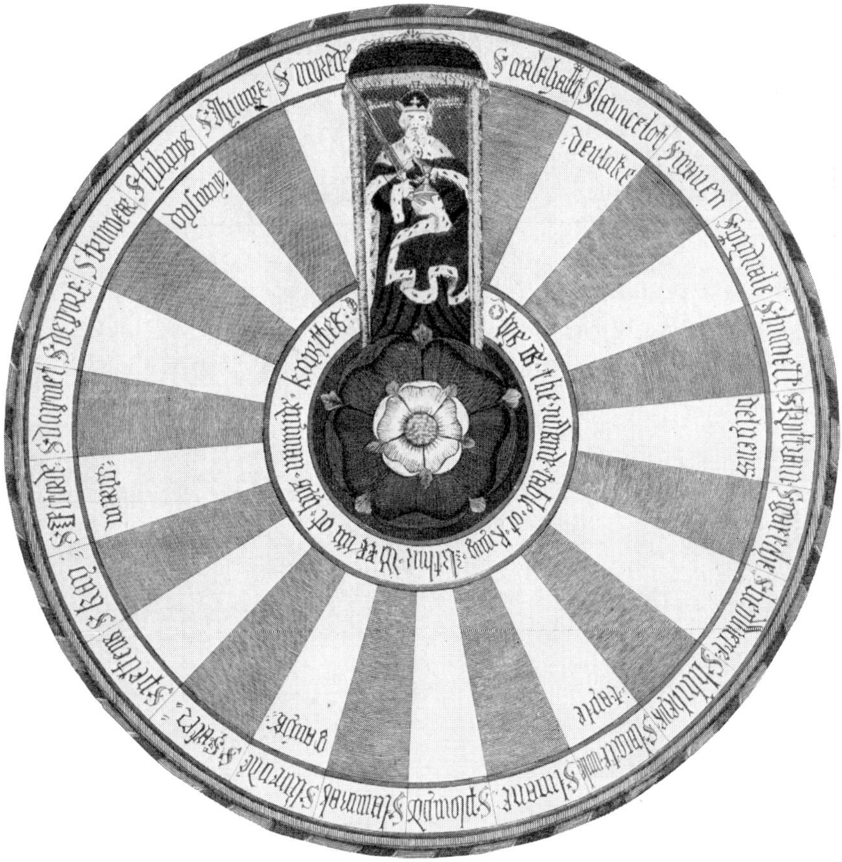

Rose Capistrano.

(Metropolitan Museum of Art)

King Arthur's Round Table, in Winchester Castle, with Tudor emblem in the center, combining the white rose of York and the red rose of Lancaster.

(Germain's)

(Photo: Conard-Pyle Co.)

Above: The Wars of the Roses. From the mural in the British House of Parliament, depicting the characters in Part II of Shakespeare's "Henry VI" in which the white rose was plucked by the York contender and the red by the representative of the house of Lancaster.

Right: The York and Lancaster Rose, by G. D. Ehret (1745).

Elizabeth I of England, from a painting attributed to Lucas de Heere. Note the roses worn at the neck, also the jewel rosettes on her costume. Elizabeth was the last of the English house of Tudor, constantly associated with the rose, England's national flower.

The evolution of the red and white rose as represented by the 1953 prize-winning Chrysler Imperial rose and the lovely white Rex Anderson.

(Jackson & Pe

The new historic Peace Rose, renamed from the French rose Gloria Dei (Glory to God) created by Francis Meilland. First appearing in this country in San Francisco, the Peace Rose was given to delegates at the V-E day celebrations in that city and is now being adopted all over the world for peace and memorial gardens.

ermain's)

(Conard-Pyle Co.)

(Chase National Bank)

Above: Cupids and roses on a historic American three-dollar bill, dated November 1, 1856.

Military medals of the Orders of the Rose: United States (left), Brazil (lower left), Finland (below).

(Jackson & Perkins)

(Chase
National Bank)

(Manley Hall)

Top: Diamond Jubilee rose. Coins, top to bottom: Elizabethan shilling (1558), with a rose at the back of Queen Elizabeth's ear. Early American coin, Rosa Americana (1722). Canadian Bouquet sou with rose, wheat, and thistle. English two-shilling piece (florin) (1938). Stamps, left to right: Austrian, Finnish, and Bulgarian.

(Lester Rose Gardens)

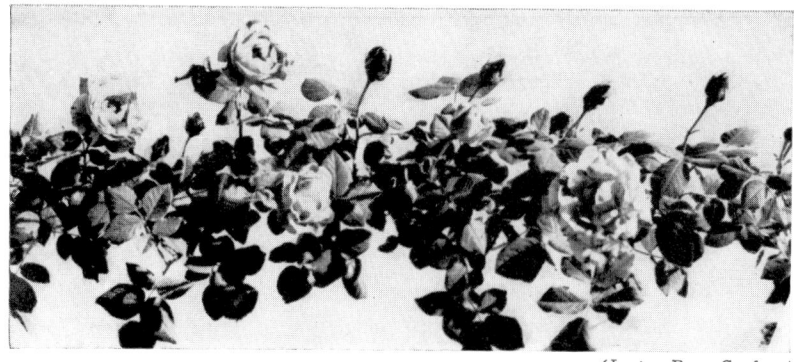

The old fashioned, historic rose Ferdinand Pichard. The tight rosette forms of the natural rose inspired the early sailors to make rose-knot designs as typified by the example below, made by W. Alford, and now in the Seaman's Institute in New York.

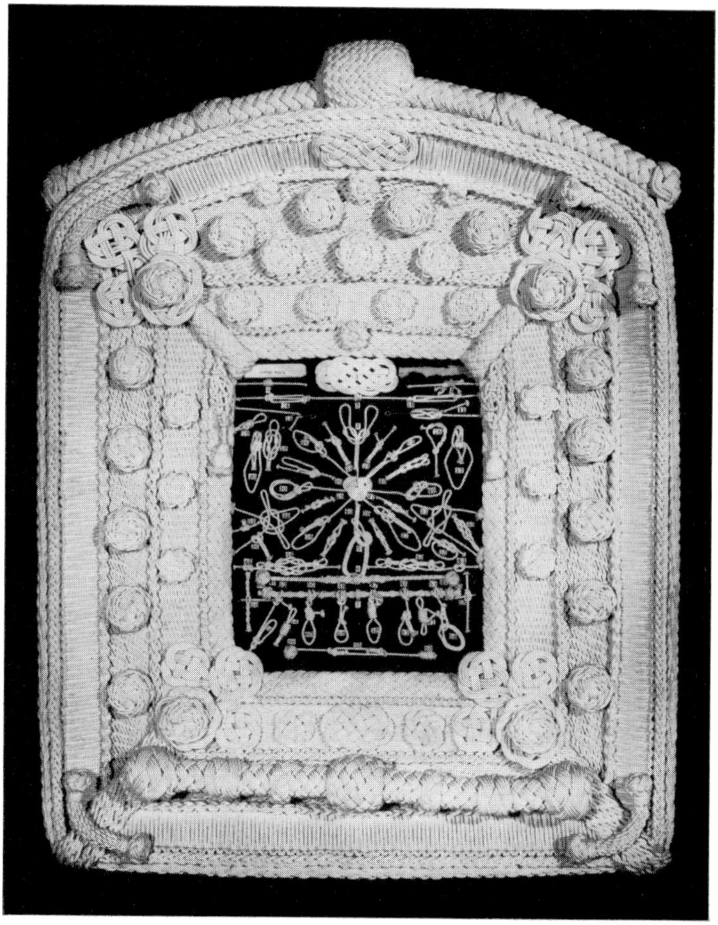

In England, King Edward I, irreverently called "Longshanks," was the first sovereign who assumed "A Rose, or stalked proper," as his badge—a golden rose in natural form. The red rose is usually assigned first to Eleanor of Provence, the queen of Henry III. The tomb of her second son, Edward, Lord of Lancaster, was covered with red roses. Edward's son was the first Duke of Lancaster and he had on his seal a branch of roses. The duke bequeathed to St. Paul's Cathedral his bed, "powdered with roses," which must have been fine indeed, but one wonders where and to what use it was put in the Cathedral.

Edward IV placed the white rose *en soleil* to commemorate his victory at the battle of Mortimer's Cross, where the sun appeared to him "like three suns and suddenly joyned altogether into one." His favorite badge was a gold collar of suns and roses with the white Lion of March hanging from it. Edward was often called "the beautifullest prince of his time" or "the Rose of Rouen," having been born in that town in 1441 or 1442.

Agnes Strickland gives one of his coronation songs, which begins:

"Now is the Rose of Rouen grown to great honour;
Therefore sing wee everyone y-blessed be that flower,
I watn ye everyone that ye shall onderstand
There sprung a Rose in Rouen that opened in England.
Had not the Rose of Rouen been, all England had been dour;
Y-blessed be the time God ever spread that flower."

Some of the animals and other flowers and objects combined with the rose in English heraldry are listed with their bearers:

Richard III: falcon with a maiden's head, falcon holding a rose.
Henry VII: Tudor rose, crowned.
Henry VIII: cock, the badge of Wales and rose.
Katherine of Aragon (first wife of Henry VIII): an open pomegranate disclosing the Tudor rose.
Ann Boleyn: a stump of a tree, a silver falcon with stiff sprays of red and white roses issuing from the tree.
Katherine Parr (sixth wife of Henry VIII): the queen's head crowned, and below the bust three tiers of rose petals.
Edward VI: Tudor rose impaling a pomegranate.

The Great Seal of Scotland was the rose, thistle, and shamrock. In the reign of James IV of Scotland, William Dunbar wrote the well-known poem, "The Thrissill and the Rois" (The Thistle and the Rose), on the affiancing of King James and Princess Margaret of England. Thus the Scottish and English emblems were joined on the royal badge of the Stuarts. Queen Anne changed the original design so that the rose and thistle were represented as growing from one stem. This badge is currently used in the

"Queen's Colour of the 2nd Battalion Scots Guards."

From France we can expect any sort of caprice. So it was that Mme. de Coigny, a French beauty, becoming tired of the romantic attentions paid her by countless beaus, had a signet engraved showing a rose besieged by insects. The motto:

"Thus it is to be a rose."

The silver, copper, and gold roses that tumble out of the numismatic collections make an absorbing study. Taken at random, there are the twelfth century coins of Hungary with rosettes, similar to the Persian stylized roses, under a cross. This combination of rose and cross was carried out in the coins of many countries. One of the most beautiful of these, a cross with four roses, was minted in France in the twelfth and thirteenth centuries. In East India during the reign of Charles I and Charles II there were roses on the rupees. Irish black money also featured a rose, and on the coin of Rhoda in Spain was a four-petaled rose. Of the British tokens issued during the sixteenth and seventeenth centuries, forty bear the imprint of the rose. The *Rosa Americana* penny pieces had a large full-blown rose in the center of a field. Three years later this same coin had a crown added to the design. These examples are only a fraction of rose coins which have been minted in various countries and centuries.

One of the early numismatic journals contains an account of ancient money and an explanation for the appearance of the rose on Rhodian coins: "Natural and uniform motive of religious belief influenced the choice of the rose as the symbol of Venus, whose daughter, by a beautiful poetic fiction, the island of Rhodes * was said to be; and, at the same time, feigned to have been espoused to the sun, the peculiar object of Rhodian worship." Roses were a constant type of the Rhodian coinage from about 400 B.C. There were seventy coins with a rose, seventeen with a rose in a square, eleven full-blown roses, one with a solar disk, and three with rosebuds, a total of a hundred and two. Further notes go on to say that the rose is frequently represented on coins of the Pangaean district and especially distinguishes the money of Traelium in Macedon. Three of these coins show Hermes and roses in combination with a thunderbolt or ivy.

Some ancient coins show the bust of Eros with winged hair, with a rose on the reverse side; or else the head of Zeus crowned with roses. Another design flanked by rosebuds is a veiled female head wearing earrings.

The only notation of a rose used on a Roman coin is made in connection with the period of Rhodian coins. "To record his victory over the Rhodians, C. Cassius Longinus, 42 B.C., the ally of Brutus in the assassina-

* The Greek for rose is *rhodon*.

142

Heraldic designs. Top left: The Marguerite of Navarre. Top right: The Crowned Tudor Rose of Henry VII with the dragon of Cadwallader and the greyhound of John Beaufort, Duke of Somerset. Center left: The Tudor rose, quarterly white and red. Bottom left: The "Rose en Soliel" of Edward IV. Bottom right: Arms of the City of Westminster, incorporating the red rose of Lancaster.

tion of Julius Caesar, places the rose on one of his denarii [coin worth 17 cents], below the Crab."

In France during the fourteenth and fifteenth centuries it was the custom for lovers to exchange *chappelets verts a la Saint-Valentin*. These chaplets of roses gradually developed into something less perishable such as jettons or marriage medals or coins. One of these bore the inscription: *"Uxor casta est rosa suavis,"* interpreted by the French as *"Une femme chaste est une rose aux doux parfumes."*

The extensive use of the rose design on English coins far surpassed other countries with the exception perhaps of Rhodes. The noble, chief gold coin of England for more than one hundred years, and one of its monetary units for nearly three centuries, was not only original and unique in its type but was so highly esteemed as to be widely circulated in other countries. Edward IV introduced an altered design, the royal or rose noble. This shows the original design of the king in the ship but with the addition of a full-blown rose on the side. On the reverse of this coin, instead of the king's initial, a rose is superimposed on a sun, Edward's emblem adopted after the battle of Mortimer's Cross. These rose nobles were struck in large numbers and several mints other than London carry their distinctive initial letter as a mint mark in the water beneath the rose, *E* for Yorke, *B* for Bristol.

Four of the rose nobles of Edward's reign weighed one ounce. There were also double rose nobles and half rose nobles. Some of the smaller pieces bore the motto *Rosa Sine Spina*. The rose noble achieved a wide circulation. Specimens occur with counter stamps of Dutch provinces, imperial Germany, Riga, and Danzig.

Henry VIII changed the numeral from VII to VIII on coins but kept his father's head on all of them. Evidently people were not used to accurate portraiture. This coin shows the crown of the double rose, *Rutilans Rosa Sine Spina*, the dazzling rose without a thorn. Queen Mary used a rose halved by the letter *H* to show, no doubt, her inheritance from her father, Henry VIII. On the majority of rose nobles in Queen Elizabeth's reign there appears a good portraiture of the queen's face framed by a ruff and crown. The rose in the illustration on page 139 is behind her head. The ship, which is stamped on the reverse side of many coins, is a true picture of the vessels sailed by Hawkins and Drake, with high stern and low bowsprit.

Canada has had a number of rose coins. The Bouquet series, one of the most interesting, is replete with roses, especially those lettered "Agriculture and Commerce of Bas Canada." The center of this coin is decorated with a sheaf of wheat, a thistle, and numerous roses.

In the United States, the one important contribution to this subject was the *Rosa Americana*, already mentioned. The history of this particular coin dates back to 1722 when the Duchess of Kendal, the king's mistress, obtained from the Earl of Sunderland a patent for the coinage of copper money for the Kingdom of Ireland, which privilege she sold for ten thousand pounds to William Wood. This same William Wood of Wolverhampton, England, thereupon commenced to coin pennies for America and Ireland. On one side was the head of George II, and on the reverse side "Rosa Americana" and date, showing a rose topped by a crown and with a ribbon beneath reading, *Utile Dulci.*

Roses have also appeared on paper money in the United States in combination with gay little cupids. Another especially fine bill from Nebraska pictures a young girl with an apron full of roses and a wreath of roses around her head.

These rose coins, heraldic banners, and crests of all nations are tangible records connected with our modern history. They prove that the rose and rose designs have always been present in the mind and heart of man and have played a very important part in his daily life. The rosettes seen on Phoenician sepulchers and on soapstone cylinders of the South African ruins at Zimbabwe are practically identical with quatrefoils and cinquefoils of heraldry. Thus the roses of feudal blazonry and primitive heraldry are definite links in the history of the world.

X

MARTYRS AND MIRACLES

. . . As thou standest there,
Thou seemest to me like the angel
That brought the immortal roses
To Saint Cecilia's bridal chamber.

HENRY WADSWORTH LONGFELLOW

In *La Rose dans l'antiquité et au Moyen Age*, published in 1892, Charles Joret shows the historical change in the attitude of Christians toward roses by contrasting the advice of two saints to their devotees. St. Paul exhorted the faithful to acquire by an exemplary life "a crown of incorruptible glory"; St. Cyprien encouraged the confessors and martyrs of his church to gain in heaven a white crown of lilies and a vermilion crown of roses. In this way the rose, which the early Christian fathers had rejected as a symbol of the pagan debauchery of the Venus-worshiping Romans, was restored to official grace; the fiats and edicts of the hierarchy of the church had not been able to overcome the folk heritage and beauty of the rose.

This restoration broke completely with teachings of such men as Clement of Alexandria who proscribed as equally abhorrent, the use of flowers and perfumes by Christians, particularly of roses and lilies. Prudence boasted that at his table neither roses nor aromatics ever appeared, and he congratulated St. Eulalie for having refused crowns of roses even as she rejected ornaments of amber and collars of gold. But the number of saints gloriously associated with roses soon outnumbered those who rejected the queen of flowers.

Although roses did not reach their height as Christian symbols until about the thirteenth century, several of the most familiar stories of roses and martyrs date from the fifth and sixth centuries. Included among them is the story of St. Benedict and the *roseto* at Subiaco in Italy. This little rose garden is still preserved; the rosebushes it contains are claimed to be the very ones whose beauty delighted the senses of the founder of the Benedictines and with whose thorns he mortified his flesh. In the picturesque language of the *Dialogues* of St. Gregory the Great, quoted by E. Cobham Brewer in his *A Dictionary of Phrases and Fables*, "when St. Benedict, afterwards Abbot of Mount Cassius, first retired to the cavern at Subiaco, he was not more than fifteen years old, and was greatly harassed by the recollection of a young woman with whom he had been in love. When the heat on him was greatest, and he felt he must return to the world, he would wallow naked among thorns and brambles till his whole body was one vast bleeding wound. It was thus by his own blood that he quenched his carnal passion."

A very similar story is told in northern Italy concerning St. Francis of Assisi, the founder of the Franciscan Order. One bitter cold day when he was shivering in his bare, stone cell, the devil came and whispered to him of the comforts and luxuries he had known before he had devoted his life to religion and charity. These pleasures, the devil added, he might enjoy again if he renounced his bleak life. Lest temptation assail him, St. Francis hastened out into the snow and, throwing off his robe, rolled in a bramble of thorns. As the thorns pricked his flesh and were tipped with his blood, each turned into a red rose. The saint gathered the roses and humbly and gratefully carried them into the chapel as an offering to the Saviour and the Madonna.

An even earlier story dating from the first century A.D. tells how the blood of the martyred St. Lucian engendered roses. Louvet, in the *History and Antiquities of the Diocese of Bouvet*, stated that these drops of blood with which the earth was soaked brought forth such quantities of red roses, "which are still to be seen, that the place of the martyrdom has been called *La Rosiere*, to signify that the blood of the martyrs is but a grain and a seed of the beautiful flowers of paradise."

The biographer of St. Aldric, Bishop of Maus, who lived from 800 to 856, claimed that God, wishing to show by some signal honor His pleasure at the virtues and devotion of his renowned servant, sent down upon him, one day when he was blessing the people, a shower of roses "which enveloped him with their perfume."

Apparently the good bishop took this sudden shower of roses as much in his stride as St. Agnes did the sudden appearance of a miraculous rose in the center of an equally miraculous platter on the table at which she and her companions were about to dine. Raymond of Capua, who wrote the authoritative life of this saint, told of how one cold day two hermits, hearing of the wonderful works and devotion of St. Agnes, came to pay her a visit. Their approach was tinged with skepticism which rapidly faded before her wisdom and humility. After a long conversation on the true meaning of the spiritual life, St. Agnes asked them to dine with her. They sat at the refectory table, but before any food was brought in, there suddenly appeared a platter, in the center of which was a beautiful rose in perfect bloom. The visiting hermits were astounded. With words of praise and thanksgiving, St. Agnes picked up the flower and addressed her guests. "Fathers, Jesus Christ has been kind enough, in the very middle of winter, when the frost has cut off all earthly flowers, to send us this rose from Paradise. This, Fathers, is a symbol of how greatly your words have refreshed my soul." After having dined, the hermits departed and carried with them this additional proof of the holiness of St. Agnes.

One of the most common and familiar types of rose miracles is that in which bread is turned into roses when the person carrying food to the poor is apprehended by hostile observers. Not the best known of these stories, though very typical of the group, revolves around Germana, Cousin of Pibrac. M. L. Veuillot, in *Vie de la Bienheureuse Germaine*, describes this incident in great detail. Germana, or Germaine, was a poor but charitable shepherdess who gave so much to the unfortunate that her mother-in-law felt certain she must be robbing their larder and hated her for it. One wintry day, the spying mother-in-law fancied she saw Germana hide food in her apron and so followed her. Two of the neighbors, happening to see both the spy and the pursued, ran after the pair to protect the shepherd girl from the abuse of the angry woman. They caught up with the woman just as she reached her daughter-in-law. When Germana was commanded to show what she was carrying in her apron so that everyone might see that she was a thief, the young girl opened her apron and from it cascaded roses. Those who witnessed the miracle recognized it as a sign of the favor found by Germana in the eyes of God, and even the hard heart of the mother-in-law was softened. Thenceforth Germana continued her calling—a life of charitable deeds.

Germana was but one of the many charitable souls of whom such miraculous incidents are related. The Reverend S. Baring-Gould, in his famous multi-volume *Lives of the Saints*, includes in his list St. Zita, St. Mathia, and St. Louis of Toulouse as well as Nicolas Tolentini, who was canonized by Pope Eugenius IV in 1446. The last one of this list was a monk who carried food, intended for the brethren of the house, to the poor. He was apprehended by the superior of the monastery, whose chidings turned to praise when the food was turned miraculously into roses which fell from the monk's garment to the superior's feet.

Probably the best known story of the transformation of bread into roses is that concerning St. Elizabeth of Hungary. Born in 1207, daughter of the king, her romance with Louis of Thuringia was a childhood one, and when Elizabeth was fifteen they were married.

During the prince's absence on one of the Crusades, his mother and sisters opposed all the charitable acts of the young bride. The prince returned at a time when famine was devastating the country, and into his

In a hallowed spot, at the cathedral of Hildesheim, Germany, grows this thousand-year-old rose bush, the oldest one known.

Santa Rosa di Viterbo, a thirteenth-century Franciscan nun. The painting is ascribed to the Spanish painter Murillo (1617-1682).

Virgin taking the first rosary from the lips of a praying monk. Woodcut from "Contemplaciones" by Gorricio de Novaria (1495).

Rosary of fifty pink roses representing Aves and five red roses representing paternosters and glorias from "Hours of the Virgin." The illumination was done in northern France during the fifteenth century.

ears poured embittered tales of how Elizabeth had rationed the people's food in order to feed certain of the poor. Losing faith in his beloved wife, he forbade her to continue these acts. One day when Elizabeth was leaving the castle with a supply of food for the sick, her husband met and challenged her to reveal what she was hiding under her cloak. As Elizabeth hesitated, fearing his displeasure, and knowing that it would be difficult to prove that the food she carried was depriving no one but herself, Louis, with an angry gesture, threw open her cloak, disclosing the basket. The food was not there. The hamper contained nothing but white roses. The penitent prince never doubted the motives of his wife again, and the miracle converted even her enemies.

A postscript to this tale is given in an article in *The Catholic World* of July, 1869. The author of "Religion Emblemed in Flowers" tells of how in Thuringia the traveler is attracted by a species of rose universally cultivated by the poorest peasant as well as the richest landowner. When its origin is questioned the answer is invariably, "Oh, that is the rose of the dear St. Elizabeth, our former queen. It was grown from one of the sprigs given to her by the angels."

A variant of this persistent type of legend, in which an offering or incriminating object was transformed into roses, is quoted by Joret in his study of medieval associations of the rose. According to Thomas de Cantipre, the pious Ada was unable to resist any appeal for help. One day when her husband was away, a leprous beggar knocked at the door, pleading for food and shelter. The good-hearted woman welcomed him and gave him food, medicine, and clean clothing. Finally she made him rest in the best bed in the house—that of her absent husband, who suddenly and unexpectedly returned, demanding entrance. In fright, Ada barred the door; but her husband, his worst suspicions aroused by this behavior, redoubled his demands to be let in. The bewildered woman finally admitted her spouse, who was by this time nearly frozen, for it was the middle of winter. Not allowing his wife to finish her halting tale, and putting the worst possible interpretation on as much as he had heard, the infuriated man dashed to his bedroom, flinging open the door. There was no one there. His bed was unoccupied, but covered with a blanket of roses.

One of the most popular legends of the early Christian Church is that of St. Cecilia, the patron saint of musicians. Cecilia, a beautiful woman of noble birth, was betrothed to Valerian. On her wedding night she revealed to him that she had a guardian angel who would protect her virginity. Valerian, though not yet converted to the Christian faith, respected her confession, but demanded to see this angel in the flesh.

Those Christians from whom he sought advice the following day bade Valerian have faith and return to his house. The dissatisfied Roman did as he was told. Upon entering his home, he heard divine music coming from his wife's chamber and saw a radiant angel standing beside her bearing two garlands of roses. Overcome with emotion, Valerian knelt at his wife's feet while the angel draped him and Cecilia with the flowers.

After Valerian had been baptized into the Christian faith, his brother Tiberius came to visit him and Cecilia, and being conscious of a scent of lilies and roses, asked how she had "untimely roses in the winter season."

And Valerian answered that God had sent them crowns of lilies and roses, but that he, Tiberius, could not see them until his eyes were opened and his body purified by baptism.

Like Valerian and St. Cecilia, St. Dorothea suffered martyrdom for her faith. Tried and condemned as a witch by Apricus, she answered his pronouncement of the death sentence, "I will suffer anything for Christ, my Lord and Spouse, in Whose garden of delight I shall gather roses and apples and be glad with Him forever."

News of her speech spread rapidly, so that on the road to the place of execution, a noble but scornful youth named Theophilus shouted, "Send me some roses from the paradise of your Christ."

At the moment of her transition, an angel appeared carrying three roses and three apples. The martyr with her dying breath commanded that they be taken to Theophilus, who, upon tasting the fruit, was converted to Christianity. Like his preceptress, he, too, ultimately became a martyr under the same religious persecution.

Roses appear significantly throughout the life of St. Rosa of Lima, patroness of America. Born in Lima, Peru, in 1586, at her confirmation she took the name of Rosa, because when an infant her face had been transfigured by a vision of a mystical rose. She became renowned for her life of prayer and self-mortification. At the age of twenty, she decided to redouble the severity of her self-chastisement and the number and degree of her penances. Thereafter she wore constantly a spiked metal crown, its needlelike, tearing points concealed by a coronet of roses.

In recognition of her life of devotion and of the many miracles attributed to her influence after her death, she was beatified by Pope Clement IX in 1667, and canonized by Pope Clement X in 1671, the first American of either continent to be thus honored. The story is told, however, that, when Clement X was asked to raise her to sainthood, he lifted his hands in horror and exclaimed, "What? Make an Indian a Saint! I'll do that when it rains roses!" Whereupon the bishop pleading St. Rosa of Lima's cause uttered a silent prayer to the Virgin and down from heaven fell a shower of roses upon the amazed pope himself.

Two of the most widely publicized of modern saints are associated with roses. When St. Bernadette, in February 1858, saw apparitions of Our

Lady in a grotto at Lourdes, she described her as "a beautiful lady with golden roses at her feet." In the summer of that same year, after many pilgrimages to the grotto, St. Bernadette saw the apparition emerge through a curtain of wild roses which draped the face of a cave and reflected the golden light that irradiated the scene. It was here that the healing spring of the Shrine of Our Lady of Lourdes was found.

In 1887, the Little Flower of the Catholic Church, the Carmelite nun St. Teresa, prophesied before her death, at the age of twenty-four, that she would let fall a shower of roses. After her body was exhumed for beatification, coffin boards and remnants of clothing were declared, by those people who were handling them to emit a pronounced scent of roses. The prophecy was apparently more accurately fulfilled later, for, writing in the *National Rose Annual* of 1927, Lewis Levy in his article, "The Rose in Religion," says that when the Little Flower of Jesus was beatified in 1926, within thirty years of her death, "three roses fell from the decorations above His Holiness' chair at the exact moment of the pronouncement of the canonization."

By far the greater number of such *post mortem* manifestations of roses are found in the early and middle periods of church history. In the *Acta Sanctorum* are found a number of these tales. When St. Lucius' grave was opened some time after his death, three roses were found growing out of his breast. As soon as someone tried to pick them they disappeared. Another tale claims that a rose was found growing from the mouth of St. Louis of Toulouse when his body was exhumed.

A similar story is related of the blessed Gandolf, priest of Milan. His faithful followers gathered one day to remove the saint's tomb from the middle of the church where it was being trodden underfoot by the crowds. While they were at work they saw a thick cloud and shortly smelled a delicious perfume that completely filled the edifice. Opening the grave of their spiritual leader they found in it a rose of marvelous beauty and exquisite aroma, as fresh, according to the chronicler, as though it had just been plucked.

A duplicate of this seemingly great miracle or mystery has taken place in modern times in connection with Nicholas Rubinstein, distinguished Russian pianist, and son of the eminent mystic who wrote the Cabala and Rosicrucian principles under the pen name of "The Ruby Stone." Nicholas died in 1881 and his body, placed in an ordinary casket without any embalming, was sealed in the vault of a monastery. In 1934, the monastery was destroyed and the body of Nicholas Rubinstein taken to a laboratory for examination.

Scientists found the body in a perfect state of preservation, with no indication of embalming fluids. But the most mysterious and significant part is, that in a position indicating that the hands had been holding it, was a fresh rose with a green stem although this flower had been in the vault for fifty-three years. Not until they took the rose from the body did it begin to decay and the body start to mummify. These facts have been published in a number of American newspapers as a scientific mystery and miracle.

Although little remains of these spontaneously engendered roses there are a few exceptions, such as the roses associated with St. Benedict and St. Francis, and in the Thuringian region, those of St. Elizabeth. Another is the Glastonbury thorn or hawthorn, a bona fide member of the rose family. The story goes that Joseph of Arimathea, after the Crucifixion, carried a staff of the hawthorn, (the thorns of Christ being part of this same plant or tree) to England where he eventually founded a primitive church. When he chose the site he thrust the staff into the ground and it promptly took root, and soon grew into a beautiful flowering thorn which blooms every Christmas. The place where Joseph and his companions rested on a hill about a mile from the present town of Glastonbury was called Weary-All-Hill, locally shortened into Warral. Until the time of Charles I, a branch of this famous tree was carried in church processions every Christmas. Ultimately it developed into two identical stems, until, during the civil wars, a Puritanical "Hew-'em-down," who thought both tree and legend savored of popery, decided to demolish it. One stem soon fell before his ax, but the blow aimed at the second stem glanced from the bark and cut off one of the hewer's legs. Because of this, only one stem of the Glastonbury thorn still stands.

A much larger rose bush is at Hildesheim, Germany, the age of which is admitted by scientists and botanists to be about a thousand years. Its origin is obscure: some trace it back to an ancient planting in honor of Freyja, the Nordic equivalent of Venus; others claim it is just a rosebush that rooted there and happened to survive. Still others say it was the bush planted by Charlemagne to commemorate a visit paid him by the ambassador of the Caliph Harounal-Rachid. But the one most favored is the legend of Emperor Louis the Pious.

In the ninth century, the site of Hildesheim was one vast forest abounding with game. It was a favorite resort of the Emperor Louis, an ardent sportsman despite his nickname "the Pious." One day the chase of a great white stag led him to the Innerste River. The stag jumped in, followed impetuously by the king. The stag escaped, but the emperor lost horse and hounds in the water and barely saved his own life. Staggering out of the chilly water, he found himself alone in an almost trackless wilderness.

At dusk, tired from seeking a way back to his companions, the erstwhile huntsman took a golden crucifix from his neck-chain and hung it on a thorn tree. Before this improvised altar he prayed for help. Then with no other protection from the prowling beasts of the forest, he lay down to sleep. In the morning when he awoke, he saw not a thorn but a rose tree standing in a heap of snow, the golden crucifix frozen to its flower-laden branches.

Almost simultaneously with the realization that a miracle had been wrought, came the sound of baying dogs and blowing horns, revealing the approach of his retinue. As the foremost came upon the scene they were amazed at the sight of their monarch praying before a beautiful rosebush. Their amazement was not lessened at his recital of its miraculous creation, and they vowed to help fulfill their emperor's command that a chapel be built on the site to commemorate his divine deliverance.

That chapel is claimed to be the beginning of the great Cathedral of Hildesheim, against whose walls grows that rosebush of ancient and divine origin. Although the stem is only two inches thick, the bush is twenty-eight feet high, covers thirty-two feet of wall, and in spite of its great age, puts forth fresh branches and green tendrils each spring. The cathedral, itself, suffered considerably from air raids in World War II but the rose bush withstood the poisonous fumes and continues to blossom through the years.

One of the most picturesque rose miracles is the creation of the rosary, which is found in the early history of the church of almost every Christian country. Brushing aside all inferences that the rosary was the logical product of a historical development, which had parallels in other religious systems, hagiographers have told and retold, with slight national variations, of the pious young man who made the Virgin an offering of a hundred and fifty roses each day. These roses he wove into a wreath for her altar. Eventually he became a monk in an austere order, and in his new way of life it bothered him that he had neither time nor opportunity to continue performing this rose devotion to his adored Lady. The abbé whom he consulted advised him instead to say a hundred and fifty aves to the Blessed Virgin each day, assuring him that they would be just as acceptable to her as his daily offering of fragrant roses.

Thereafter at a certain hour, the young monk knelt in front of the altar of the Saviour's mother, repeating the requisite numbers of aves. One day he was sent on a long journey; and when the hour for his daily devotions arrived, he found himself in a lonely wood where, unknown to him, thieves were hiding. The young monk stopped, knelt in the path and began his prayers. The robbers, circling closer, were about to attack him when they were stopped by a heavenly light that enveloped the kneeling figure. The now frightened thieves watched while a beautiful, glowing woman appeared and stood beside the young monk. Reaching down, she took from his praying lips a hundred and fifty roses which she gracefully wove into a garland. As she handled the roses, they grew smaller and smaller. When the garland resembled a string of beads, she placed it about the neck of the kneeling worshiper and then disappeared from the scene as miraculously as she had entered it. And thus, according to legend, the first rosary was created.

Three rose miracles in connection with the Virgin follow a definite pattern, although they occurred in three different countries and periods. The first was in Guadalupe in 1531, the second at Fatima in 1917, and the last at Lipa in 1948. In the first instance, a humble Indian, baptized Juan Diego, was on his way to attend Mass. Passing a small, bare hill, he saw a white cloud float down and turn into an arc of scintillating light which sent out the colors of the rainbow. In the midst of this resplendence appeared a beautiful Indian woman, the Virgin Mary.

"Go to Bishop Zumarraga," she said, "and tell him I wish a church built on this hill."

Juan hurried to the city but the bishop did not believe the story. Impelled by inner forces, Juan returned to the hill the following evening. The Virgin appeared again, giving him the same message. When Juan made his second trip the bishop was impressed but told Juan to "tell the lady she must send some token so I will know she is the Virgin."

When Juan went to the hill for the third time and saw the Virgin, he repeated the bishop's message. The Virgin told him to go to the very top of the hill and gather roses there. Juan was astonished at this request as the hill had always been bare, but he obeyed and found roses growing in profusion. He filled his apron or *tilma* with them and was told to take them to the bishop.

When Juan opened his *tilma* to deliver the roses to the bishop, the miraculous image was found, imprinted on the coarse fabric. It was a full-length picture of the Virgin. The bishop was so impressed that he made plans for a church to be built as speedily as possible on the appointed hill top. This very picture, a mystery to scientific investigation, hangs above the altar of the Church of Our Lady of Guadalupe. It represents the most venerated object in all Mexico and is the reason for vast and strenuous yearly pilgrimages on the part of the deeply religious people.

The second miracle took place in Portugal, in the parish of Fatima. Three children, Jacinta, Francis her brother, and their cousin Lucy were tending sheep on a hill outside the town. Hearing the Angelus bell the three little shepherds knelt down and recited the rosary together. When they finished, a blinding flash of lightning made them fearful of a storm. As they prepared to drive the sheep home, they saw an apparition of the Holy Mother. She besought them to recite their rosary every day to obtain peace for the world. Also, to come on the thirteenth of each month

Apparition of the Virgin of Guadalupe (from "A Treasury of American Folkways" by Frances Toor [Crown]).

for six months at this same hour until at the end of that time, in October, she would tell them her wish.

The children's story met with doubts and suspicion, but even the threat of imprisonment could not change their faith. In the months that followed, those who were converted to their belief went with them on their pilgrimage. On these occasions only the children were granted the grace of seeing the Virgin, while those who were pure in heart witnessed the vehicle (the glory of light) that carried her to earth and the showers of rose petals.

The thirteenth of October was wet and gloomy, a day to test anyone's faith. But the Virgin appeared and gave her message to the children, which was to build a chapel and to recite the rosary every day. Since that time a church has been built and the shrine is currently the scene of vast pilgrimages.

The third miracle of the Virgin occurred on September 12, 1948, on the Feast of the Most Holy Name of Mary, in Lipa, in the Philippines. A sister was walking in the garden of the Carmelite Monastery when she heard a woman's gentle voice say, "Fear not, my child. Kiss the ground. Whatever I tell you to do you must do. For fifteen consecutive days come to visit me here." The sister did not see anyone, she only heard the voice.

Faithful to the Virgin's request, the sister returned to the garden each day and was rewarded by the sight of the Virgin, who left rose petals in place of her apparition. The sister was next instructed to have a statue of the Virgin placed in the garden and to recite a rosary there every day. When this was done, rose petals were strewn in the cells of the monastery or on the staircases. Some of these petals showed a faint outline of the Virgin.

On the final day of the Virgin's appearance she besought the people to pray and help spread her devotion, saying that all she had asked at Fatima she was repeating, for people to become more religious. Her final words were that if her wishes were not complied with, this would be the last time she would appear on earth.

These three miracles and the message of the rose have affected the lives of millions of people, creating within them new strength, hope, and faith. It is interesting to note also that in each instance the Virgin appeared to a poor person, and one with a pure heart. Her plea, given first to a man, then a child, and last to a woman was always the same, for increased prayer and holiness in the world.

XI

FAIRY TALES

The joy of travel has the same renewal as Medea's philtre, and it is delightful to be enchanted by all the glory and blessing God has created. Kiss the fresh rose, the innocent child's mouth, say your thoughts in natural words and it will not be misunderstood here.
HANS CHRISTIAN ANDERSEN, "Letter from Spain"

THE SO-CALLED fairy tales of Hans Christian Andersen, the Brothers Grimm, Oscar Wilde, and other authors, most of whom are unknown, represent a partial mixture of folklore and fable, added to by their own highly inventive genius. Frequently, too, these tales borrow from the proverbs of the Old Testament and the parables of the New. The writers mentioned not only made constant descriptive reference to the rose, but often used it as a symbol, in much the same manner as the great masters did in their allegorical and religious paintings.

Although supposedly written for children, one suspects that many of the tales were created to entertain or console the child still dwelling in the adult heart. The stories of these writers are uniquely refreshing, well plotted, richly philosophical, and primed as a rule with a surprise ending.

In their day these same authors were singularly honored. When Hans Christian Andersen visited England, he was entertained by royalty, and Jenny Lind, who refused all invitations from the outside world, received him "like a dear brother."

Andersen must have had the rose uppermost in his mind at all times for even in his conversations he mentioned the flower constantly. At one of Queen Victoria's birthday balls, he described the English women as "flower-like and lovely standing like rose petals in the press." In his diaries

he wrote of his love for Louise Collin and sadly called her his "last rose."
In "The Moorish Girl," he had Niama say:

> "I have the faith:
> That the Prophet's Paradise and Christ's Heaven
> Are, like nature, but one realm,
> And that all the roses of love,
> Which blossom there, send forth with equal strength
> The same fragrance to Christian and Moor."

He places the rose on as many pages as he can in his fairy tales, just as he pressed them (and other flowers) to enclose in letters to his friends. "Thumberline's cradle," for example, "was a smartly varnished walnut shell with a rose-leaf to cover her." And in "Little Ida's Flowers" there walked first of all into the hall, two beautiful roses with little gold crowns on their heads; they were the king and queen. The grand duke's palace in "The Bronze Boar" boasts of "a garden under the penthouse roof where thousands of roses bloom in winter."

The Dancer in "The Steadfast Tin Soldier" is described as "wearing a dress of clearest gauze, and a narrow blue ribbon that looked like a scarf, over her shoulder; and in the middle of this ribbon was a shining tinsel rose as large as her whole face." The day after the Dancer and the Tin Soldier had been swept up by the servant maid and burned, all that was left of him was "melted tin in the shape of a little heart," and nothing of the Dancer but the tinsel rose "burned as black as coal!"

Symbolism is added to the descriptive use of the rose in "The Wild Swans." There Elsie searches for her eleven brothers all of whom have been transformed into feathered kin. After many trials, which end in the heroine's being tied to a stake to meet a witch's fate, her brothers suddenly appear to claim her. Then "a wonderful fragrance, as of millions of roses, spread around. Every faggot surrounding the stake had taken root and shot out branches, and a great hedge of red roses had grown up. At the very top was one pure white blossom, shining like a star. When this white rose was broken off and placed on Elsie's breast she awoke with joy and peace in her heart."

Another delightful Andersen creation is "The Snail and the Rosebush." The substance of the story is as follows:

In the center of a garden surrounded by a hedge of hazel stood a Rosebush in full bloom. Under this lay a Snail, who thought he had a great deal within him—since he had himself.

"Wait till my time comes," he said, "I shall accomplish something more than to yield roses, or bear hazelnuts."

Illustrations by Sir John Tenniel for Carroll's "Alice's Adventures in Wonderland" (above) and "Through the Looking Glass" (right)

161

"I expect a great deal from you," said the Rosebush. "May I ask when it will appear?"

"I shall take my time," replied the Snail philosophically, observing the world from within himself.

Year after year things went on just the same way. The Rosebush bloomed anew, the Snail came forth, and whenever the Rosebush asked him what he had given to the world, he now would answer, "What have I given? I spit upon it! It is nothing to me. Bear your roses; beyond that you cannot go! I have my public within myself. I am going into myself, and there I shall stay. The world is nothing to me!"

"How sad it is!" said the Rosebush. "However much I might desire it, I cannot creep into myself. I must always spring forth into roses. The petals fall and the wind carries them away! But I saw one of my roses laid in the housewife's psalm book; one of my roses found a place on the breast of a beautiful girl, and another was kissed in joy by a child. It did so much good; it was a true blessing. That is my memory, my life!"

The years rolled by. The Snail now was dust in the dust; the Rosebush was earth in the earth. The rose of remembrance in the psalm book had fallen to dust, but in the same garden bloomed new rosebushes; in the same garden lived other snails, who had a great deal within them.

And should we read the story of the extrovert and introvert again from the beginning, "it will never be different."

One of the most beautiful and mystical of Andersen's stories is "The Snow Queen." At the beginning of the story we find Kay and Gerda happily playing together beside the rosebushes which grew in flower boxes on the roof. The little girl had but recently learned a psalm, and she sang it to the little boy, and he sang it to her:

> "Where roses blow in the flowery vale
> There we the Child Jesus shall hail."

When they had finished, they held each other by the hand, kissed the roses, and then looked up at the sun, speaking to it as if the Christ Child indeed were there.

One day when the two little friends were playing around on the roof, Kay suddenly cried, "Ouch, I felt a sharp pain in my heart. And now something flew into my eye!" This was a fragment of glass from an evil mirror which immediately distorted his vision and made everything look small and mean.

"Stop crying, Gerda!" he said. "You look ugly like that. And that rose is worm-eaten, and this one is quite crooked! They're ugly roses!" Whereupon he kicked the box in which they grew and tore off two of the most beautiful blooms.

Under the wicked influence of the glass splinter, Kay continued to be rude and naughty, and when winter came he spent most of his time far-away, sledding on his own. One day, stopping a moment to play with Gerda, he brought out a magnifying glass, held up the corner of his blue coat and let the snowflakes fall upon it.

"Now look through the glass, Gerda," he said. "These little stars with points look more wonderful than real flowers! And there's not a single fault in them!"

As days pass, Kay is seen less and less. Completely under the spell of the Snow Queen, whose heart is but cold logic and fact, he abandons Gerda and the roses, flying off with the queen to a distant and icy land.

Heartbroken at his disappearance, Gerda sets off in search of him and comes to the flower garden of the "Woman Who Could Work Enchant-ments." The old woman is immediately desirous to keep Gerda, and realiz-ing that if the girl sees the roses in the garden she will remember her little playmate, she takes her staff and pointing it at the rosebushes causes them to sink into the earth.

All goes well with the plan until one day Gerda, sitting in the garden, notices that the prettiest flower on the old lady's sunbonnet is a rose. The sight makes her start crying, and as her tears moisten the earth, the rose tree that had been sunk at this spot springs up in full bloom. This of course puts Gerda in mind of the beautiful roses at home and her little playmate. As she kisses them, the roses explain that Kay is not dead. "You see, we have been in the ground where all the dead are, but Kay was not there."

So Gerda once more sets out on her search and finally meets a little Robber Girl who informs her that Kay is in Lapland at the Castle of the Snow Queen.

Meanwhile, Kay, in the grounds of this castle, spends most of his time playing with pieces of flat ice, making icy puzzles of Reason. To him these figures are of the highest importance because of the fragment of the evil mirror still lodged in his eye. He plans out the figures to form words, but he can never make the word he wishes for most—*eternity*.

When Gerda finally arrives at the castle, she finds Kay the moment she enters the portals. He cries out with delight, for, at the sight of her, he is able at last to spell the word *eternity*.

Gerda throws her arms around his neck and weeps as she sings:

> "Where roses blow in the flowery vale
> There we the Child Jesus shall hail."

Kay bursts into tears also, and, as he weeps, the splinter of glass comes out of his eye.

Suddenly everything is as it had been, and the two return home, glowing with warmth and happiness. An older Kay and Gerda look into each other's eyes, all at once understanding the song. There they sit, grown up, yet still children at heart. It is summer, and the roses on the roof blow gently in the breeze.

A deeply symbolic tale of Andersen's is "The Loveliest Rose in the World": he writes that there once reigned a queen in whose garden were to be found the most glorious flowers imaginable. Above all others, the monarch loved roses, a great quantity growing in many different colors against the walls of her castle. Some even grew tall enough to creep through the windows of her chamber, where one day, surrounded by sorrowful attendants and physicians, the queen lay dying.

"There is still one thing that can save her," said the wise man who had been sent for. "Bring her the loveliest rose in the world, the rose that is the symbol of the purest, brightest love. If that is held before her eyes ere they close, she will not die."

Forthwith both young and old came from every side bearing the most beautiful specimens they could find. But the wise man shook his head, saying, "They have not named the right flower. It is not the rose that springs from the hearts of youthful lovers, not the bloom that sprouts from the blood of the hero who dies for his country. Nor is it the flower for which man devotes many a sleepless night—the magic flower of science."

At length the queen's little son came into the room.

"Mother," cried the boy, "only hear what I have read."

And as he read of Him who suffered death upon the cross, a glow spread over the cheeks of the queen. From the leaves of the Book there bloomed an ethereal rose, growing out of the blood of Christ which had been shed to save mankind.

"I see it!" she said. "He who beholds this, the loveliest rose on earth, shall never die."

The rose figured in many a description by the Brothers Grimm. In "Spindle, Shuttle and Needle," for example, we find the following lines: "Suddenly the shuttle sprang out of the girl's fingers and flew away and began to weave a long, narrow carpet bordered on each side with roses and lilies. This carpet led the young Prince to her door and he was enchanted by what he saw; for in the doorway the young girl was standing in her plain little dress, but everything about her glowed like a rose on a bush . . ."

The story, "Snow White and Rose Red," written by the same authors tells of a poor widow who lived in a small cottage in front of which grew two rose trees. She took such good care of the trees that they blossomed all summer long, one with white and the other with red roses.

The widow had two children, both girls; and because they reminded her of the beautiful roses in her garden, she called one Rose Red and the other Snow White. In the summertime, Rose Red kept house. She always got up at sunrise and before she did anything else, she would pick a white and a red rose and set them at her mother's bedside for a morning greeting.

After their adventures in the forest, during which the two girls befriend a bear who turns out to be a prince in disguise, Snow White marries the Prince and Rose Red marries his brother. The mother goes along to live with them, taking her two rose trees with her.

A plausible explanation of this tale has been rendered by a student of Rudolph Steiner. Steiner, himself, believed that "in the rose there live the forces of our earliest memories and this is why people have always had such a great love of roses."

One day, in a Steiner school at Wynstones, near Gloucester, this particular fairy tale was performed on the stage when a certain Mr. Glas was present. After seeing a second performance, he said that the real meaning of the story was suddenly revealed. Later N. Glas wrote and published *Snow-White and Rose-Red, The Meaning and Exact Rendering of Grimms' Fairy Tale*. According to him, Snow White is the brain and nerve force in the body whereas Rose Red constitutes the blood . . . and, as in the words of the tale, Snow White and Rose Red never want to be parted from one another. Rose Red expresses it impulsively, "Not as long as we live."

In the fairy tale, the various stages of life are portrayed. At first, while the children are living in complete innocence, there is absolutely no fear. The Guardian Angel is quite near, sheltering the children from the abyss. But, when the time of bodily maturity is approaching, the angel can no longer watch with the same intensity. So the bear who "pokes his huge black head through the door" occasions great fear. This bear is a clumsy being, but it is seen at once that he is not wicked. The soul forces which desire to take hold of the human being at the time of sexual ripeness are at times unruly, because they long for union with the body. This sex expression is personified by the bear; outside he is hairy and black but the voice that comes from him is good-natured, wishing above all to dispel the fear that he has brought into the house. The following collection of symbols presented at that moment are excellent: the stillness of the house, then when the bear steps inside, "the little lamb bleated, the little dove fluttered and Snow White hid behind her mother's bed." Later on, the treasures of the earth that the two girls discover—the sack of gold, the bag of pearls, and the sack of precious stones—indicate a purpose beyond that of a desire simply to amuse the reader. This particular interpretation may not, of course, express the Grimms' own symbolism, but it suggests interesting possibilities of analysis of this type of fairy tale.

Oscar Wilde had a greater awareness than most people that as we grow older we forget how to read significant meanings into ordinary happenings, consequently he tried to rekindle the fire of imagination. One of the many symbols he employed in his writings was the rose, which to him was so much more than just a flower. A more or less complete exposé of his sentiments is found in the pages of *De Profundis,* which he wrote in prison.

Wilde's fairy tales are among the most heart-rending and most beautifully written of any. Always the poet, the rhythm of his lines, the use of exotic words and Oriental-sounding phrases create such vivid imagery that the pages require no illustrations. Although it is said that he wrote these tales for his two sons, they seem, inevitably, to be the concrete expressions of the secret heartaches and bitter disillusionment this ill-starred soul suffered in life. Each is a cry, a poignant confession.

"The Nightingale and the Rose" tells the story of a young student who must bring his love a red rose in order to have her dance with him that night at the prince's ball. The nightingale overhears his lament and begs of the rosebush under the student's window to yield one red rose. But the rose tree replies, ". . . the frost has nipped my buds. . . . If you want a red rose . . . you must build it out of music by moonlight, and stain it with your own heart's-blood. You must sing to me with your breast against a thorn . . . and your life-blood must flow into my veins, and become mine."

"Death is a great price to pay for a red rose," the bird replies. ". . . Yet Love is better than Life, and what is the heart of a bird compared to the heart of a man?"

And so as the bird sang on the topmost spray of the rose tree, there bloomed a marvelous rose, petal for petal followed as song followed song. Pale it was at first, "so the Nightingale pressed closer against the thorn, and the thorn touched her heart," then these songs grew wilder and wilder, "for she sang of the Love that is perfected by Death, of the Love that dies not in the tomb.

"And the marvelous rose became crimson. . . . Crimson was the girdle of petals, and crimson as a ruby was the heart."

"The rose is finished now," cried the tree. But the Nightingale made no answer, for she was lying dead on the ground.

The young student cries out in delight when he sees the rose and after picking it he hurries to the professor's house.

The professor's daughter frowns when she sees the rose. "I am afraid it will not go with my dress," she says, "and, besides, the Chamberlain's nephew has sent me some real jewels, and everybody knows that jewels cost far more than flowers."

". . . You are ungrateful," the young student answers angrily; and he

"The Mother and the Rose Bush." This mural illustrating Hans Andersen's story was painted by Fritz Syberg for the Hans Christian Andersen Museum at Odense, Denmark. In order to find her child in the winter forest, a mother is requested to warm the rose bush with her heart's blood. As the thorns pierce her flesh the bush suddenly blossoms and tells the way her young son went.

The Rose Prince, from a painting by the Swedish artist Olle Hjortzberg. This Eastern fairy tale tells of a young prince who, in order to gain admittance to a certain castle, conceals himself in a basket of roses destined for the lady of his affections (see page 171).

(Photo: Conard-Pyle Co.)

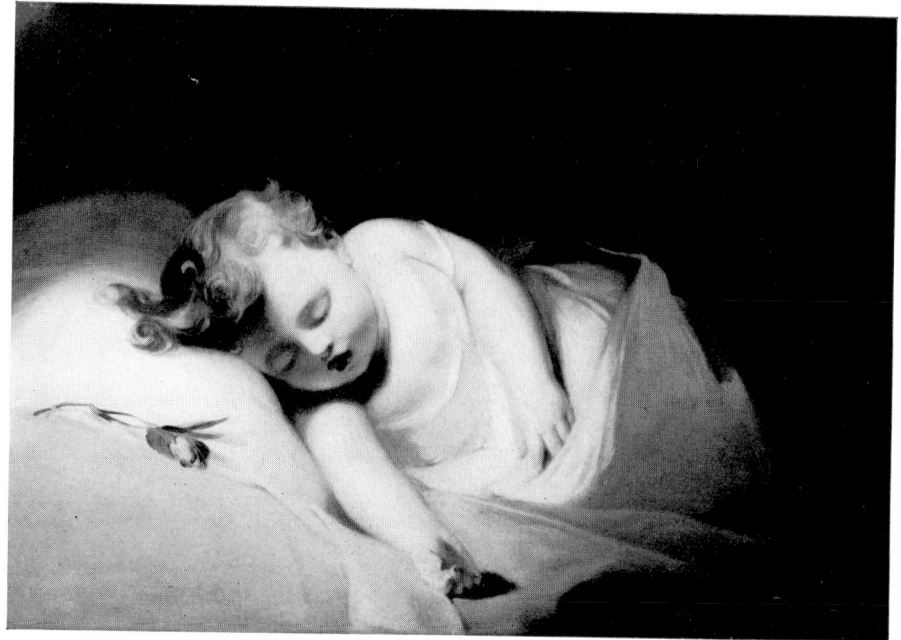

Above: "The Rose-bud," a romantic painting with a fairy tale quality by the American artist Thomas Sully (1783-1872). At left: Bud of the Fred Howard rose.

Illustration by Vera Bock for "Oscar Wilde Fairy Tales"
(Peter Pauper Press).

throws the rose into the street where a passing cart crushes the petals under
its wheels.

"What a silly thing Love is," said the student as he walked away,
". . . making one believe things that are not true. . . . I shall go back
to Philosophy and study Metaphysics." And he returned alone to his attic
room.

"The Birthday of The Infanta" is another of Wilde's tragic tales. A
typical descriptive passage concerns the Infanta's costume: "Pink and pearl
was her great gauze fan, and in her hair, which like an aureole of faded
gold stood out stiffly round her pale little face, she had a beautiful white
rose."

When the little Dwarf was brought to her birthday party, his tricks
so amused her that she took from her hair the beautiful white rose, and
partly for a jest, or to tease the Camerera, threw it to the Dwarf across the
arena. He took the whole matter quite seriously and pressing the flower
to his rough, coarse lips, put his hand upon his heart.

Later, when the Dwarf heard that he was to dance a second time that day before the Infanta, he was so proud that he ran out into the garden kissing the white rose in an "absurd ecstasy of pleasure." But when he hears the White Rose Tree exclaim: "He has actually got one of my best blooms! . . . I gave it to the Infanta this morning myself, as a birthday present, and he has stolen it from her," he leaves the garden to search for the Infanta.

Inside the palace he finds the throne room, but cares nothing for all its magnificence. "He would not have given his rose for all the pearls on the canopy, nor one white petal of his rose for the throne itself." Then, suddenly, he sees in a huge mirror the reflection of a hideous image which puzzles him until, taking from his breast the beautiful white rose, he kisses it. "The monster had a rose of its own, petal for petal the same! It kissed it with like kisses, and pressed it to its heart with horrible gestures." Seeing this, the Dwarf gave a wild cry of despair and fell sobbing to the ground, tearing the white rose to pieces. The sprawling monster did the same and scattered the faint petals in the air.

From these two stories we get a picture of the symbolic meaning that Oscar Wilde sensed in the nightingale's rose of passion and the Infanta's white rose of purity. Out of his sensitivity to sound, color, and symbols came the golden texture of his writings.

Although Andersen, the Grimms, and Wilde are the most famous known writers in this field, the fairy rose did not blossom only in their hands or respective countries. China tells us of a different color rose in "The Blue Rose Fairy Tale."

Long ago there lived an Emperor who had but one daughter. Beautiful, wise, and gifted, the Princess could chant the songs of the great poets better than any scholar in China, young or old. The Emperor was aging and wished to see his daughter married. To prove his worth the suitor must find "the blue rose."

The first suitor, a rich merchant, ordered his shopkeeper to dye a rose deep blue. The second, a courageous warrior, went to the king of the Five Rivers and had the king's servants carve a full-blown rose out of a blue sapphire. The third, the Lord Chief Justice, had an artist make a porcelain bowl with a blue rose painted on the surface, so delicate in color that it appeared like a living flower plucked from heaven. But none of these offerings were considered satisfactory.

That evening, when the Princess was in the garden, a young minstrel came and sang to her. Then, before she returned to the palace, he declared his love. With tears in her eyes she explained about the blue rose. To her surprise the minstrel only smiled, promising to bring one to her father the following morning.

170

When the minstrel appeared in court with a white rose, picked from the royal garden, the Emperor said to his daughter, "This penniless singer has dared to bring what he claims is the blue rose."

The Princess looked at the rose, then at the minstrel. The love she saw in his eyes made her blush and, turning to her father, she said: "But this is without doubt, the blue rose."

The Lord Chief Justice and all the court protested angrily, "It's white." But the Princess repeated, "I say the rose is blue!"

The Emperor, knowing well that her perception was keener than anyone's in the kingdom, proclaimed that if the Princess thought the rose was blue—blue it was!

So the Princess and the minstrel were married and lived happily ever after.

In the German book of heroes there is a story of a rose garden at Worms surrounded by a single silken thread. In this garden lived the Princess Chrymshilde. In order to protect herself from the giants in the surrounding forest, she promised a chaplet of roses and a kiss to anyone who would successfully defend the garden and slay an attacking giant. Hildebrandt, a knight, was successful in this mission, and while accepting the roses he, rather ungallantly, declined the kiss. Later on, another defender, a monk, met with equal success. He not only took the kiss, but begged for one apiece for all the members of his confraternity. To this the Princess consented, but only after the valiant monk had "fulfilled his task" of giant-slaying—one for every kiss.

There is a simple little tale based on an Eastern legend called "The Rose Prince." According to the fairy story, a handsome young prince fell madly in love with the youngest daughter of the Sultan. Admittance to the royal palace was denied him, however, and the doors were guarded both day and night by picked men. Nothing daunted, the young prince racked his brains to find not only a way of entering the chamber of his beloved, but of doing it in the most romantic way possible outside of combat—which in this case, against such odds, would have meant certain death. Finally he hit upon an idea. He ordered an enormous basket filled with roses, and concealed himself in the bottom of it as it was brought to the castle. Once safely delivered, out skipped the gallant prince to declare his love. As in all fairy tales, love triumphs over every obstacle and the two eventually are married and live happily ever after.

From India, the Hindu tale of "Vishnu, Brahma and a Rose," shows the feeling this flower evoked in many Orientals.

One day when Vishnu had come down to earth and was bathing in a pool, a lotus opened its petals and Brahma stepped out from its center. Pointing proudly to his lotus, Brahma proclaimed it to be the most beautiful flower in the world.

"It is lovely," agreed Vishnu, "but in my paradise there is a lovelier flower, pale as the moon, with perfume so sweet that no fragrance on earth can compare with it."

"Show me a flower lovelier than the lotus," Brahma said unbelieving, "and you shall have my place as chief god."

Vishnu summoned the serpent Shesba, and in a flash they were carried through space to the god's paradise. Here Vishnu led Brahma through beautiful gardens to a bower, the four columns and roof of which were fashioned of gleaming mother-of-pearl. And there, as in a shrine, grew a slender rosebush with but one blossom of great size. Its petals were creamy white and its delicate odor was the sweetest Brahma had ever known.

"This," said Vishnu, "is the fairest flower that grows."

Brahma bowed his head and admitted that there was no flower as lovely as the rose and graciously ceded his place to Vishnu as chief god.

When he returned to the lotus, the flower, learning what had happened, turned green with envy. And this green tinges her petals to this very day.

In Scandinavia, the rose is under the special protection of trolls and dwarfs. The king of the dwarfs, we are told, once dwelt in a garden of roses which was surrounded by a silver fence with four golden gates. It was well known throughout this section of the country that any mortal rash enough to enter this garden would lose an arm or a leg. But as these were magic roses, with the power to grant a man three wishes if he held them, the temptation was too great for some to resist.

One moonlit night while the dwarfs were making merry at the king's palace in the very center of the garden, two bold young men climbed over one of the golden gates. No sooner did they stand among the roses, than an arm of one and a leg of the other fell off. In terror, they turned to rush out, but the legless one, limping behind, remembered to stop long enough to snatch a rose off one of the bushes. Once over the gate, his first wish was to have his leg back again. Then he wished for his friend to recover his arm. Last of all, he wished for them both to be wealthy.

These three wishes were granted, and their success made the king of the dwarfs so angry that in his fury he caused the palace and magic garden to disappear and he and his followers went off in haste to live under the hills. Here we are supposed to find them still, wandering about, watching zealously over all rosebushes.

One of the most famous fairy tales in which the rose figures symbolically is *Beauty and the Beast*. A rich merchant had three daughters, the eldest two being greedy and ugly, while the youngest one was so naturally good and lovely that she was called Beauty. There came a day when the merchant's luck turned against him and, having lost nearly all his money, he was obliged to live with his daughters in a tiny cottage. While the elder sisters did nothing to help, Beauty willingly did the housework and waited upon them at the same time assisting her father in every way she could.

One day a letter arrived, telling the merchant that a job awaited him in a distant town. Overjoyed, he prepared to set out, and asked his daughters what they would like him to bring back for them upon his return. The elder sisters requested beautiful dresses and jewels, while Beauty, knowing how poor her father was, and thinking it would cost him nothing, asked for a beautiful rose—if he could find one.

After receiving his order for work, the merchant prepared to return home, but taking the wrong turn, was soon lost in a large forest. A terrible storm arose, and climbing a tree to see if he could discern any light that would indicate some nearby dwelling in which he could find refuge for the night, he finally finds his way to a magnificent and brilliantly lit castle. Seeking admittance he finds the door open and no one visible. Helping himself to food conveniently laid on the table, he next discovers a comfortable bed awaiting him and falls asleep upon it. To his surprise in the morning, there is a new suit of clothes carefully laid out for him. As he wanders out into the garden he sees the most perfect rose tree, which of course reminds him of his youngest daughter's request. Upon stealing the most radiant rose, he is startled by the presence of the ugliest and most terrifying beast he ever laid eyes upon. Because of the merchant's seeming ingratitude for the hospitality shown him overnight, the Beast threatens him with death. When, upon bended knee, he implores forgiveness for his indiscretion, the Beast agrees to spare him on one condition—that he promise to send him the first living thing he sees upon his return home. Thinking it was sure to be his dog, the merchant agrees, only to find that his first sight is Beauty, running up the drive to welcome him home.

In despair of his ill fortune, the merchant resolves to return to meet his death, but Beauty, upon hearing of his adventure, insists upon going with him. The beast agrees to spare both if Beauty is left with him at the castle, where he promises no harm shall befall her.

Beauty at first is terrified and shudders involuntarily every time she sees the Beast. But finally, seeing how this wounds him, she is filled with compassion, realizing that the Beast is really gentle and kind beneath the hideous exterior with which he is burdened. She promises to return if he will but permit her to visit her father once more. The Beast, desperately in love with her, reluctantly gives his consent, and in her absence, pines by the rose bushes, the blossoms of which remind him of her.

In the joy of her reunion with her father, Beauty forgets her promise to return at the end of a week, until one night she dreams that the Beast is dead, and soon awakens with tears in her eyes. Hurriedly dressing, she places a magic ring on her finger, given her by the Beast before she left him, and is immediately transported to the castle. Here she finds the Beast out in the garden by the rose bushes, nearly dead. Fearing she would never return, he had eaten nothing since her departure. "I could not live without you," he confesses, with tears in his eyes. Whereupon Beauty implores him to get better and promises to marry him if he will but live "for it is surely better to be kind and gentle than to have a handsome face, and indeed I love you." Immediately a wonderful change comes over the Beast, and to Beauty's amazement he changes into a young and handsome prince. Rising and taking her hand, the young man explains that a wicked fairy had cast a spell over him which could not be removed until some gentle girl promised to marry him, ugly as he was.

These tales of enchantment are only a few of the great number that have made use of the rose in one or another way. Other notable examples in which the rose plays one of the leading parts are: "The Neighboring Families" by Hans Christian Andersen, "The Rose from the Grave of Homer," and "Thorwalden's Grave." There is also the famous reference to the painting of the rose bushes in *Alice in Wonderland*. Although this delightful fantasy is not a fairy tale in the true sense, mention should be made here of Carroll's classic which delights adults as much as children.

XII

PROSE AND POETRY

And the rose like a nymph to the bath addrest,
Which unveiled the depth of her glowing breast,
Till, fold after fold, to the fainting air
The soul of her beauty and love lay bare. . .

PERCY BYSSHE SHELLEY

A DELIGHTFUL STORY is told about Shelley when he lived in a little rose-covered cottage at Lynmouth and produced some of his finest, most imaginative work. Here, it is said, his favorite amusement was to blow soap bubbles. Pipe in hand, he would seat himself in the doorway beneath climbing roses and send forth a cloud of shimmering spheres. Floating airly upward they reflected every changing tint, especially the pink of the roses and the blue of the sky. It was in those days that his friends called him the "Elf King."

In this idyllic setting the flow of poetic words no doubt came unsought. Emerson knew the truth of this form of inspiration. He knew that hills and mountains and sky can talk to man if he will but listen; that flowers have a definite language. He suggests this in the line:

"Speaking by the tongues of flowers."

Centuries before these authors lived, the rose played a part in sayings which have since been handed down as proverbs in many different countries. The combination of time and roses, for instance, is mentioned in almost every language, from the simple rendition of the Portuguese, "Time brings roses," to the more complicated German version, "Time brings roses but not the rose tree."

The following list contains some of the best rose proverbs and has been selected as a fair representation of various nations:

175

ALBANIAN	"The rose came out and hid the violet."
ARABIC	"A sponge to wipe out the past, A rose to make the present sweet: And a kiss to salute the future."
CHINESE	"The rose has thorns only for those who would gather it."
EGYPTIAN	"A rose fell to the lot of a monkey." (said of persons little deserving their good luck.)
ENGLISH	"If you lie upon roses when young, you'll lie upon thorns when old."
GEORGIAN	"The nightingale sings as beautifully on thorns as on roses."
GERMAN	"Roses for a brief space and thorns for eternity is folly."
INDIAN	"Only the nightingale understands the rose."
LATIN	"To do good to the ungrateful is to throw rose water into the sea."
SLOVAKIAN	"Time and patience bring roses."
SWISS	"Time brings roses but first of all buds."
TURKISH	"Man is harder than stone and more delicate than the rose."

Far too many rose stories and literary references, both long and short, have been written through the centuries to attempt here the mention of more than a few. One of the most delightful, of course, was the book *The Rose and the Ring* by William Makepeace Thackeray. This is an adult burlesque fairy tale. The fun arises from the fact that the magic rose which belongs to Prince Bulbo of Crim Tartary and the magic ring worn by the Prince Giglio of Paflagonia make their possessors seem both lovely and lovable. Unfortunately, the loss of these objects shows the two princes as they really are.

Referring to the rose in his *All Trivia*, Logan Pearsall Smith entertainingly writes, "Most of all I envy the octogenarian poet who joined three words, 'Go lovely rose!' so happily together that he left his name to float down through Time on the wings of a phrase and a flower."

And later in this same book he remarks:

"Oh, dear, this living and eating and growing old, these doubts and aches in the back, and want of interest in Nightingales and Roses!"

Emerson, in his essay on "Self-Reliance," points out that "Man is timid and apologetic; he is no longer upright, he dares not say, I think, I am, but quotes some saint or sage. He is ashamed before the blade of grass or the blowing rose. These roses under my window make no reference to former roses or to better ones; they are what they are; they exist

The rose. A symbolical and poetic study by Ansel Adams.

Rose Nocturne
(Armstrong Nurseries)

Such color as the curtained bee would know
Drowsed in the bedstead of a crimson rose,
Such color as the vineyard speck might swim
Deepened in the full Burgundian glass.
Such color as the unborn Juliet feet
Nursed in the reddest vein in Shakespeare's heart.

Christopher Morley

Rose Helen Traubel, named after the famous opera star.

with God today. There is no time to them. There is simply the rose; it is perfect in every moment of its existence. Before a leaf-bud has burst its whole life acts; in the full-blown flower there is no more; in the leafless root there is no less."

One of the most unique rose books was written by a scholarly sea captain, Samuel A. Binion. In compiling the text he spent several years perfecting a picture alphabet, a sort of rose code, using leaves, buds and full-blown roses to spell out Christian names. This art is called phyllanthography and a charming rose picture is made for each name.

To list and evaluate all the books, essays, and articles that have been written from the standpoint of rose gardens and culture would be a work in itself. Many books contain one or two chapters on the appearance of the flower in art, its meaning in religion, its use in customs, and other general information interesting to the average reader as well as the garden enthusiast. Some of these are so delightfully written that they furnish a welcome escape from the present world tension. The following selection, while not comprising all the best ones in this category has been made from the point of view of those which can be seen in most public libraries:

A Rose Odyssey, J. H. Nichols
Floral Symbolism, Elizabeth Haig
My Friend the Rose, Francis E. Lester
A Book about Roses, Dean Hole
Rose Recipes, Eleanor Sinclair Rohde
Sun Dials and Roses of Yesterday, Alice Morse Earle
The Rose, Its History and Culture, S. B. Parsons
The Rose Upon Her Briar, Helen Temperly
The Book of Flowers, Katherine Tynan and Frances Maitland

It has been roughly estimated that there are more than four thousand rose songs. Some of these are familiar to everyone such as "My Wild Irish Rose," "Roses of Picardy," "The Last Rose of Summer," "Only a Rose," "In the Time of Roses," and "Rose of My Caravan." The folk song, "Bendemeer's Stream," brings to life the haunting beauty of the flower:

> "There's a bower of roses by Bendemeer's stream
> And the nightingale sings 'round it all the day long;
> In the times of my childhood 'twas like a sweet dream
> To sit 'mid the roses and hear the bird's song."

We should certainly add to this list two songs by Stephen Foster whose recently completed shrine is at White Springs, Florida: "This Rose Will Remind You," and "Ah, May the Red Rose Live Alway."

Poets have immortalized the rose since time immemorial. Ordinary words such as fall to the lot of more lowly flowers such as the daisy or buttercup are seldom used. Nearly always we find the rose as regal, queenly, noble, jeweled, marvelous, mystical, or secret. Her flower is compared to a gorgeous urn or a radiant cup of gorgeous hue; and she appears in crimson dress or scatters shreds of velvet silk upon the grass. The sweetbriar is white as the wing of a dove with breasts of beaten gold, and its fragrance is inimitably sweet.

Sir Philip Sidney wrote: "Nature never set forth the earth in so rich tapestry as divers poets have done, neither with so pleasant rivers, fruitful trees, sweet smelling flowers, nor whatsoever may make the earth more lovely," and of all the "sweet smelling flowers" none has been mentioned so many times as the rose. Poets have constantly employed her beauty to add warmth and color to philosophic lines and verses, to further romance and sentiment, or to emphasize some mystic meaning. And in a lighter vein, as with everything else symbolically beautiful, their wit has been aimed at the rose.

Thomas Hood recalls the rose sentimentally in "The House Where I Was Born":

> "I remember, I remember
> The roses, red and white."

Lord Byron warns us philosophically to:

> "As soon seek roses in December . . . as ice in June."

Dorothy Parker in "One Perfect Rose" questions with puckish humor:

> "Why is it no one ever sent me yet
> One perfect limousine, do you suppose?
> Ah no, it's always just my luck to get
> One perfect rose."

while Oliver Wendell Holmes says in "My Aunt" (who was evidently a spinster lady):

> "One sad, ungathered rose
> on my ancestral tree."

The first poet disciple of the rose was Homer. But in the *Iliad* and the *Odyssey* he borrows the brilliant colors of the rose to point the rising of the sun. Aurora, according to him, has fingers of roses, and perfumes the air with their scent. Few, if any, literary men are more celebrated than this traditional epic poet of Greece for beauty of conception or interesting

*Illustration by J. Reschofsky for "L'Églantier" by Princess Bibesco
(courtesy, "France Illustration").*

similes inspired by natural objects.

In Sappho's academy for the instruction of young girls in music, poetry, singing, and dancing, they made wreaths of roses and violets and composed verses. These were used in the processional dances and songs for the festivals of the gods. Sappho sent these lines to one of her most loved pupils:

> "When many a wreath of violet
> And rose in timely garlands set
> Thou twinest sitting by my side."

She also wrote "Ode to the Rose":

> "Would Jove a Queen of Flowers ordain,
> The Rose, the Queen of Flowers, should reign.
> The Grace of Plants! The Pride of bowers,
> The Blush of Meads, the eye of flowers,
> Her sweets the breath of love disclose,
> Cythera's favorite bloom she glows.
> What flower is half so lovely found,
> As when, with full-blown beauties crowned,
> The Rose each ravished sense beguiles
> And on soft amorous Zephyr smiles?"

Sappho's love of the flower prompted Diogenianus to write:

> "No honey for me, if it comes with a bee,
> But, Sappho, of thee
> Few flowers, yet they are roses all."

Other Greeks such as Anacreon, Bion, Theocritus, and Apollodorus relate various fables respecting the origin of the rose and how it obtained the bright color for which it is distinguished. Anacreon, like Sappho, composed an entire ode in praise of his favorite flower:

> "The Rose is the honour and beauty of floures,
> The Rose is the care and love of the Spring,
> The Rose is the pleasure of th' heavenly Pow'rs.
> The Boy of Faire Venus, Cythera's Darling
> Doth wrap his head round with Garlands of Rose
> When in the dances of the Graces he goes."

These other lines are also attributed to him:

> "Friends! Form your accents with mine, in singing the season of flowers, and the Rose of Spring."

"The Rose is the sweet perfume which the mouths of the gods exhale; the joy of mortals, the loveliest ornament of the Graces in the flowery season of love, and the dearest delight of Venus."

"The Rose is the object of the songs of the poets, the favorite plant of the Muses."

"Though she wounds us with her thorns, we gather her with pleasure. What delight to hold this flower consecrated to love, and to breathe its sweet odours!"

"Our poets sing of the rosy fingers of Aurora, the rosy arm of the Nymphs, the cheeks of Venus tinted with Roses."

"The Rose is useful to the sick; she braves the duration of years; agreeable even in decay, she preserves the perfume of her youth."

"What shall I say of her origin? When the Sea formed from her froth and displayed on her waves the beautiful Venus, brilliant with dew; when Pallas sprang forth armed from the brain of Zeus, the earth brought forth this admirable plant, a new masterpiece of nature. Eager to hasten her blooming, the gods watered her with nectar, and then this immortal flower elevated herself majestically on her thorny column."

The rose progression in poetry moved on from Greece to Rome where Virgil, Ovid, Horace, and Juvenal extolled the beauty of the flower. From thence we turn to Persia, and Shiraz, "the fairest gem of Iran, the 'Abode of Knowledge,' the home of poets, roses and nightingales . . . once a capital city of the historic province of Fars. Here Magick was first hatched; here Nimrod for some time lived; . . . and here a series of two hundred kings have swayed their sceptres. Future historians will add 'here lived Sadi and Hafiz.'"

But before the birth of either Sadi or Hafiz, Omar Khayyam wrote of the rose in his *Rubáiyát*,

> "Look to the Rose that blows about us—'Lo,
> Laughing,' she says, 'into the World I blow!
> At once the silken tassel of my Purse
> Tear, and its Treasure on the Garden throw.'"

Then came Sadi, one of the most illustrious of Persian poets. This great attachment to the rose was due in part to the circumstances attending his liberation from slavery. His master, it seems, had promised him his liberty but tarried in fulfillment of the promise. Sadi went to him one day with a rose in his hand and said to his master, "Do good, while yet thou hast the power, for time is fleeting, and the season of power is often as transient as the duration of this flower. Do not delay longer the fulfillment of thy promise, O my master!" These words so struck his master that he liberated Sadi at once.

Reference to the rose is made on almost every page of Sadi's *Rose Garden*. "On Gratitude," he writes, "He produced the rose for you from the thorn." "On Repentance," concerning the death of a child, "Marvel not if the rose blooms out of his dust, for many a one endowed with roselike body sleeps in the ground." "On the Ways of Dervishes," he explains that "Everything that you behold is exclaiming the praises of God, as is well known unto the understanding heart. Not only the nightingale and the rose-bush are chanting the praises of God, but every thorn is a tongue to extol Him." "Excellency of Contentment" records the advice of a father to his son, "O Son, heaven has befriended you this time, and good fortune has been your guide so that you have been able to pluck the rose from the thorn and to extract the thorn from your foot." In "The Effect of Education" we read: "He ought to submit to violence from an enemy who wishes to enjoy a friend, because the treasure and the dragon, the rose and the thorn, sorrow and gladness are linked together."

The tomb of Hafiz, the third great Persian poet, is not far from the Koran Gate and in the center of the gardens of Shiraz which provided him with many themes and songs. Today, Shiraz has little to show except the glory of the Tang Pass, the Regent's Bazaar, and her gardens of cypress. She lives in the aura of her poets' graves. This is especially true in the evening when a cloud of dust hangs over the little city like golden gauze; and the evening breezes carry the scent of the rosebushes in the gardens. Then classical Shiraz has not merely an honored past, it has a glorious present.

Hafiz was loved and honored during his lifetime perhaps more than any other. His poems are tapestries. Beauty, Love, Youth, and Joy are held captive by his roses and nightingales for eternity! Odes 14 and 49 are given here:

"O Love, the very perfume of the rose,
   As the dew carries it about the sward,
   Smiting my senses like an unseen sword,
  Out from the rose-bush of your bosom blows;
   And lo! the very nightingales are mad,
   Frenzied with singing—just as though they had
  Looked one delirious moment in your face."

I sometimes think that never blows so red
The Rose as where some buried Caesar bled

(From the "Rubiyat of Omar Khayam," illustrated by Edmund J.
Sullivan; Avon Edition.)

"Now that the rose-tree in its dainty hand
Lifts high its brimming cup of blood-red wine,
And green buds thicken o'er the empty land,
Heart, leave these speculations deep of thine,
And seek the grassy wilderness with me.
Who cares for problems, human or divine!"

Poetry, in the East, is held in such veneration that the name of "legitimate magic" or the expression "to string pearls" has been given to the composition of verse. The illustrations or illuminations could be likened to "rose magic." The works of the favorite poets are generally written on fine, silky paper, the ground of which is powdered with gold or silver dust; the margin composed of a rose motif and nightingale. The beautiful line edgings, the powderings of gold, and the margin miniatures are exquisite. Often the paper is of flower or fruit tints, pale lemon yellow, light orange, lilac, and every tint of rose, since white paper offends the Persian eye. Some of these volumes were scented with attar of roses. The copy of the poems of Jami, last of the classic poets of Persia, in the Bodleian Library at Oxford even after four centuries is still fragrant with the original rose perfumes.

The Western poets have never been such constant disciples of the rose, although Ronsard, the first French poet who sang of this flower did receive the honor of having a rose named for him. His "Lines to His Mistress" are well known:

"And gather in their blushing prime,
The roses of your youth!"

Many interesting stories are told of this particular poet. "In France, since the reign of Philip Augustus, rose water was carried in large vases to baptisms. The day of Ronsard's birth, when he was carried from the Chateau de la Poissonnière to the church, the nurse let him fall. Another young lady, in trying to help, overturned on the baby's head a large quantity of rose water, so that the day of his birth might have been the day of his death. This incident was considered a presage of the good odour with which France would one day be filled by the flowers of his learned writings."

As a poet he received great honors and pensions from Henry II and Francis II. Charles IX added priories and abbacies and Queen Elizabeth presented him with a set of diamonds. Mary, Queen of Scots, was so delighted with Ronsard's beautiful poetry that she sent him a magnificent rose of silver, valued at five hundred pounds, with this inscription, "A Ronsard l'Apollon de la source des Muses."

The SICK ROSE

O Rose thou art sick.
The invisible worm.
That flies in the night
In the howling storm:

Has found out thy bed
Of crimson joy:
And his dark secret love
Does thy life destroy.

*William
Blake
(1757-1827)*

Thomas Moore and William Butler Yeats perpetuated the rose in Irish verse. The poetry and prose of the latter is so replete with rose symbolism that this material is reserved for the next chapter which treats the subject more fully. Thomas Moore's most familiar passages about the rose are:

> "You may break, you may shatter the vase, if you will,
> But the scent of the roses will hang round it still."

> " 'Tis the last rose of summer.
> Left blooming alone."

> "Rose of the garden, such is woman's lot.
> Worshipped while blooming, when she fades, forgot!"

The historical use of the rose in England made the native poets especially conscious of this flower. Shakespeare, already quoted several times in this book, was one of the first, and he mentions the rose more than a hundred times in his plays and sonnets. Such lines as these are typical:

> "From fairest Creatures we desire increase,
> That thereby Beauty's Rose might never die."

Robert Herrick, seventeenth century English poet, loved flowers so much that one of the critics who knew him personally complimented him by saying: "Many flowers just grow to illustrate quotations from his works." He wrote many rose poems, the best known of which perhaps is:

> "Gather ye rosebuds while ye may,
> Old Time is still a-flying,
> And the same flower that smiles today
> Tomorrow will be dying."

John Milton, another of the world's most distinguished poets, mentions the rose in his lament on blindness:

> ". . . Thus with the year,
> Seasons return, but not to me returns
> Day, or the sweet approach of ev'n or morn
> Or sight of vernal bloom, or summer's rose."

And to Robert Southey the rose appeared again as a mystical flower in the lines:

> "The Rose expands
> Her paradise of leaves."

Lord Byron, Shelley, Keats, and later Tennyson, the Brownings, and Swinburne, all frequently mention the rose in separate lines or in entire poems, and each reveals something of his character by the way he used the symbol. For instance, Byron states: "The roses of love glad the garden of life," while Shelley is nostalgic in the lines:

> "Why must I think how oft we two
> Have sate together near the river springs . . . .
> While the musk-rose leaves, like flakes of crimson snow
> Showered upon us, and the dove mourned in the pine
> Sad prophetess of sorrows not our own."

Robert Browning refers to the rose as

"This glory garland round my soul."

and Elizabeth Browning expresses a feminine interest in her poem, "A Dead Rose":

"O Rose, who dares to name thee?
No longer roseate now, nor soft nor sweet,
But pale and hard and dry as stubble wheat,
Kept seven years in a drawer, thy titles shame thee."

Some poets, not content with their own creations, have borrowed from others. Robert Bridges, poet laureate of England, does this in *The Testament of Beauty*:

"Thus Shakespeare, in the sessions of sweet silent
thought
gathering from memory the idealization of love,
when he launched from their dream-sheds those golden
sonnets
that swim like gondolas i' the wake of his drama,
fashion'd for their ensignry a pregnant axiom,
and wrote: From fairest creatures we desire increase
that thereby Beauty's Rose might never die."

In the United States, we find another devotee of the rose in Henry Wadsworth Longfellow. A student of Dante, Longfellow's "Marble Rose of Rome," the Colosseum, is similar to Dante's Paradise, "in form of a white rose." And in his *Golden Legend* we read:

"As thou standest there,
Thou seemest to me like the angel
That brought the immortal roses
To Saint Cecilia's bridal chamber."

Edgar Allan Poe is easily recognizable in these lines "To Helen":

"There fell a silvery-silken veil of light,
With quietude, and sultriness, and slumber,
Upon the upturned faces of a thousand
Roses that grew in an enchanted garden,
Where no wind dared to stir, unless on tiptoe—

191

Fell on the upturn'd faces of these roses
That gave out, in return for the love-light,
Their odorous souls in an ecstatic death—
Fell on the upturn'd faces of these roses
That smiled and died in this parterre, enchanted
By thee, and by the poetry of thy presence."

The delicate humor of another American, Emily Dickinson, is charmingly manifest in:

"God made a little gentian;
It tried to be a rose
And failed, and all the summer laughed."

Don Marquis contributes humorously:

"Publishing a volume of verse is like dropping a rose petal down the Grand Canyon and waiting for the echo." ("The Sun Dial")

Last but not least there is of course that famous line from Gertrude Stein's *Sacred Emily:*

"Rose is a rose is a rose is a rose."

Even from this brief survey we can see that the number of poets who have put into words the emotions many of us feel when we look at a rose is legion, and all have contributed rich remembrances to our daily lives. Oscar Wilde in the conclusion of his introduction to the verses of a young poet, *Rose Leaf and Apple Leaf,* added this suggestion: "In some such way as this we could gather up these strewn and scattered petals of song into one perfect rose of life!"

XIII

SYMBOLISM AND MYSTICISM

The Rose, wherein, the Word Divine made itself flesh . . .

DANTE

SYMBOLISM, the visible sign of an invisible reality, is a natural and universal language. In man's desire for beauty, inherent to a great or lesser degree in every human heart, he found that the rose came as close to his concept of perfection as any other material object. The miraculous unfolding and maturing into full bloom and fragrance, followed by the flower's drooping and final decay and dust, represented the cycle of human life. Its colors are not without significance either, white suggesting purity, and red either the passion of love or the blood of martyrs.

The lotus, which ranks second in popularity, has limited symbolic virtues and grows in few sections of the world. Its fragrance is negligible; its blossoming period of short duration. The rose, on the contrary, is versatile, lending itself readily to symbolism in religious ceremonies, the rituals of secret orders or societies and the mysticism of writers, poets, and painters in all countries and centuries.

The similiarity of the framing or spelling of the word *rose* in so many different languages is claimed by some authorities as further proof or evidence of divine purpose. The word *rose*, from the Greek, means red. It is connected with *rota*, a wheel, which resembles the outline of a rose. In English, French, Danish and Norwegian the name rose is the same. In other countries it is very similar:

Rosen	German
Rosa	Italian, Spanish, Portuguese, Latin
Roja	Russian
Rocza	Hungarian
Roza	Polish

Rhodon	Greek
Rhos	Celtic
Roose	Dutch
Ros	Irish

In the preceding chapters many symbolic uses of the rose have been given, demonstrating the significance and influence of this universal symbol. Few sections of the world have escaped its power or influence. In Guatemala, Central America, the priests of the age-old Cult of Chuch Kajan of the Mayakiche Indians carry bags over their shoulders, containing rose petals, resin, and candles. The petals are used as an important part of their rituals, which have been performed since the dawn of history.

The Slavic people, with picturesque symbolism, used to acknowledge their remembrance of souls lost at sea. During the season of roses, wreaths were woven of leaves and blossoms interspersed with small candles. After lighting the candles, the wreaths were launched from the banks of the Vistula River and left to drift out to sea. This ancient and pagan custom was a gesture to the mighty entity which could both take and give life. Similar rose wreaths with lighted candles were also offered for one or more living members of the family then sailing in far off waters. The many traditional ceremonies or rituals of this type have built up in the hearts and minds of all peoples a religious and sentimental response to the rose.

In tracing rose symbolism back to some of its beginnings we find that the Egyptians, Greeks, and Romans regarded the rose as a symbol of human love. There was, however, one striking exception when Amenhotep IV, Pharaoh of Egypt in 1360 B.C., placed these words on papyrus: "Suffering is the golden cross upon which the rose of the Soul unfoldeth." This was the beginning of the deeper, the esoteric meaning of the rose symbol which has increased in significance throughout the centuries. In Christianity, the symbol was accepted directly after the death of Christ, but we find little record of it in the church until the beginning of the Renaissance. In *The Lost Language of Symbolism* Harold Bayley states that "the rose being regarded as the Heavenly Spirit of the Highest was by the mystics identified with Jesus Christ, of whom Vaughan writes:

> " 'Tis now clear day: I see a rose
> Bud in the bright East and disclose
> The pilgrim Sun."

Other Christian interpretations point to the five petals of the red rose as representing the five wounds of Christ, and the white rose, the Virginity of the Blessed Virgin.

Like the early Greeks, the Persians connected the rose with love, but in a deep sense, for the Persian word for rose is *Gul*, which means "the mighty God." Such quotations in their literature as "the face of my Beloved is a rose" would suggest a divine connotation. In France, the emphasis is more simply upon romance, the rose traditionally symbolizing Venus—and the same love which Hafiz had immortalized so perfectly in such odes as:

> "Love, thou art fair, as delicate as dew
> Upon a rose-leaf thy young freshness is."

Dante was perhaps the first poet who attributed the highest form of mysticism to the rose, making it the symbol of Paradise or Heaven, "brighter than a million suns, immaculate, inaccessible, vast, fiery with magnificence, and surrounding God as if with a million veils."

He makes further references in the *Divine Comedy*:

> "So ranged above the Light on every side
> Thousands of thrones themselves I saw regard,
> Numerous as they who have returned from earth.
> And if the last grade in itself collects
> So great a light, what must be the expanse
> Of this Rose to the farthest of its leaves?
> My vision by the breadth or by the height
> Was not bedazzled, but embrased the whole—
> The mode and vastness of that blessedness."

> "Into the yellow of the eternal Rose,
> Which blows, and spreads in tiers, and renders up
> Odours of praise to the aye vernal Sun,
> Like one in silence, but in wish to speak,
> Beatrice led me . . ."

Dante's use of symbolism in regard to the rose is discussed by H. Flanders Dunbar in her *Symbolism in Medieval Thought and Its Consummation in the Divine Comedy*:

"The vision that sees in a yellow rose the solution of the drama of life and death is not native to this generation. Modern culture, formed in the rise of the scientific method, finds itself in a position to smile at the naiveté that sees in a flower at once an expression of philosophic truth, the goal of a career, and the fulfillment of social and political theory. Dante's Celestial Rose is readily banished to the realm of poetic conceit or buried among the ashes of time-worn symbolisms, while contemporary thought puzzles genially over an almost obsolete tradition: seeking in its fossils, disclosures of the phenomena of mind, and ignoring their living role organic in the enigma of genius.

"No longer, as in the 13th and 14th centuries, is a rose a natural and appropriate expression of the deepest that is known. Once a luminous eternity unfolding without pause its myriad petals, each the throne of a radiance-vestured soul, it offered up perpetually as perfume the incense of creation's praise. As it mirrored, like the crystal sea, the Threefold Glory in whose radiance it was bathed, over its angelic multitudes, glowing and shadowless, like bees ascended and descended bearing blessings from the sun. *In this Celestial Rose has been discerned a statement of truth far more accurate than any possible to the unaided power of science, although demanding foundation in the most rigorous discipline of the intellect. . . .* For Dante, symbolism constituted not only the natural, but the most adequate expression."

From these and other records of esoteric acceptance of the rose as a symbol of creation and life, we can see how the astonishing rose windows may have come to be incorporated in the Gothic cathedrals. The greatest example undoubtedly is the one at Chartres, where, in connection with the other interrelated works of men with extraordinary inner convictions and powers, it radiates an eternal symbolic message to those seeking revelation in the path of religion. Whether or not there is any direct connection with the East, where symbolic rose windows are also to be found in church architecture appears not to be definitely established. Among the many analogous beliefs, however, is that of the Brahmins who say that the Almighty has his abode in the heart of a rose.*

William Blake, who steeped himself in religious study, made some of the most interesting illustrations for the *Divine Comedy*. These reflected an inevitable mystical concept, the one of the yellow rose perhaps being the most beautiful. This is called "The Queen of Heaven in Glory," from "Paradise," Canto XXXI. On each of the unfolded petals is sketched the faint outline of a female figure, the petals building up, as a pyramid, toward the center which supports a seated figure with Mary printed above her head. She is encircled with tiny angels which resemble bees. There are also scattered throughout the petals a book of Homer, the Bible, and several other objects difficult to decipher—at least in the present state of the original.

The mystical rose was fostered in Germany by Goethe. *The Mysteries* written by him tells of the pilgrimage of Brother Mark to a secret Brotherhood. On his arrival at the gate of the monastery he sees above the entrance not only the cross but another symbol, a garland of roses. He naturally asks this question:

* Usually referred to as a Silver rose.

196

Rose window (or wheel of Fortune), symbolizing eternity, in the Gothic cathedral at Amiens. Fourteenth Century. Below: Symbolic rose copied from the old fashioned French cabbage rose. The petals of four roses are used around the central blossom. (Courtesy, Patricia Easterbrook Roberts.)

Symbolic rose made of gold, originally used in early
Christian church ceremonies. It was the custom to present a golden rose to an illustrious person, or group, conspicuous for loyalty to the Holy See. A description of
this custom is given on page 101.

"Madonna and Child in Rose Arbor" by Stephan Lochner (?-1451). A rose trellis, symbolizing heavenly joy and delight, stands behind the central figure. The roses in the Madonna's crown signify divine love, while the brooch, featuring a unicorn, represents maidenly purity.

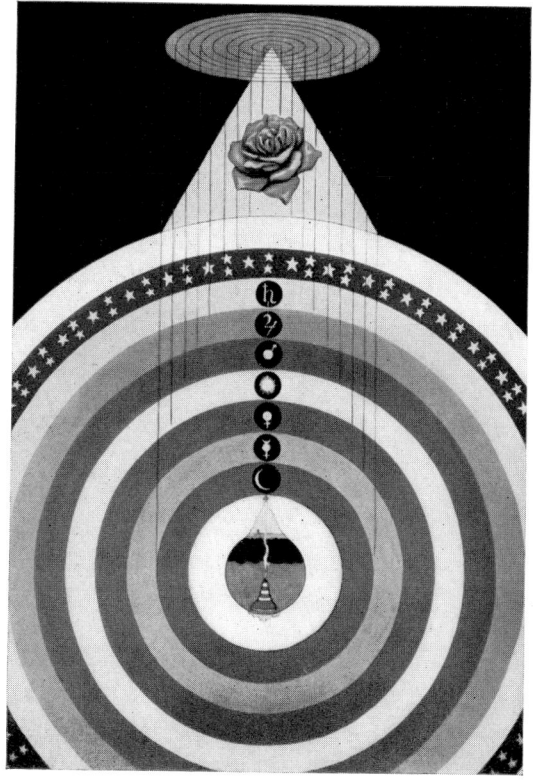

Above: Sketch by William Blake (1757-1827) for Dante's "Divine Comedy." "What must be the expanse of this Rose to the farthest of its leaves?" The Queen of Heaven in glory is sketched at the top of the symbolic rose.

Right: A key to Dante's "Divine Comedy." As the soul climbs the seven steps of Purgatory it is cleansed of the seven mortal sins and ascends through the seven spheres. In the eighth the soul receives spiritual truths and in the ninth is absorbed into the celestial mysteries.

> "Who added to the cross the wreath of roses?
> It is entwined by blooming clusters dense,
> Profusely spreading just as though they could
> Endow with softness e'en the rigid wood."

The poem depicts the principles of Christianity in the profoundest manner, and Brother Mark sees what the Rosy-Cross must overcome:

> "A dragon is enthroned with fiery wings;
> And here between his jaws a bear is holding
> An arm from which the blood it loses springs,
> Both shields, in distance corresponding quite,
> Hung next the Rosy-Cross to left and right."

In the end, Mark witnesses the festival of Light, Life, and Love:

> "He clearly sees their wonderful apparel,
> The white resplendent garments which they wear.
> Their girdles made of intertwining roses,
> The wreaths of flowers in their curly hair;
> They seem to come from some nocturnal dances."

These three youths with their symbolic roses whom Brother Mark sees as in a dream are the eternal three. They are the rejuvenating spiritual powers.

The rose symbol used by Robert Southey was the silver rose of India. According to one of the traditions of the East, there stands on Mount Calasay, the Hindu Olympus, a table upon which lies a silver rose bearing among its petals the two holy servants of the Most High whose duty it is to "Praise God without ceasing." Another explanation describes Mount Calasay as a table on which lies a silver rose that contains two women as bright and fair as pearls. In the center of this rose is the triangle, or residence of God. In *The Curse of Kehama,* Southey describes Mount Calasay:

> "Lo, there the Silver Bell,
> That, self-sustain'd hangs buoyant in the air!
> Lo! the broad table there, too bright
>   For mortal sight,
> From whose four sides the bordering gems unite
>   Their harmonizing rays,
> In one mid fount of many-colour'd light.
> The streams of splendor, flashing as it flows,
> Plays round, and feeds the stem of yon celestial rose!
> Where is the sage whose wisdom can declare
> The hidden things of that mysterious flower,

That flower which serves all mysteries to bear?
　The sacred triangle is there,
　Holding the Emblem which no tongue may tell;
　Is this the Heaven of Heaven, where Seeva's self doth dwell?"

At this point, Glendoveer, the most beautiful of the good spirits, seeks to remove the curse of Kehama:

"So saying, up he sprung,
And struck the bell, which self-suspended hung
　Before the mystic Rose
From side to side the silver tongue
Melodious swung, and far and wide
Soul thrilling tones of heavenly music rung,
　Abash'd confounded,
It left Glendoveer . . . yea all astounded
In over-powering fear and deep dismay;
　For when that Bell had sounded,
　The Rose, with all the mysteries it surrounded,
The Bell, the Table, and Mount Calasay,
　The Holy Hill itself, with all thereon
Even as a morning dream before the day
　Dissolves away, they faded and were gone."

The use of the rose in many experiments conducted by the alchemists intensified the symbolic power of the rose in the affairs of man. In Rosenberg's book *Rhodoligia* is a claim relative to the supernatural qualities of the rose besides its curative properties. He asserts as a positive fact, supported by several authorities which he quotes, the remarkable regeneration or resurrection of the rose. He further states that notwithstanding the many marvelous things which we already know with respect to the improving, forcing, changing, and multiplying of roses, we have yet to describe the most surprising of all, namely its regeneration, or the reproduction or resurrection of that flower from its own ashes. This is called the Imperial Secret, because Emperor Ferdinand III purchased it from a foreign chemist at some fabulous price. The concluding sentence regarding the experiment ends with, "Finally all this material being placed in a glass vessel, with a certain quantity of pure dew, forms a blue powder, from which, when heat is applied, there springs a stem, leaves and flowers, and a whole and perfect plant is formed from its own ashes."

In a letter dated March 20, 1859, Longfellow recognizes this claim: "For my own part, I am delighted to hear the birds sing again. Spring always reminds me of the Palingenesis or recreation of the old alchemists, who believed that form is indestructible and that out of the ashes of a rose, the rose itself could be reconstructed if they could only discover the great secret of Nature."

Again, hidden among the pages of one of the volumes of his poems are the following lines:

> "And the wild-Roses of the promontory
>   Around me shuddered in the wind, and shed
>   Their petals of pale red.
>   There was an old belief that in the embers
>   Of all things their primordial form exists,
>   And cunning alchemists
>   Could recreate the Rose with all its members
>   From its own ashes, but without the bloom,
>   Without the lost perfume.
>   Ah me! what wonder-working, occult science
>   Can from the ashes in our hearts once more
>   The Rose of youth restore?"

Another tale of alchemy concerns the rose nobles of the reign of Edward I or Edward IV. It is a tale of magic. The coin, it seems, was exquisitely fine and beautiful and so much gold was used in the whole coinage that the word quickly spread that it had been produced by the aid of magic. William Camden (1551–1623) says of the early coin:

"Our alchemists doe affirm as an unwritten verity that the gold thereof was made by multiplication or projection alchemicall of Raymond Lully in the Tower of London."

Because of this, the rose nobles were held to be a sort of amulet. It was thought that the possession of one hindered the theft of a purse containing it. Both Edward I and Edward IV were firm believers in the magic arts, particularly alchemy, and either of these two kings might have produced this coin.

Both Elizabeth and Robert Browning concerned themselves with unusual qualities of the rose. Encased in the deep mysticism of Robert Browning's *Transcendentalism* are these lines:

> "As Swedish Boehme never cared for plants
>   Until it happed, a-walking in the fields,
>   He noticed all at once that plants could speak,
>   Nay, turned with loosened tongue to talk with him.
>   That day the daisy had an eye indeed—
>   Colloquised with the cowslip on such themes.
>   We find them extant yet in Jacob's prose.
>   But by the time youth slips a stage or two

While reading prose in that tough book he wrote,
(Collating, and emendating the same
And settling on the sense most to our mind)
We shut the clasps and find life's summer past.
Then, who helps more, pray, to repair our loss—
Another Boehme with a tougher book
And subtler meanings of what roses say,—
Or some stout Mage like him of Halberstadt,
John, who made things Boehme wrote thoughts about?
He with a 'look you!' vents a brace of rhymes,
And in there breaks the sudden rose herself,
Over us, under, round us every side,
Nay, in and out the tables and the chairs
And musty volumes, Boehme's book and all,—
Buries us with a glory, young once more,
Pouring heaven into this shut house of life."

Elizabeth Browning was moved by a different form of mysticism in connection with the rose in her *Lay of the Brown Rosary*. This poem is the lament of a young girl whose struggle involves the thought of an earthly love instead of the love of Heaven, the mystical rose tree which bears seven times seven.

"To choose perhaps a love-lit hearth,
        instead of love and heaven—
A single rose for a rose-tree which
        beareth seven times seven?
A rose that droppeth from the hand,
        that fadeth in the breast,
Until in grieving for the worst, we
        learn what is the best!"

Sir Edwin Arnold, in *The Light of Asia*, describes the spiritual awakening of the young Prince Siddārtha, or Buddha. Because of the prophecy made at his birth—that the young prince "shall tread the sad and lonely path of self-denial and of pious pain"—his father, the king, exerts every effort to keep him from this fate. When indications of his saintliness begin to appear with his questioning:

"And when the rose dies where are gone
        Its scent and splendor?"

his father takes him on a tour of his realm so that he may feast his eyes on their great wealth. As they drive past the painted temples and fabulous gardens, the young Siddārtha notices only how "the swart peasant sweats for his wage, toiling for leave to live. And how he urged the great-eyed oxen through the flaming hours, goading their velvet flanks. How lizard fed on ant, and snake on him," and

> "Looking deep, he saw
> The thorns which grow upon this rose of life."

His soul was full of pity for the sickness of this world which he would heal!

On their return from this expedition, which had proved so unsuccessful, the king and his council try other means to avert the tragic prophecy. They build a Palace of Love, where Siddārtha will be kept the prisoner of his wife, the beautiful Yasōdhara. Here, "no mention should be made of death, or age, sorrow, or pain, or sickness," to the extent that:

> "Every dawn the dying rose was plucked,
> The dead leaves hid, all evil sights removed."

And night and day there were provided for him a band

> "Of nautch girls, cup bearers, and cymballers,
> Delicate, dark-browed ministers of love,
> Who fanned the sleeping eyes of the happy Prince,
> And when he waked, led back his thoughts to bliss
> With music whispering through the blooms, and charms
> Of amorous songs and dreamy dances, linked
> By chime of ankle-bells and wave of arms
> And silver vina-strings; while essences
> Of *musk* and champak, and the blue haze spread
> From burning spices, soothed his soul again
> To drowse by sweet Yasōdhara; and thus
> Siddārtha lived forgetting."

But in the young prince's happy home of love, where he knew naught but bliss and happiness, save

> "... as when sleepers roam dim seas in dreams,
> And land awearied on the shores of day,
> Bringing strange merchandise from that black voyage
> ... oftimes, when he lay with gentle head
> Lulled on the dark breasts of Yasōdhara,
> He would start up and cry, 'My world! Oh, world!'"

and "the pity in his look was awful, and his visage like a god's." In his ears the music of wandering winds bewailed the peace, the rest they never found. Thus was Siddārtha reminded that love could not last while the suffering world awaited deliverance. And one night, rising with a heart filled with sadness, he bade farewell to the roses of his court, " 'I will depart,' he spake, 'the hour is come!' " and to his wife, " 'Thy tender lips, dear Sleeper, summon me to that which saves the earth but sunders us.' " Thus the Devas claimed Siddārtha, and going out alone into the world where "thorns grow upon this rose of life," he spends his days in good works and long hardships until finally, his destiny fulfilled, he returns in glory as Buddha.

The Irish poet, William Bulter Yeats, regarded the rose as a symbol of intense spiritual significance, borrowing from William Blake such symbols as the secret rose, and quoting Blake directly in, "O Rose thou art sick." The flower is the Rose of Battles, "beauty grown sad with its eternity;" it is the Rose of the Knights of St. John. In "To the Secret Rose," Yeats begins:

> "Far off, most secret, and inviolate Rose
> Enfold me in my hour of hours; where those
> Who sought thee at the Holy Sepulchre,
> Or in the wine-vat, dwell beyond the stir
> And tumult of defeated dreams; and deep
> Among pale eyelids heavy with the sleep
> Men have named beauty. Your great leaves unfold
> The ancient beards, the helms of ruby and gold
> Of the crowned Magi . . ."

and ends:

> "I too await
> The hour of thy great wind of love and hate.
> When shall the stars be blown about the sky,
> Like the sparks blown out of a smithy, and die?
> Surely thine hour has come, thy great wind blows,
> Far off, most secret, and inviolate rose?"

"The Rose upon the Rood of Life" (rood is a cross or crucifix) shows not only the beauty of his poetic craftsmanship but the degree of spiritual attainment that Yeats must have arrived at in his life. He undoubtedly believed that the rose was the heart of God. Because of this idea, many of his stories and poems are strangely prophetic:

> "Red Rose, proud Rose, sad Rose of all my days!
> Come near me, while I sing the ancient ways:

206

"Come near, that no more blinded by man's fate,
I find under the boughs of love and hate,
In all poor foolish things that live a day,
Eternal beauty wandering on her way.

"Come near, come near, come near—Ah, leave me still
A little space for the rose-breath to fill!
Lest I no more hear common things that crave;
The weak worm hiding down in its small cave,
The field mouse running by me in the grass,
And heavy mortal hopes that toil and pass;
But seek alone to hear the strange things said
By God to bright hearts of those long dead,
And learn to chant a tongue men do not know.
Come near; I would, before my time to go,
Sing of old Eire, and the ancient ways;
Red Rose, proud Rose, sad Rose of all my days."

A collection of his stories was to have appeared in the publication entitled *The Secret Rose*, but Yeats's publisher took a distaste to them, although later a number were printed out of this collection, in particular, the "Doctrine of Alchemy" and the "Initiates' Experience at the Temple of the Alchemical Rose." Another story, "Out of the Rose," tells the adventures of one of the Knights of St. John who fought the Powers of Corruption in the world and died in the service of the Rose. According to the knight, the Heart of the Rose is the Kingdom of God. His last words as he stretches out both arms toward the west are, "Oh Divine Rose of Intellectual Flame, let the gates of thy peace be opened to me at last!"

Yeats's use of the rose undoubtedly inspired several Irish poets of modern times. In Sean O'Casey's play, *Red Roses for Me*, is the song:

"A sober black shawl hides her body entirely,
Touch'd by th' sun and th' salt spray of the sea
But down in th' darkness a slim hand, so lovely,
Carries a rich bunch of red roses for me."

In the same play are numerous touches of the rose symbol of Ireland and the Church: "Are you catalogued too, with the Catholic Young Men going about with noses long as a snipe's bill, stripping the gayest rose of its petals in search of a beetle?"

One of our modern poets, Phelps Putnam, adds to the material on symbolism, although he does not come to any conclusions. His poem "Hasbrouck and the Rose," is filled with fascination:

"Hasbrouck was there and so were Bill
And Smollet Smith the poet, and Ames was there.
After his thirteenth drink, the burning Smith,
Raising his fourteenth trembling in the air,
Said, 'Drink with me, Bill, drink up to the rose.'
But Hasbrouck laughed like old men in a myth,
Inquiring, 'Smollet, are you drunk? What rose?'
And Smollet said, 'I drunk? It may be so;
Which comes from brooding on the flower, the flower
I mean toward which hour by hour
I travel brokenly; and I shall know
With Hermes and the alchemists—but hell,
What use is it talking that way to you?
Hard-boiled, unbroken egg, what can you care
For the enfolded passion of the Rose?'
Then Hasbrouck's voice rang like an icy bell:

" 'Arcane romantic flower, meaning what?
Do you know what it meant? Do I?
We do not know.
Unfolding pungent rose, the glowing bath
Of ecstasy and clear forgetfulness;
Closing and secret bud one might achieve
By long debauchery . . .
Except that I have eaten it, and so
There is no call for further lunacy.
In Springfield, Massachusetts, I devoured
The mystic, the improbable, the Rose.
For two nights and a day, rose and rosette,
And petal after petal and the heart,
I had my banquet by the beams
Of four electric stars which shone
Weakly into my room, for there
Drowning their light and gleaming at my side
Was the incarnate star,
Whose body bore that stigma of the Rose.
And that is all I know about the flower;
I have eaten it . . . it has disappeared.
There is no ROSE.'

"Young Smollet Smith let fall his glass; he said
'Oh Jesus, Hasbrouck, am I drunk or dead?' "

It is reasonable to suppose that much of the interest and inspiration with reference to the rose which poets and artists brought to life came from their association with one of the orders whose symbol was the rose and the cross. These societies found it necessary to function secretly in many countries because of the intolerance either of the church or state. The rose and cross is the dual male and female aspect, the cross being the male and the rose the female, or wisdom and love in the same order. This symbol occurs in most of the mystical societies of Christendom and Islam. The information that has been uncovered in this particular branch of research is extremely interesting.

One of the most popular and enduring of these early societies are the Rosicrucians. Their initiates were attracted to this order not only by the teachings but by the beauty and significance of their emblem, the rosy cross. Old Thomas Fuller in his *Worthies* wrote of it thus: "Sure I am that a Rose is the sweetest of flowers, and a cross accounted the sacredest of forms or figures, so that much of eminency must be imparted in their composition." This simple thought was shared by many who felt that the blending of two such significant forms, the rose and the cross, must in itself confer dignity on the order.

In *The Shadowy Waters*, W. B. Yeats has one of his characters attempt a description of this rose and cross:

> "I can see nothing plain; all's mystery.
> Yet, sometimes there's a torch inside my head
> That makes all clear, but when the light is gone
> I have but images, analogies,
> The mystic bread, the sacramental wine,
> The red rose where the two shafts of the cross,
> Body and soul, waking and sleep, death, life,
> Whatever meaning ancient allegorists
> Have settled on, are mixed into one joy.
> For what's the rose but that; miraculous cries,
> Old stories about mystic marriages,
> Impossible truths. But when the torch is lit
> All that is impossible is certain,
> I plunge in the abyss."

A very old and mystical Rosicrucian symbol is the alchemical and hermetic rose cross. The petals of the great rose in the center of the cross are twenty-two in number and represent the twenty-two letters of the Hebrew cabalistic alphabet. The seven petals in the middle stand for the seven planets and the seven double letters of the cabalistic alphabet, while the three inner petals represent the elements air, fire, and water. There is also the rose cross proper with its five petals in the very center of the large cross.

Evidence of this society and its members can be found in many books. One of the first accounts of the sect in popular writing was the *Romaunt of the Rose*. Although seemingly a picture of youth and chivalry, there was a deeper meaning. It was deemed by the Rosicrucians to be the allegorical masterpiece of the society. The double language of love and alchemy satirized the monks and gave a complete specimen of hermetic philosophy.

Throughout Chaucer's works, especially his *Romance of the Rose*, which is similar to the earlier *Romaunt*, are many veiled allusions. In order to have written these, Chaucer must have been familiar with this or some kindred society. It was claimed that his friend John Gower, the poet, was a Rosicrucian. His monument at St. Saviour's Southwark shows him crowned with roses, and with the "three virtues" at his feet.

The Rosicrucians ingeniously discovered similar emblems and proofs in Dante's *Divine Comedy*. One of the high prophets wrote: "The Paradise consists of a series of Cabbalistic circles divided by a Cross like Ezekiel's pentacle. A Rose blossoms in the center of this cross." Dante was perhaps the first to publicly and categorically reveal the rosy cross of the Rosicrucians.

A distinct impression of Rosicrucian ideas is found in *The Rape of the Lock*; indeed, Pope says plainly that he composed his poem "On a new and odd foundation, the Rosicrucian doctrine of spirits." But the sylphs and gnomes and salamander of his fanciful brain often had pursuits and manners other than those of the Rosicrucian philosophy.

The masques of the times of James I and Charles I, and Shakespeare, also, show the existence of Rosicrucianism and its influence. In the *Sonnets* are the lines:

> "Why should poor beauty indirectly seek
> Roses of Shadow, since his Rose is true?"

A footnote in one of the early editions reads: "We seek the Reformation of the whole wide world. The *Fama* was the ethical text book of the Rosicrucians whose symbol was the Rose crucified on the Cross. Francis Bacon is known to have been the Imperator of their Secret Order." The sonnet line: "Time's Best Jewel from Time's Chest lie hid?" has the following pertinent footnote: *"Time's Best Jewel* The Rose, Symbol of the Secret Rosicrosse Literary Society. *Time's Chest* . . . the outer Case of Masonry in which the Jewel is preserved. Free Masonry is neither more nor less than Rosicrucianism as modified by those who transplanted it to England.—De Quincey."

Francis Bacon introduced the symbol of the rose with an esoteric or Masonic significance. German philosophers also declare that the actual

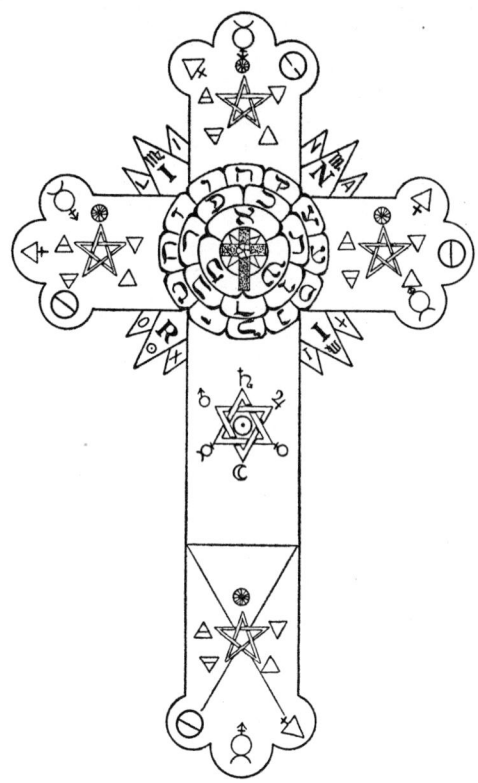

The Hermetic Rose Cross.

source of Freemasonry ran through the secret Society of the Rose. It is the central figure in the Eighteenth Degree of the Scottish Rite of Freemasonry. All these facts and suppositions build up to give an increasing power and purpose to rose symbolism. They picture the redemption of man through the union of his lower temporal nature and his higher eternal self.

In the religious traditions of the Orient, a mystic rose is found in an allegorical garden. The Brahmin paradise features a silver rose. Buddha and the Hindu god, Indra, both suffered for robbing paradisaical gardens of a flower. The emblem of Mohammed's eyes was considered to be a rose. The garden of King Midas, who turned to gold all that he touched, was filled with roses of sixty petals. The Peruvian Eve of the Garden of Eden sinned not for plucking an apple, but a rose. The Mexican Eve also gathered a rose.

This garland of symbolic roses encircles the globe. For example, in the religious ceremonies of the Mexica tribes it is customary for the women to carry roses in their hands and the men to wear garlands of the same flower around their necks. In England, especially at St. Paul's in London, it was once the custom for priests to be crowned with roses. "On June 30, 1405, when Bishop de Walden was installed there, he and the Canons of the Cathedral walked in solemn procession, wearing garlands of red roses," and the Armenian custom, Burning with Roses, is another excellent example of the use of the rose as a symbol.

A colorful rose ceremony stemming from an early European tradition is conducted every year in the Manheim Church of Pennsylvania. Here a gift of one red rose is paid, on the first Sunday in June, to one of the descendants of the Stiegel family in exchange for the original church. The ceremony is called the Feast of Roses, similar to the beautiful line of poetry written by Moore: "The valley holds its feasts of roses." Baron Stiegel was a German Lutheran and was therefore familiar with the intense rose symbolism of his native land.

Martin Luther, of whom Browning wrote:

> "Grand rough old Martin Luther
> Bloomed fables, flowers on furze,
> The bitter the uncouther:
> Do roses stick like burrs?"

had for his crest a rose containing a heart with a cross in the center. The seal of the Evangelical Lutheran Theological College in Madras, India, is a combination of the lotus, rose, and cross. The pond in which the lotus floats, represents India, and the lotus itself, Sarasvati, Goddess of Knowledge. From an invisible rock under the surface of blue water rises a golden cross in the center of which is the Luther rose, golden rays emanating from it in all directions. This snow-white rose with five petals on a golden ground has a red heart, in the center of which is a small black cross signifying, according to the old German rhyme, that the heart of a Christian is walking on roses only when it is living under the cross.

Rudolph Steiner's use of the rose symbol is a black cross and red rose for cognition of the higher worlds, and Mary Baker Eddy speaks of the rose as "the smile of God" or "a monument of Deity."

In his description of the ritual witnessed by an initiate in the temple of "The Alchemical Rose," Yeats wrote superbly:

"The dance wound in and out, tracing upon the floor the shapes of the petals in the Rose overhead, and to the sound of hidden instruments; and every moment the dance was more passionate, until all the winds of the world seemed to have awakened under our feet. After a little I grew weary and sank into a half-dream, from which I was awakened by seeing the petals of the great Rose, which no longer had the look of mosaic, falling slowly through the incense-heavy air, and, as they fell, shaping into the likeness of living beings of extraordinary beauty. Their dance now took on a more and more definite shape, so that I was able to distinguish beautiful Grecian faces and august Egyptian faces, and now and again a divinity by the staff in his hand or by a bird fluttering over his head. And soon every mortal foot danced by the white foot of an immortal, and in the troubled eyes that looked into untroubled, shadowy eyes I saw the brightness of uttermost desire, as though they had found at length, after unreckonable wandering, the lost love of their youth."

Theodore Parker also sums up in a practical, down-to-earth manner:

"Every rose is an autograph from the hand of God on His world about us. He has inscribed His thoughts in these marvelous hieroglyphics which sense and science have, these many thousand years, been seeking to understand."

In the letters of Rainier Maria Rilke is this sentence: "Rose, oh pure contradiction, desire to be no one's sleep beneath so many lids." And the present-day mystic poet, T. S. Eliot "gives Reality that is eternally underlying all things," in these lines:

> "All manner of things shall be well
> When the tongues of flame are in-folded
> Into the crowned Knot of the fire
> And the fire and the rose are one."

And, finally, there is that profound sentence uttered by an old monk, recorded in the *Diary* of E. O. Boyle, who wrote:

"Strange that such a little Rose should live on for well-nigh half a century, calmly putting forth its leaf and bloom summer after summer, whilst so many of the men and women who knew it once have passed away. It somehow makes me think of the old monk, pointing to the frescoes on his convent walls and saying, *These are realities, we are the shadows.*"

ACKNOWLEDGMENTS

THE AUTHOR wishes to thank all the museums, libraries, artists, and photographers who have contributed so much of the material in this book, including the Metropolitan Museum of Art, American Museum of Natural History, the Library of Congress, the Vatican Library, the Pierpont Morgan Library, and the New York and Miami public libraries. Special thanks are also due to the American Rose Society; Roses, Incorporated; Paul Thurston; L. Richard Guylay and Associates; the National Rose Society, London; the Chrysler Corporation; Mount Pleasant Press and Mr. P. M. Parthemere, the American Order of Rosicrucians; Hispanic Society of America, the American Numismatic Society and to the embassies and legations of Italy, Germany, Finland, Denmark, France, and Great Britain.

The following nurserymen, allied organizations, and personnel have been especially helpful: Armstrong Nurseries and H. C. Swim; Lester and Tillotson Rose Gardens; Germain's and Dr. Walter E. Lammerts; the Conard Pyle Company; Jackson and Perkins Company, and Eugene Boerner; Pedro Dot, Barcelona; Francis Meilland, Tassin-Les-Lyon.

In addition, the author wishes to thank Bryan Holme, for the arrangement and design of the book; and Joan Wickham, Mrs. Theodosia La Barbera, the late Dr. J. Horace McFarland, Fleur Cowles, Mrs. Helen Hutson Weber, Richardson Wright, Frank S. Hedge, Roberta Lord, Patricia Easterbrook Roberts and the late Robert Pyle for their help and encouragement.

BIBLIOGRAPHY

A *Book about Roses,* by Dean Hole
A *Book of Roses,* by J. Ramsbottom
A *Catalogue of Greek Coins,* the British Museum
A *Dictionary of Miracles,* by E. Cobham Brewer
A *Group of Eastern Romances and Stories,* by W. A. Clouston
America's Garden Book, Louise Bush Brown
American Journal of Numismatics, by Alfred E. Frey
An *Encyclopedic Outline of Masonic, Hermatic, Cabbalistic and Rosi-crucian Symbolical Philosophy,* by Manly P. Hall
Armenian Legends and Festivals, by Louis A. Boettiger
A *Rose Odyssey,* by J. H. Nichols
Bagatelle and Jardins, Bagatelle Library, Paris
Beautiful Flowers and How to Grow Them, by Horace J. Wright
Bouquets and Bitters, by Julia Meade
British Garden Flowers, by George M. Taylor
Carolina Gardens, by E. T. H. Shaffer
Child Life in Colonial Days, by Alice Morse Earle
China Collecting in America, by Alice Morse Earle
Early Poems and Stories, by W. B. Yeats
Emerson's Essays, by Ralph Waldo Emerson
English Coins, by George C. Brooke
Floral Symbolism, by Elizabeth Haig
Flower Lore and Legend, by Katharine M. Beals
Flowers and Flower Lore, by Rev. Hilderic Friend
Flowers and Their Pedigrees, by Grant Allen
Flowers as Food, by Florence White
Flower Songs for Flower Lovers, by Rose Porter
Foreign Imitations of the English Noble, by Herbert B. Ives
Garden Flowers in Color, by Glendon A. Stevens
Garden Poetry, by Sylvia Spencer
Gardens in South Africa, by Dorothea Fairbridge
Gardens in Spain, by C. M. Villiers Stuart
Grace of Guadalupe, by Frances Parkinson Keyes
Handbook of Christian Symbols, by Erskine Clement Waters
Handy Book of Curious Information, by William Shepard Walsh
Handy Book of Literary Curiosities, by William Shepard Walsh

Hans Christian Andersen Fairy Tales, by Hans Christian Andersen
Hennessey on Roses, by Roy Hennessey
Heraldry and Floral Forms, by Herbert Cole
Herbal Simples, by Fernie
Magic Gardens, by Rossetta E. Clarkson
Melanges de Numismatiques, by F. de Sauley
Modes and Manners, by Max Von Boehn
Motif-Index of Folk Literature, by S. Thompson
My Friend the Rose, by Francis Lester
Mystical Life of Jesus, Spencer Lewis (American Order of the Rosicrucians)
Myths and Legends of Flowers, by Charles M. Skinner
Numismatic Graeca, by L. Anson
Odes of Hafiz, by Hafiz
Old Roses, by Mrs. Frederick L. Keays
Old Time Gardens, by Alice Morse Earle
One Hundred and One Legends of Flowers, by Elizabeth Todd Nash
Oscar Wilde's Tales, by Oscar Wilde
Oxford Dictionary of Quotations
Parsons on the Rose, by S. B. Parsons
Poems and Fragments, by Sappho
Poetry of Flowers, by Kirtland
Racial Proverbs, by Selwyn Gurney Champion
Real History of Rosicrucians, by Arthur Edward Waite
Rhodologia, by J. Ch. Sawer
Rose Alchemiea, by W. B. Yeats
La Rose à Travers les Ages
Rose Annual (various years), compiled by the American Rose Society
Rose Garden of Persia, by Louisa Stuart Costello
Rose Recipes, by Eleanor Sinclair Rohde
Roses and Rose Gardens, by Walter P. Wright
Roses in Art, by E. A. Bunyard
Roses of the World in Color, by J. Horace McFarland
Les Rosiers
Ros Rosarum Poems
Saints and Their Emblems, by V. and F. Drake
Southey's Poems, by Robert Southey
Standard Dictionary of Facts, by Henry Woldmar Knoff
Stories and Legends of Garden Flowers, by Vernon Quinn
Study in Symbolism, by M. F. Howard
Sun Dials and Roses of Yesterday, by Alice Morse Earle
Symbolism in Medieval Thought and Its Consummation in the Divine Comedy, by H. Flanders Dunbar
Symbolism of the Rubiyat of Omar Khayyam, by J. S. Pattinson
Symbolism of Heraldry, by C. Cecil Wade
The Academy of Armory, by Rendell Holme
The Book of Flowers, by Katherine Tynan and Frances Maitland

The Book of Perfumes, by Eugene Rimmel
The Book of Roses, by Louis Durand
The Book of the Rose, by Rev. A. Foster Melliar
The Earth Speaks, by Princess Atalie
The Fauna and Flora on the Coin-Types of Ancient Rome, by Frances Guecchi
The Flower Family Album, by Fischer and Harshberger
The Fragrant Notebook, by G. Arthur Coan
The Gardener's Day Book, by Richardson Wright
The Gardener's Travel Book, by Edward Irving Farrington
The Golden Bough, by James George Frazer
The Magic of Herbs, by C. F. Leyel
The Mary Calendar, by Judith Smith
The Pentamerone of Graubattista, translated from the Italian of Benedetto Croce
The Rose, by H. B. Ellwanger
The Rose and Islam, by Samuel and M. Zwerner
The Rose and the Ring, by William Makepeace Thackeray
The Rose Book, by H. H. Thomas
The Rose Garden, by William Paul
The Rose's History and Culture, by S. B. Parsons
The Rose upon Her Briar, by Helen Temperly
The Science and Art of Perfumery, by Edward Sagarin
The Secret History of Francis Bacon, by Alfred Dodd
The Story of Gardening, by Richardson Wright
To Persia for Flowers, by Alice Fullerton
Traite de Numismatique du Moyer Age, by Arthur Enzel
Up from the Earth, by Sylvia Spencer

INDEX

Aben-Zohar, 72
Accomplisht Cook, 92
Actuaris, Johannes, 73
Ada, story of, 151
Adam of Cobham, 62
Adams, Ansel, 177
Addenbrooke, Joseph, 48
Africa, Cape Gardens of, 120
Agnes, Saint, 147-148
Albertus Magnus, 67-68
Al Borak, 12-13
Alchemical rose, 212
   cross, 209
   temple of, 207
alchemists, use of rose by, 202, 203
Aldric, Saint, 147
Alexandra, Queen, 58
Alice in Wonderland, 174
allergy to roses, 83
All Trivia, 176
Amenhotep IV, 194
American Beauty rose, 100, 128
American Rose Society, 50, 123
Amiens, Cathedral, 197
amulet:
   of rose hips, 60
   of rose nobles, 203
Anacreon, 7, 36, 96, 184, 185
Anakit, festival of, 101
Anderson, Hans Christian, 159, 164, 167,
   174
angels and roses, 34
Angelus, Saint, 33
Anglicus, Bartholomeaus, 81
Antony, Mark, 17-18
Aphrodite, 7, 8
Apollo, 8
Apollodorus, 184
Arabia:
   distillation in, 73
   perfume trade of, 72
Arabian Nights, 83
arbor of roses, 118
arcanum regium, 86
Armenia, burning with roses, 101, 212

arms, coats of, 143; *see also* heraldry
Arnold, Sir Edwin, 119, 204
aromatic prophylactics, 85
art, 31-58
   designs on various objects, 35
   grill work in cemeteries, 35
   illustrations in books, 36, 53, 54
     hymnals, 53
   music, 57
   paintings, 32-35
   portraits of rose, 54, 57, 58
   present-day use of rose, 58
   rose design:
     on china and porcelain, 35
     on glass, 36
     on coffins, 35
   sculpture, 31-32
   valentines, 36
   woodcuts, 53
Arthur, King, 127
attar (otto) of roses, 17, 70
   appearance of, 75
   books scented with, 188
   discoveries of, 73-74
     European, 73-74
   external use of, 84
   extraction of, 75
   naming of, 73
   process of making, 75-76
   pure, 75
   scientific distillation of, 75
Audubon, John James, 43
Austrian rose, 95
Aventine, Rome, rose garden on, 110, 118-
   119

Bacon, Francis, 210-211
Bacon, Friar, 93
Bacchus, 8, 14
Baden-Baden, rose festival at, 119
Bagatelle Rose Gardens, 108
Barbarossa, 103
Baring-Gould, S., 148
Basile, Giambattista, 66
baskets of roses, as gifts, 94

battlefield, and roses, 125
Bayley, Harold, 194
"Beauty and the Beast," 165, 172-174
bed coverlets, rose design in, 36
Belgium, midsummer festival, 103
"Bendemeer's Stream," 181
Benedict, Saint, 146
Bernadette, Saint, 152-153
Bible, the, 196
  on incense and perfume, 71
Biltmore Estate rose garden, 122
Binion, Samuel A., 181
Bion, 184
Birth of Venus, 9
"Birthday of the Infanta, The," 169-170
Blake, William, 53, 98, 189, 196, 200, 206
blood rose, 12
Blow, Richard, 52
Bluebeard stories, 62
"Blue Rose Fairy Tale, The," 170-171
blue rose tree, Russian tale of, 64
blush rose, 8
bob of gold, 79
Bock, Vera, 74
Boehme, 203
Boleyn, Anne, 29
Book about Roses, A, 181
Book of Flowers, The, 181
Book of Physic, 25
Book of Wisdom, 32
books and the rose, 36, 53-54, 57-58, 176-181
  recipe books, 25, 84, 86, 91
  rose borders in, 53
Botticelli, Sandro, 7, 9, 31, 51, 105
Boucher, François, 40, 57, 78
Bouquet Room, White House, 129
Boyle, E. O., 213
Brahma, "Vishnu, Brahma and a Rose," 171-172
Brand, John, 60
Brazil Order of the Rose, 129
Breda rose, 120
briar rose, 11, 15, 64
  creation of, 11
"Briar Rose," 66
Bridges, Robert, 191
Britain; *see also* England:
  London election of Lord Mayor, 94
  medicinal use of rose in, 80-81
  Wars of the Roses, 94, 134
British Perfumer, The, 76
"Bronze Boar, The," 160
Brown, Thomas, 105

Browning, Elizabeth, 190, 191, 203, 204
Browning, Robert, 125, 190, 203-204, 212
Brummell, Beau, 79
Brutell, L'Heritier de, 54
Buddha, 204
Bulgaria:
  ritual to protect cattle from evil eye, 65
  source of attar, 75
Burns, Robert, 21-22
Burton, Sir Richard F., 83
Byron, Lord, 96, 182, 190

cabala, the, 16
cakes, rose-flavored, 92
Canada, rose coins of, 144
canker rose, 63
Canterbury Tales, The, 66
Cape Gardens of Africa, 120
Carrol, Lewis, 174
carvings:
  on coffins, 35
  on fountain pipes, 35
Cashmere, exporter of attar, 75
cathedrals:
  Gothic, rose windows in, 196
  sculptured roses in, 32
Catholic Church, rose ceremonies of, 98, 101-102
Cecilia, Saint, 151-152
celestial rose, 201
  Dante's, 195, 196
cemeteries, rose motif in, 35
Central America, rose symbolism in, 194
Ceremony of the Rose, 21
chaplets of roses, 95
Charlemagne, 32, 154
Charles II, King, 21
charms, 59-68
  German, 60
  good luck, 64
  Greek, 60
  love philters, 59, 60
  Persian, 59-60
  and portents, 59-68
  rose water as, 16
  for safe childbirth, 65
chastity, rose as test of, 61
Chaucer, Geoffrey, 26, 53, 54, 210
Cherokee rose, 12, 124, 128
  design, 36
childbirth, and rose, 65-66
china, rose design on, 35
China:
  Cherokee rose from, 124
  fairy tales of, 170-171

China (cont.):
  names of roses, 28
  rosaries in, 98
  rose gardens in, 120
  rose-scented teas, 74
  wild roses in, 124
Christ:
  fragrance, "sweet odor of," 102
  the loveliest rose in the world, 164
  rose as emblem of, 23, 194
Christ Child, 53
  paintings of, 34
  red rose associated with, 63
Christians:
  change of attitude toward rose, 140
  legends of rose, 11, 14
  symbolism, rose in, 31-33
Christmas rose, creation of, 11
Chrymshilde, Princess, 171
churches and chapels:
  roses in, 98, 101-102
  sculptured roses in, 32
Clement of Alexandria, 146
Clement X, Pope, 152
Cleopatra, 17-18, 19, 71
climbing rose, medicines from, 91
coffins:
  rose emblems on, 24, 35
  roses on, 98
coins:
  magic, 203
  stylized roses on, 139, 142, 144, 145
cold cream, invention of, 81
Coleman, Mrs. Wesley, 124
Collection of Roses from Nature, A, 57
Collin, Louise, 160
Colombe, Jean, 53
colors of roses, 13, 63; see also under in-
      dividual colors
complexion, rose as aid to, 66
conception, and rose, 65-66
Condamine, Robert de la, 105
confessionals, and rose, 94
conserve of roses, 91
Constantine the Great, golden rose of,
      101
Contemplaciones sobre el Rosario, 53
  crown of roses, 32-33
conventionalized design, 35
Coolidge, Calvin, Jr., 129
Coral Gables, Florida, test garden at, 123
coronet of roses, 152
cosmetic use of rose, 81
"Cottage Girl, The," 60-61
crests, rose, 212

Crete, early painting of rose, 54
crimson rambler, 28
cross:
  hermetic rose, 211
  rose and, 142, 209
crown of thorns, 34, 63
crowns of nobility, rose emblem on, 130-
      131
crowns of roses, 98
  to alleviate pain, 84
  Christian fathers, 146
  midsummer festival, 103
  symbol of joy, 32
  worn by priests, 212
Crucifixion, red rose and, 64
Crusaders, 65, 72, 121
cult of rose, 26
Cunningham, Ann Pamela, 129
Cunningham, Robert and Louisa, 128
Cunto de li Cunti, 66
Cupid, 14, 15
cures; see medical use of rose
currency, 138, 139
Curse of Kehama, The, 201
cushions, rose-filled, 18
customs and fashions, 93-104
  baskets of roses, 94
  Chinese, 120
  competitions, games, festivals, 102-104
  death due to rose custom, 104
  flower language, 95
  imprisonment due to rose custom, 104
  marriage customs, 95-96
  roses and graves, 96-98
  roses and the church, 98, 101-102
  roses near confessionals, 94
  rose suspended from door, 94
  of Slavic peoples, 194
Cyclopedia of Perfumery, 72
Cyprian, Saint, 146

damask rose, 85, 121
  attar from, 75
  scent of, 70
Dante, Alighieri, 53-54, 193, 200
  Divine Comedy, 195, 196, 200
  mysticism of, 195
"Dead Rose, A," 191
Deas, Lizzie, 15
death:
  roses and, 63, 96-98
  in service of rose, 207
Decameron, The, 66
de Heere, Lucas, 135
Delhi, Palace of, India, 35

Delile, Dr., 108
De Profundis, 166
De Quincy, Thomas, 210
Design, and the rose, 35, 53-54
 carved on benches, 94
 carved on ceilings, 94
 on coins, 142, 144-145
Diaghilev, 27
Diana, 8
Dickinson, Emily, 192
Diego, Juan, 156
Dijon group of roses, 70
Diogenianus, 184
distillation, 70, 71, 72, 73
Djihan-Guyr, A'thr, 73
Divine Comedy, 53-54, 195, 196, 200
 Rosicrucian emblems in, 210
"Doctrine of Alchemy," 207
dog rose, 70
 superstition, 63
 syrup from hips of, 81
Dominican fathers, 118
D'Orbessan, 32
Dorothea, Saint, 33, 152
Dot, Pedro, 123
Doughty, Charles M., 74
"drinkable gold," 86
drinks of roses; *see* food and drink
Drummond, Sir William, 132
Dubray, V. G., 42
Dunbar, H. Flanders, 195
Dunbar, William, 141
Dutch Masters, rose used by, 120

Earle, Alice Morse, 81, 181
East Indian Companies, 121
Eddy, Mary Baker, 212
Edgartown Cemetery, Martha's Vineyard, 35
Edward I, King, 141
Edward III, King, 130
Edward IV, King, 141
Egyptian tomb decoration, 37
Egyptians and rose, 17
 floral scents, 71
 funereal use of rose, 96
Eleanor of Aquitaine, 96
Eleanor of Provence, 141
Eliot, T. S., 213
elixir of roses, 86
Elizabeth I, Queen of England, 24, 35, 79, 86, 93, 127, 144, 188
Elizabeth of Hungary, Saint, 148
Elizabeth of York, 126

Elizabeth Park rose garden, Hartford Connecticut, 123
emblematic use of rose:
 festival of Anakit, 101
 on shields, 125
embroidery (silk), 46
Emerson, Ralph Waldo, 175, 176
England:
 Church of, 101
 names of roses, 28
 poetry, 182, 190
 rose, national emblem of, 108
 rose gardens in, 108, 117
English rose, 121
Eros, god of love, 16
Esdras, description of heaven, 105
essence of roses, 21
essential oil of roses; *see* attar of roses
Eve, Peruvian and Mexican, 211
evil eye, rose as protection against, 65
evil omen, rose as, 62
Eyck, Hubert van, 33, 35
Eyck, Jan van, 33

fairy tales, 159-174
 German, 164-165, 171
 of Grimm brothers, 159, 164-165
 of Hans Christian Anderson, 159-164
 of Near East, 171-172
 of Oscar Wilde, 159, 166-170
faithfulness, rose as test of, 61-62
Fama, text book of Rosicrucians, 210
family names, Rose, Rosen, Rossett, Roosevelt, 132
fashions; *see also* customs and fashions:
 roses behind ear, 93
 rosettes in shoes, 93
Fatima, miracle of, 156, 157
Feast of Roses, 212
festivals:
 Baden-Baden, 119
 Bulgarian, 75
 midsummer, 101, 103
Fête de la Rosiers, 103
Fête-Dieu, 98
Finland's Order of the White Rose, 129
Firuzabad (*see* Shiraz)
FitzGerald, Edward, 97
Flemish tapestries, 21, 37
Flora, 8
Floral Symbolism, 181
flower language, 95
Fluvius, Lucius, 104
food and drink:
 conserves, 91

food and drink (cont.):
  food turned to roses, 148, 151
  pickled rosebuds, 91
  rose cakes, 92
  rose-flavored tea, 74, 83
  rose hips as food, 80-81
  rose-petal jam, 83
  rose syrup, 81, 95
  rose-water drink, 95
  rose wine, 83-84
  sweets, 92
Foster, Stephen, rose songs of, 181
Fragonard, Jean Honoré, 57, 99
fragrance of rose, 69-79; see also perfumes and scents
France:
  names of roses, 28
  perfume industry in, 76
  poetry, 188
  rose as symbol of romance, 195
  rose water industry in, 73
Francis of Assisi, Saint, 33, 147
Frazer, Sir James George, 65
Freemasonry, rose as symbol of, 210-211
French Perfumer, The, 76
Freyja, 14, 94, 154
fruit scent, in roses, 70
Fuller, Thomas, 209

Galen, inventor of cold cream, 81
Gandolf, priest of Milan, 153
gardens, 105-124
  of adoration, 105
  African, 120
  battle of Shipka fought in, 125
  Bulgarian, 125
  in Calcutta and Singapore, 121
  Chinese, 120
  early New England, 121
  Egyptian, 17
  English, 108, 117
  first municipal rose display, 123
  French, 106, 108
  German, 119, 171
  Italian, 118-119
  L'Hay garden, 106
  medieval, 120-121
  monastery, 120
  natural, 105
  peace, 123
  Persian, 117
  private, 105
  public, or test, 105
  rose hybridizers, rosarians, nurserymen, 123

gardens (cont.):
  roseto at Subiaco, Italy, 146-147
  by Saluda River, 128, 129
  Spanish, rose plots, 118
  Swiss, 119
  test, 123
  types of, 105-106
  United States, 122-124
  wild, 124
  at Worms, story of, 171
gardeners, medieval, 120-121
garlands of roses, 18, 156
  German, 103
  Greek, 103
Garter, Knights of the, 130, 131
Gautier, Théophile, 27
geneology of rose, 107
Genus Rosa, The, 57-58
George, Saint, Order of, 130
Gerard, John, 80
  herbals of, 84-85
Germaine, story of, 148
Germany:
  fairy tales of, 164-165, 171
  legends of, 14, 15, 94
  mystical rose of, 196-201
  rose gardens in, 119
  rose symbolism in, 212
  superstitions, 60
Ghazipur, palace of, 18
Glas, N., 165
glass, rose design on, 36, 49
Glastonbury thorn, Joseph of Arimathea, 154
Gloria Dei rose, 123
goa stones, 85
Goethe, The Mysteries, 196
Golden Bough, The, 65
Golden Dawn rose, 70
Golden Legend, 191
golden rose:
  form and symbolism of, 101-102
  origin of, 101
Gothic cathedral (Rose window), 197
Gozzoli, Benozzo, 35
Grant rose, 12
Grasse, France, perfume industry in, 76
Gravereaux, Jules, 106, 107
graves:
  miracles from, 152-154
  use of rose on, 93, 96-98
grave-tree superstition, 63-64
Gray, Henry Peters, 19
Great Britain; see Britain

INDEX

Greece:
ancient, liquor of, 84
floral scents of, 71-72
funereal use of roses, 96
garlands of roses, 103
heraldic use of rose, 132
legends of rose, 7-8, 14, 15
names of roses, 28
poetry, 182, 184-185
Gregory the Great, Saint, 147
grill work in cemeteries, 35
Grimm, Jacob and Wilhelm, 66
fairy tales of, 159, 164-165
Guadalupe, miracle of, 156
gulab (rose water), 73
Gul-i Bakarvali, 67
Gulistan, Sadi, 73, 74-75, 83

Hafiz, 60, 73, 117, 186, 188, 195
Hagedorn, *Cynosbatologia*, 86
Haig, Elizabeth, 181
Hampton, Dr., 70
Harpocrates, god of silence, 93
"Hasbrouk and the Rose," 208
Hat design, 100
hawthorn, 154
Heber, Bishop, 18
Hebrew cabalistic alphabet, 209
Hebrew legends, 8, 11, 14, 72
hedge rose, 81
hedges of roses, 120
in religious paintings, 34
Heizmann's Nursery, Switzerland, 119
Heliogabalus, 18
Heneage, Lady, 82
Henry IV, King of France, 125-126
Henry VII, King of England, 127
Henry VIII, King, 29, 127, 141, 144
heraldry, 131-132, 143
coats of arms, 143
English, 130, 141
French, 142
Greek, 132
postage stamps, 131
Scottish, 141
herbals of Gerard, 84-85
hermetic rose cross, 209, 211
Herodotus, 69
Herrick, Robert, 7, 14, 190
Hershey Rose Garden, 114, 122
Hesz, David, 60
Heywood, John, 84
Hildesheim, Cathedral, 149
Hildesheim, rose bush 1000 years old, 154, 155

hips, rose, 63
amulet of, 60
of dog rose, 63
as food, 80-81
powder and syrup from, 81
vitamin C content, 80
Hjortzberg, Olle, 167
Hole, Dean, 181
Holme, *The Academy of Armory*, 22-23, 130
Holmes, Oliver Wendell, 182
Holy Trinity, three roses for, 22, 33
Homer, 71, 132, 182, 196
Hood, Thomas, 182
Hours of the Virgin, 53
House of Frescoes, Knossos, Crete, 54
"House Where I Was Born, The," 182
Hugo, Victor, 98
hundred-leaved rose, 69, 76
Hunt, Leigh, 16
Huysum, Jan van, 54
hybridizers, rose, 123
Hyde Park, rose garden at, 129
hymnals, the rose in, 53

Ibn Khaldun, 72
Iliad, The, 182
illustrations in books and manuscripts, 36, 53-54, 57-58, 176-181
Blake's, for *Divine Comedy*, 196
Imperial Order of the Yellow Rose, United States, 129, 130
Imperial Secret, 202
incense, early use of, 71
India:
fairy tales, 171-172
perfume trade of, 72
rose in, 18, 21
roses as medicine in, 81
silver rose of, 196, 201, 211
Intarsia design, 52
International Rose-Test Garden, 123
"In the Time of Roses," 181
Irish poetry, 189
iron chest (German), 38
Italy, rose gardens in, 118-119
Jackson & Perkins Nursery, 115
Jacobites, white rose of, 127
Jacqueminot rose, 69
James IV, of Scotland, 141
Jami, rose-scented book of, 188
jemelloes, 92
Jericho, rose of, 60, 65
Jersey Beauty rose, 70
jewelry, 50

Jonson, Ben, "To Celia," 25
Josephine, Empress of France, 21, 42, 54
  rose garden of, 108
Joseph of Arimathea, Glastonbury thorn,
  154
Josselyn, John, 121
Judas, 11

Katherine of Aragon, 29
Keats, John, 190
Keller, Helen, 123
Kelmscott Press, rose border, 53, 54
Kew, Royal Botanic Gardens of, 117
King Arthur's Round table, 133
king and queen of roses, 103
Kipling, Rudyard, 69
kissing comfits, 92
Knighthood, and rose, 22-23, 125
Knights of St. John, rose of, 206
Knights of the Garter, 130

Laetare Sunday, 102
Lake Mohonk, New York, rose garden,
  122
Lancaster, Pennsylvania, Red Rose City,
  128
Lancaster and York, houses of, 126
Langles, Louis M., 73
"Last Rose of Summer, The," 181
Lawrance, Mary, 41, 54, 57
Lawrance, Sir Thomas, 89
Lay of the Brown Rosary, 204
"Legend of the Knight of Cologne," 53
legends of rose:
  American Indian, 12
  Christian, 11, 14, 67-68
  color, 13-14
  German, 14, 15
  Greek, 7-8, 15, 93
  Hebrew, 8, 11, 14
  Mohammedan, 12-13
  Roman, 7-8, 93
  thorns, 11, 12, 15
Leo IX, Pope, 101-102
Lester, Francis E., 57, 181
Levy, Lewis, 153
Leyel, C. F., 74
L'Hay rose garden, 106, 107
Light of Asia, The, 119, 204
Lillie, Charles, 76
Lind, Jenny, 159
Lindley, John, 57
Lipa, miracle of, 156, 158
literature, 175-192
"Little Ida's Flowers," 160

Lives of the Saints, 148
Lochner, Stephen, 199
Longfellow, Henry Wadsworth, 54, 146,
  191, 202
Longpre, Paul de, 54, 57
Lord Roberta, 123
Louis, Guillaume de, 26
Lost Language of Symbolism, The, 194
lotus symbolism, 193, 212
Louise Van Houtte rose, 76
Louis of Toulouse, Saint, 148, 153
Louis the Pious, Emperor, 154
love, rose as symbol of, 194, 195
love philters, 17, 21, 59-60
Low, Rabbi, 72
Lucien, Saint, 147
Lucius, Saint, 153
Luther, Martin, 212
Luther rose, 212
Lyons, rose garden at, 108

McFarland, Dr., 123
Madelon, 11
Madonna of Guadalupe, Order of, 129
Maitland, Frances, 181
Malmaison, rose garden at, 108
Malta, roses of, 18
Manheim Church, Pennsylvania, 212
"Marble Rose of Rome," 191
Marie, Archduchess, 21
Marie Antoinette, 54
Marienroschen, 14
Marie Van Houtte rose, 76
marriage customs, 95
Martini, Simone, 32
martyrs, roses and, 146-147, 152
Mary, Queen of Scots, 188
Mary Magdalen, Saint, 64
Mary Tudor, Queen, 144
Masonry, symbol of rose in, 210-211
Mathia, Saint, 148
mea rosa, 94
Mectilda, Saint, 71
Medul, John Cook, 50
medals, military, 138
Medici, Lorenzo de, 118
Medici, Marie de, 82
medicinal use of rose, 18, 66-67, 72, 80-92
  to alleviate pain, 84
  arcanum regium, 86
  attar of roses, 74
  for black plague, 85
  books on, 84, 86, 91
  for colds or catarrh, 80
  dried roses, 84, 85

medicinal use of rose (*cont.*):
  for hangovers, 84
  to heal inflammations, 86
  during medieval epidemics, 85
  as ointment, 84-85
  for overindulgence, 86
  Penn's recipes and formulas, 25
  Provins rose, 80
  as purge, 85
  safeguard against infection, 85
  to staunch blood, 85
  for 33 fatal diseases, 86-87
  as tonic, 80
  during World War II, 80-81
Meilland, Francis, 123
Memorial Park, Peace, Jacksonville, Florida, 123
Mendel, Dr., test garden, Coral Gables, Florida, 123
Meun, Jean de, 26
Mexica tribes, religious ceremonies of, 212
Mexico, story of Eve, 211
Midas, King, rose of, 211
Middle Ages, rose superstitions, 64
midsummer, and rose, 60-61
  festivals, 65, 101, 103
Milto, legend of, 81-82
Milton, John, 15, 190
miracles, 147-158
  appearance of rose on platter, 147
  blanket of roses, 151
  creation of rosary, 155
  food turned to roses, 148, 151
  Hildesheim rosebush, 154-155
  mystical rose, 152
  post mortem manifestations, 152-154
  rain of roses, 152, 153
  roses from blood of martyr, 147
  Saint Cecilia, 151-152
  Saint Dorothea, 152
  shower of roses, 147
  thorns turned to red roses, 147
  three roses, 153
  of the Virgin, 156-158
Mohamet II, 73
Mohammed, 74, 211
  birthplace of, oasis of flowers, 74
Mohammed Achem, 73
Mohammedan legends of rose, 12-13
Monastery gardens, 120-121
Moore, Thomas, 189
Morley, Christopher, 179
Morris, William, 53
Mortimer's Cross, battle of, 141
Mosque of Omar, 72

Mosque of Saint Sophia, 73
moss rose (Rosa muscosa), 40
  origin of, 11
  as portent, 61
Mother and the Rose Bush, The (Fairy tale), 167
Motif, rose; *see* design
mottoes, rose, 132
Mount Calasay, 201, 202
Mount Vernon, restoration of, 129
Mumtaz Mahal, 21
Murillo, Bartolomé Esteban, 33, 149
Museum L'Hay, 106
music, and perfume, 79
Muskechives, 92
musk-scented roses, 70
  attar from, 75
"My Aunt," 182
My Friend the Rose, 181
Myrithis, Egyptian magician, 17
Mysteries, The, 195, 196-201
mystical rose, 152
mystical societies, 209
mysticism, 53-54
  of Robert Browning, 203
  of writers, poets, painters, 193
mystic rose, 202
myths; *see* legends of rose
"My Wild Irish Rose," 181

names of roses, 28, 122
  hedge roses, 120
Napoleon, 21, 28, 108
Near East:
  attar of roses, 73
  fairy tales of, 171-172
  perfumes of, 72, 73, 74
  rose windows in, 196
"Neighboring Families, The," 174
Nero, 18
  guests smothered with roses, 104
  love of the rose, 118
New England:
  gardens of settlers, 121
  wild roses in, 124
New Psalter of the Virgin Mary, 53
Nichols, J. H., 181
nightingale, and rose, 13
"Nightingale and the Rose, The," 166, 169
Nijinsky, Waslaw, 20, 27
Nimrod, 11
Northern countries, roses of, 124
Nostradamus, 85
Nour-Djihan, Princess, 73

INDEX

Novaria, Caspar Gorricio de, 53, 56, 150
nurserymen, 123

O'Casey, Sean, 207
"Ode to the Rose," 184
odophone, 79
Odyssey, The, 182
oil of roses; see attar of roses
old-fashioned roses, 120
old roses, scent of, 79
old rose scent, 70
Omar Khayyam, 28-29
  tomb of, 97
"One Perfect Rose," 182
"Only a Rose," 181
Orangerie, the, 111
Order of the Garter, 130, 131
Order of the Rose, 16, 22
orders and societies, 209
Orders of the Rose, military, 129
O'Shaughnessy, Arthur, 16
Our Lady of the Flower, 34

painters, 54, 57
  mysticism of, 193
Paintings, 32-33
  Dutch masters, 120
papal heraldry, 132
paper money, roses on, 145
Paracelsus, 86
Park de la Tête d'Or, 108
Parker, Dorothy, 182
Parker, Theodore, 213
Parry, Ernest John, 72
Parsons, Alfred, 57-58
Parsons, S. B., 80, 181
Paul, Saint, 146
Peace Conference, at Lake Mohonk, 122
Peace Memorial Park, Jacksonville, Florida, 123-124
Peace rose, 123, 124
Peace Rose Garden, Abilene, Texas, 124
Pedro, Emperor of Brazil, 129
Penn, William, 25
Pentamerone, 66
Pepys, on rose wine, 84
perfumes and scents, 69-79
  compared to music, 79
  early making of, 70-72
  early trade in, 72
  of Elizabethan days, 79
  first classification of, 70
  industry of today, 75-76
  Lillie's recipes for, 76, 79
  meaning of perfume, 71

perfumes and scents (cont.):
  odors of various roses, 69
  salt in making of, 71
  symbolic of divine love, 71
Permet, 74
Persia:
  legend of rose, 11
  love of rose, 60
  perfume trade of, 72
  poetry, 185-186, 188
  rose, flower of, 69
  rose as symbol of love, 194-195
  rose gardens in, 117
  roses as medicine in, 81
  sacks of rose blossoms, 74
Peru, story of Eve, 211
petals of rose:
  aid to slumber, 86
  burning of, 72
  chemical analysis of, 80
  in church, 98
  cure for plague, 85
  dried:
    preparation of, 86
    steeped in wine, 84
  jam from, 83
  sandwiches, 92
  smoke from, 65
  steeped in liquids and oils, 71
  steeped in sweet wine, 71
  sweet bags, 86
Peter, Saint, tomb of, 101
phyllanthography, 181
pickled rosebuds, 91
Piesse, Septimus, 79
Pieta, 34
Pigouchet, Philippe, 36
pink roses, 63, 70, 122
  Castilian, 122
Pisano, Giovanni, 32
Pliny, 70, 76, 85, 104
Plymouth rose, 25
Poe, Edgar Allan, 191-192
poetry, 182-192
  English, 182, 190
  French, 188
  Greek, 182, 184-185
  Irish, 189
  Persian, 185-186, 188
  Roman, 185
  United States, 191-192
poets, mysticism of, 193
pomanders, 79, 85
pomegranates and roses, 35
Pomet, Historie des Drogues, 91

Pompadour, Mme. de, 57, 76
porcelain, rose design on, 35-36
portents:
  British, 63
  charms and, 59-68
  of death, 63
  Italian, 62
  of misfortune, 62-63
  rose of Jerico, 60
portraits of rose, 54, 57
postage stamps, rose on, 131
potions, rose, 59-60
potpourri, 87
potpourri, recipe for, 86
potted roses, 91-92
powder of roses, 68
Powell, Mrs. Edward, rose, 70
priests crowned with roses, 212
prose:
  books, 176-181
  proverbs, 175-176
Provence rose, 121
proverbs, 175-176
Provins rose, 80, 93
Putnam, Phelps, 207-208
Pyle, Robert, 123

Queen Elizabeth I, 135
Queen's Delight, A, 91
Queer, the Quaint, the Quizzical, The, 60

Rabelais, on superstition, 59
Radegonde, Saint, 121
Ram, *Little Dodoen*, 86
Rape of the Lock, The, 210
recipes:
  dried rose petals, 86
  Lillie's, for perfume, 76, 79
  for making rose scent, 71
  palsy drops, 91
  in Penn's *Book of Physic*, 25
  pickled rosebuds, 91
  potted roses, 91-92
  rose conserves, 91
red, for passion, 193
Redouté, Pierre Joseph, 43, 54, 108
red rose, 13, 14, 58, 85, 166
  ceremony of, Manheim, Pa., 212
  in church, 101
  conserve, 91
  as evil omen, 63
  medicinal use of, 84
  as rent, 127
Red Roses for Me, 207
Reinisch, E. F., 122

rent in roses, 127
Reschovsky, J., 183
resurrection of rose from ashes, 202-203
Resurrection rose, 60, 65
Rhazes, 72
Rhodanthe, 8
Rhodian coins, 142
Rhodoligia, 86, 91, 202
ribbon roses, 93
Rilke, Rainer Maria, 213
Robertson, Lexie Dean, 124
Rohde, Eleanor Sinclair, 79, 181
Romance of the Rose, 9, 19, 53, 210
Roman de la Rose, Le, 26, 53
Romans:
  coins of, 142
  floral scents of, 72
  lavish use of roses, 18
  legends of rose, 7-8
  poetry, 185
Romaunt of the Rose, 210
Ronsard, Pierre de, 188
Roosevelt, Franklin Delano, 129
rosa Americana penny, 142, 144
rosa arvensis, 70
rosa Banksia, 70
Rosa centifolia, 69, 76, 79
Rosa Flos Veneris, 93
rosa gallica, 30, 96
rosa Hollandia, 82
Rosa Mundi, grave of, 96
rosa muscosa (moss rose), 40
rosa nitida, 124
Rosa of Lima, Saint, 152
rosarians, 123
rosarie de l'Hay, 106, 107, 110
rosaries, origin of, 98, 155-156
rosa rubiginosa, 70
rosary, 150
rosa sancta, 96
rosa solis, 83
Rosa Wichuraiana, 113
rose:
  antiquity and ancestry of, 7
  Briarcliff, 90
  cabbage, 197
  Capistrano, 133
  centifolia, 38
  Chrysler Imperial, 136
  in different languages, 193-194
  evil-smelling, 12
  Ferdinand Pichard, 140
  First Love, 20
  "flower of flowers," 84
  Fred Howard, 168

rose (cont.):
  golden, 198
  Helen Traubel, 180
  Margot Kister, 89
  Mary Margaret McBride, 109
  meaning of word, 193
  Mission Bell, 90
  Mrs. Sam McGready, 89
  Nocturne, 178
  Peace, 137
  Pinkie, 88
  Provins, 43
  queen of flowers, 7
  Ramond Bach, 89
  Rex Anderson, 136
  Sutter's Gold, 87
  Tafetta, 77
  Tallyho, 46
  as universal symbol, 194
  York and Lancaster, 134
Rose, Thomas, 35
Rose, Its History, Poetry, Culture, and Classification, The, 80
Rose, Its History and Culture, The, 181
Rose and the Ring, The, 176
rose-blossom tea, 92
rosebuds, 32, 95, 168
  sacks of, in Arabia, 74
rose bush, world's largest, 112
rose bush, world's oldest, 149
rose code, 95, 181
Rose de Mai, 76
"Rose from the Grave of Homer, The," 174
rose gall, 66
Rose Garden, 186
rose garden, medieval, 109
rose garden, Oakland Municipal, 113
rose garden, Queen Mary's, 111
rose garden by the sea (N. H.), 116
Rose Garden Song, 119
rose hips; see hips, rose
rose knots, of sailors, 23, 140
Rose Leaf and Apple Leaf, 192
rose medallion, 35-36
Rosemont, South Carolina, 128
Rosenborg, Rodologia, 86, 91, 202
Rosenkavalier, Der, 27
rose nobles, and alchemy, 203
Rose Odyssey, A, 181
Rose of Bakawali, 67
Rose of Battles, 206
"Rose of Eden, The," 69
"Rose of My Caravan," 181

rose petals; see petals of rose
rose plot, in Spain, 118
"Rose Prince, The," 171
rose prints (fairy tales), 167
Roseraie de L'Hay, 106
Rose Recipes, 181
"Rose Red, Snow White and," 165
Rose rock and mineral, 10
"Roses of Picardy," 181
Rose Sunday, 102
rose syrup, 95
rosettes:
  on sepulchers, 145
  in shoes, 93
Rose Upon Her Briar, The, 181
"Rose upon the Road of Life, The," 206
Rose Vogue, 78
rose water (gulab):
  birthplace of, 72
  in canal, 73
  as charm, 16
  of Cleopatra, 71
  cure for fainting, 83
  early trade in, 72-73
  emblematic use of, 101
  fountains of, 18
  glycerine and, 81
  industry in Europe, 73
  in marriage customs, 95-96
  purification with, 72-73
  trench filled with, 18
  as tribute, 72
  used in baptism, 188
  weapon of mock warfare, 103
rose windows, in Gothic cathedrals, 196, 197
Rosicrucians, 209
  philosophy of, 210
Rossetti, Dante Gabriel, 34
Rossi, Geronimo, 73
Rosy-Cross, the, 201
Rubaiyat rose, 29
Rubinstein, Nicholas, 153
Ruby Stone, The, 153
rug, needlepoint, 49
Ruskin, John, 35, 58
Russia, rose legend, 64

Sacred Emily, 192
Sacrum Book of Hours, 53
Sadi, 185, 186
  Gulistan, 73, 74-75, 83
sailing ships, cuttings carried in, 121
St. Paul's, in London, 212
Saints, and the rose, 32-33, 71

Saladin, 72, 73
Salency, rose girl of, 103
San Dominico Hotel, rose garden, 118
sandwiches, rose-petal, 92
San José, California, rose garden, 122
Santa Rosa di Viterbo, 149
Sappho, 7, 14, 184
Satan, and briar rose, 15
Scalamandre, 51
Scandinavian countries:
　fairy tales of, 172
　roses in, 124
scarabee, allergic, 83
Scented Garden, The, 79
sculpture, rose in, 31-32
　on ceiling, 94
secret rose, 206, 207
"Self-Reliance," 176-177
sex of rose, 7, 209
Shadowy Waters, The, 209
Shakespeare, William, 24, 59, 65, 69, 70,
　93, 126, 190, 191
Shelley, Percy Bysshe, 175, 190
Sherman, General, 25
shields, rose mottoes on, 132
Shipka, battle of, 125
Shiraz, 72, 117, 186
shower of roses, 18
Siddartha, Prince (Buddha), 119, 204
Sidney, Sir Philip, 182
Signorelli, Luca, 35
Silver Rose, 27
　of India, 196, 201, 211
Slavic people, and rose symbolism, 194
Sleeping Beauty, story of, 119
Smith, Logan Pearsall, 176
"Snail and the Rose Bush, The," 160
"Snow White and Rose Red," 164-165
societies and orders, 209
Society of the Rose, 102
Solon, 71-72
songs, rose, 181
Southey, Robert, 8, 11, 190
Spain:
　rose plots in, 118
　woodcuts, 53
Spectre de la Rose, Le, 20, 27
spellbound flowers, 89
spicy-scented roses, 70
"Spindle, Shuttle and Needle," 164
Sprenger, Jacob, 53
stained-glass windows, rose motif in, 32
stamps, 139
Standish, Rose, 25

Star Rose Gardens, West Grove, Pennsylvania, 123
Stauffer, F. H., 60
"Steadfast Tin Soldier, The," 160
Stein, Gertrude, 192
Steiner, Rudolph, 165, 212
Stiegel, Baron, 36
　ceremony of the rose, Manheim, Pa., 212
Strabo, Walafrid, 84, 121
Strauss, Richard, 27
Strickland, Agnes, 141
Stuarts, royal badge of, 141-142
sub rosa, origin of term, 93-94
Sullivan, Edmund J., 187
Sully, Thomas, 168
Sun Dials and Roses of Yesterday, 81, 181
superstitions, and rose, 59-68
　British, 63
　Bulgarian, 65
　Christian, 67-68
　colors of roses, 63-64
　conception, from eating rose leaf, 65-66
　German, 60, 63, 65
　Greek, 60
　Italian, 62, 65
　Middle Ages, 64
　Persian, 59-60
　pre-Christian, 65
　Russian, 64
　safe childbirth, 65
　science and, 59
　Transylvanian, 65
sweet bags, 86
sweetbriar rose, 12, 65, 121
　in poetry, 182
Swinburne, Algernon Charles, 190
Switzerland:
　rose nursery in, 119
　white rose, prize for virtue, 103
symbolism, and the rose, 35, 53-54, 64
　beginnings of, 194
　Christian, 31, 194
　cycle of human, 193
　in fairy tales, 159-174
　golden rose, 101-102
　Greek, Roman, Egyptian, 194
　Holy Trinity, 33
　Jericho rose, symbol of safe childbirth, 65
　orders and societies, 209
　religious, 193
　and pagan debauchery, 146
　in paintings of Virgin, 33-34
　rose and lotus compared, 193

symbolism (cont.):
    rose as abode of spirit, 64
    roses engraved on tombstones, 97
    silver rose, 27, 196, 201, 211
    Slavic, 194
    supernatural happenings, 67-68
    three symbols, German, 119
Symbolism in Medieval Thought and Its Consummation in the Divine Comedy, 195

Tabb, Father, 97
table setting, 87
Tadema, Alma, 18
Taj Mahal, 18, 19
tapestry (Franco-Flemish), 37
Tea:
    rose-blossom, 92
    rose-scented, 74, 83
tea rose, 70, 76
Temperly, Helen, 181
Tennyson, Alfred Lord, 190
Teresa, Saint, 153
Testament of Beauty, The, 191
Thackeray, William Makepeace, 176
Theocritus, 184
Theophilus and Saint Dorothea, 152
Theophrastus, 71
Thompson Indians, superstitions of, 65
thorns, 34
    on rose of life, 205
    legends of origin, 11, 12, 15
    "passion of Christ," 102
    Saint Benedict and, 147
    symbols of fear, 95
Thorwaldsen, Bertel, 97-98
"Thorwaldsen's Grave," 174
"Thumberline," 160
Time's Best Jewel, 210
Time's Chest, 210
tincture of roses, 71
Tobar, Alfonso da, 34
"To Helen," 191-192
Tolentini, Nicolas, 148
tombs, decorated with roses, 97, 141
tombstones, rose motif on, 35
Topeka, Kansas, rose garden, 122
"To the Secret Rose," 206
Transcendentalism, 203
Transylvanian ritual, 65
Trask, Spencer and Katrina, 122-123
tribute of roses, 103
Tristan and Iseult, 21, 182
troubadours, 23
truthfulness, rose as test of, 62

Tsing-moi-gin-hwa, Chinese rose, 74
Tudor rose, 24, 127
Tun Li-Ch'en, 92
tussie-mussie (Victorian bouquet), 17, 94-95
Tynan, Katherine, 181

Ulrich Brunner rose, 76
under the rose, use of term, 94
United States:
    poetry, 191, 192
    rose, as state flower, 128
    rose gardens in, 122-124, 128-129

valentine, 48
valentine design and designers, 36
Valerian, 151-152
Vanderbilt, George W., 122
Vartavar, burning of the rose, 101, 212
Venus, 7-8, 13, 17, 71, 81, 93, 142, 146, 195
Venus and Adonis, 59
Verres, 18, 67
Victoria, Queen, 159
Vier, Don, 49
Villa d'Este, 118
Villeneuve, Armand de, 73
Vincent, Saint, 33
vinegar of roses, 85
Virgin Mary, 53
    in art, 32, 33-34
    "enclosed garden of," 105
    Marienroschen of, 14
    rose miracles and, 155
    rose-wreathed statue of, 98
Virgin of the Rose, 32
"Vishnu, Brahma and a Rose," 171
vitamin c, in rose hips, 80

wallpaper, 52
Wars of the Roses, 24, 94, 125, 126-127
Weber, Richard, 27
Weinachtsrose, 60
Western world, names of roses, 28
white rose, 13
    for purity, 193
    prize for virtue, 103
    unexpected blossoming of, 63
Wilde, Oscar, 64, 83, 192
    fairy tales of, 159, 166-170
wild rose, 63, 70, 203
    in China, 124
    prairie, 128
    Saint Bernadette and, 153
"Wild Swans, The," 160
"William and Margaret," ballad of, 64

INDEX

Willmot, Ellen Ann, 57-58
wine, rose, 18, 83-84
witchcraft, and rose, 64, 65
woman, and rose, 16-17
Wood, William, 145
woodcuts, 53
wood engravings, 53
Worthies, 209
wreaths of roses, 98, 101
Wright's Chaste Wife, The, 62
writers, mysticism of, 193

Yaddo, Saratoga, New York, rose garden at, 122

Yeats, William Butler, 31, 189, 206-207, 209, 212
yellow rose, 13, 95
  symbolism of, 195
York, Pennsylvania, White Rose City, 128
York and Lancaster, houses of, 126

Zevio, Stefano da, 39
Zillah, 8, 11
Zita, Saint, 148
Zoroaster, 11, 71
Zurburan, Francisco de, 34